Best Practices for Therapy

Empirically Based Treatment Protocols

Dear Mental Health Professional:

This protocol is part of the *Best Practices for Therapy* series that is designed to provide mental health practitioners empirically based treatment programs. We have edited this series to be clear and user-friendly, yet comprehensive and step-by-step.

The series offers high quality, consistently formatted protocols that include everything you need to initiate and complete treatment. Each session is outlined in detail with its own agenda, client education materials, and skill-building interventions. Each session also provides sample instructions and therapist-client dialogues.

The therapist protocol you are using corresponds with an available client manual that is designed to be used concurrently. Your protocol has all the handouts, worksheets, homework assignments, in-session treatment exercises, and didactic material that is in the client manual. Also included are pre- and post-assessments, and an overall program evaluation. An appendix contains a treatment plan summary (now required by many managed care companies).

Ten *Best Practices for Therapy* protocols are currently available or in development. They include protocols for PTSD, GAD, OCD, panic disorder/agoraphobia, specific phobia, social phobia, depression, anger management, BPD, and eating disorders.

We wish you every success in using this program with your clients.

Sincerely,

Matthew McKay, Ph.D.
John Preston, Psy.D.
Carole Honeychurch, M.A.

OVERCOMING SITUATIONAL AND GENERAL ANGER

■

A Protocol for the Treatment
of Anger Based on Relaxation,
Cognitive Restructuring,
and Coping Skills Training

Jerry L. Deffenbacher, Ph.D.,
and Matthew McKay, Ph.D.

Best Practices for Therapy
Empirically Based Treatment Protocols

Publisher's Note

This publication is designed to provide accurate and authoritative information in regard to the subject matter covered. It is sold with the understanding that the publisher is not engaged in rendering psychological, financial, legal, or other professional services. If expert assistance or counseling is needed, the services of a competent professional should be sought.

Distributed in Canada by Raincoast Books

Copyright © 2000 by Jerry Deffenbacher and Matthew McKay
New Harbinger Publications, Inc.
5674 Shattuck Avenue
Oakland, CA 94609

Cover design by Poulson/Gluck Designs
Edited by Carole Honeychurch
Text design by Michele Waters

ISBN-10 1-57224-204-3
ISBN-13 978-1-57224-204-3

Printed in the United States of America

New Harbinger Publications' website address: www.newharbinger.com

12   11   10

10   9   8   7   6   5

Contents

Overview of Anger

Overview of the Disorder

Biologically, anger is a part of the basic fight/flight mechanisms. Becoming angry and ready to fight off real threats can serve very adaptive, evolutionarily meaningful functions. For example, the aroused, aggressive individual might fight off a predatory animal or attacking human and live to see another day. When the arousal system breaks down, however, anger may become excessive. Dysregulation in serotonergic and noradrenergic systems can predispose some people to overreact with anger and impulsive, potentially aggressive behavior.

But biology-driven anger problems are rare. Basic biological systems are shaped powerfully by psychological and social forces, and there is little evidence of anger- or aggression-based biological preparedness in humans. That is, what the individual becomes angry about, the intensity of that anger, the forms of expression shown, and the targets of that expression are *mostly learned*. Early parent-child interactions model and reinforce a great deal about anger and its expression, and the family continues to be a strong socialization force shaping the nature and expression of anger. Early peer experiences, but particularly peer socialization processes during adolescence, also exert strong influences on how anger will be experienced and expressed. Schools, religious institutions, the media, and other cultural forces all communicate information, norms, and sanctions that shape the experience and expression of anger.

Some socialization experiences lead to very adaptive anger responses. Many people develop appropriate mild to moderate anger reactions to provocative situations and respond to that anger with a flexible repertoire of behavior that is self-enhancing, respectful of the rights of others, and oriented toward the resolution of problems.

On the other hand, learning can he hijacked. Socialization experiences may teach the individual that a number of situations are highly insulting, attacking, and threatening, when in fact they may be negative but not especially aversive. Nonetheless, the person will be mobilized to respond to the perceived threat by simply blowing up. Moreover, many socialization experiences model and reinforce high levels of anger and aggression. As a result, high levels of anger and dysfunctional behavior become normalized ways of handling difficulties. Over time, these experiences are consolidated into social-emotional-behavioral scripts that become highly automatic (though dysfunctional) ways of responding.

The treatment approach outlined in this protocol is based on the assumption that the components of the anger response can be identified and that new learning experiences can be developed to provide the individual with alternative scripts and ways of responding. An individual's anger at a moment in time is a function of the complex interactions of three domains: 1) one or more triggers or eliciting stimuli; 2) the person's pre-anger state, which consists of both momentary and enduring elements; and 3) appraisal processes.

Triggers and Precipitants of Anger

Anger may be elicited by one or more of the following three triggers: 1) specific sources of provocation; 2) events that trigger significant anger-related cognitions, memories, and images related to earlier traumatic events; and 3) internal states and experiences.

In the first class of triggers, anger is set off by a specific event or condition. Some triggers involve particular events, such as being stuck in traffic or seeing others mistreated. Others involve specific people and their behaviors, such as a supervisor's reprimand or a significant other's critical comments. Still other cases of anger arousal involve specific objects, such as a car that will not start or another piece of equipment that is malfunctioning. Anger also may be triggered by relatively impersonal events like weather that interferes with plans for outdoor activities or one's favorite sports team losing badly. Finally, anger may be triggered by one's own behavior or characteristics, such as failing at an important task or being significantly overweight and out of shape. In all of these cases some relatively definable event or condition appears to elicit anger. Moreover, the individual can often specify the relationship between the condition and the resulting anger, stating something on the order of "X makes me mad."

In the second class of triggers, anger *appears* to be elicited by specific situations. However, the degree of anger aroused is more stimulated by the angry thoughts, memories, and images the situation brings to mind than the situation itself. Some of the strongest anger reactions of this type are experienced by people with posttraumatic stress disorder. For example, a woman experienced intense rage and a nearly uncontrollable urge to hit her husband when he asked her to dance and put his hands on her hips. After considerable exploration, it was revealed that the way her husband had touched her hips triggered off associations to how her father had touched her hips during incest as a child. In another case, a worker became very angry and belligerent when given nearly any type of negative feedback by a specific supervisor. While acknowledging that he didn't like negative feedback, the worker reported that his response was way out of proportion to the nature of the feedback, and that he didn't react this way to other supervisors. Self-monitoring of his reactions and of his supervisor's behavior revealed that the tone of his supervisor's voice and mannerism of frowning over his right eye reminded the angry man of his father—a critical and physically abusive man. Clinically, less severe but important parallels abound. For example, one member of a relationship may become angry with a partner because his or her behavior is reminiscent of an earlier negative relationship. A person may overrespond to criticism because of their history of receiving criticism as a youngster.

Often, people with this type of anger trigger are not clear about the extent of the connection between their anger and the stimuli that apparently elicited it. They may be confused because the degree or type of anger reactions seems out of proportion, yet they nonetheless experience anger (and, in some cases, other negative emotions) when exposed to trigger conditions. It may take a period of interviewing, self-monitoring, and/or self-reflection for the client to identify the underlying self-dialogue, memories, and images that are much more responsible for the anger than specific external events.

In the third class of triggers, anger is not aroused so much by external conditions as by internal events occuring inside the angry person. One of the most common of these triggers is feelings or emotions other than anger that tend to set off the anger response. For example, the person may become angry when feeling rejected, dismissed, ashamed, embarrassed, or hurt. That is, some condition elicits one or more of these emotions, which, in turn, trigger anger. Another example would be an individual who makes a social error and feels very embarrassed. This painful feeling of embarrassment generates anger with himself and at the people involved for witnessing his pain. A person may feel hurt by a partner's comment and, in an effort to avoid feeling the pain of the perceived slight, may retaliate angrily. For others the internal triggering events are less emotional and more cognitive. One of the most common cognitive precipitants is worrying or ruminating about past or potential negative events. The person becomes more and more angry as past injustices, mistakes, and misdeeds are turned over and over in their head. For example, a woman who felt she had been overlooked for a promotion and treated unfairly in past performance reviews spent several hours a week in angry rumination about her mistreatment. In another case, a man who had experienced a sudden relationship breakup spent most of his evenings in angry brooding, jealousy and thoughts of revenge. In both cases, anger is secondary to experiencing negative emotions or cognitive events. People may differ in the degree of insight they have into their anger triggers. It may take some self-monitoring or assessment interviewing to clarify the nature of the cognitive or emotional anger-trigger.

Pre-Anger State

Transient and more enduring processes within the individual also influence the presence and course of anger. These characteristics may be thought of as filters that screen incoming information in ways that lower or raise the threshold for anger and influence the intensity and form of anger expression.

Immediate Pre-Anger State

One important element is the individual's immediate cognitive-emotional-physiological state at the time of an anger-related stimulus (i.e., what the person is thinking, feeling, and experiencing physically). If an individual is in a calm, relaxed state or experiencing positive thoughts and feelings, he or she is much less likely to become angry. In addition, the individual is more likely to utilize effective cognitive and behavioral coping skills. However, a negative pre-anger state lowers the threshold for anger, and the person enmeshed in this state is likely to respond with more intense anger and aggressive or dysfunctional behavior.

Prior anger is one very important element of the immediate pre-anger state. If the person is already angry or frustrated, even if it has nothing to do with current precipitants of anger, the individual is more likely to respond with anger and to respond more intensely (Zillman 1971; Zillman and Bryant 1974). Angry individuals are often able to describe this phenomenon (e.g., "I was already mad when I walked in the door. She didn't really have a chance"; or "My fuse was already lit"; or "The pump was already primed.")

The impact of the immediate cognitive-emotional-physiological state, however, isn't limited to anger. A long line of research by Berkowitz (1990) has shown that nearly any negative state can affect the probability and intensity of an anger reaction. For example, being fatigued, sick, hungry, stressed, hurried, anxious, depressed, or hung over can influence the anger reaction. Such negative states appear to increase the presence and power of aversive thoughts, images, feelings, and memories. These, in turn, lower the threshold for anger. Individuals may be relatively unaware of experiencing these conditions and how the conditions influence their anger. Clients often report being confused about and sometimes dismayed at their reactions. Variability in responding often holds the key to understanding. Exploring why the individual responds with no or minimal anger on one occasion, but with much stronger anger on another may reveal that the problematic anger often occurs when the person is tired, sick, preoccupied, and the like.

Enhancing the client's awareness of pre-anger conditions and guiding them to monitor these conditions closely may become an important target of intervention. Cognitive and relaxation coping skills can then be used to modify the pre-anger state. For example, one working mother who often became angry with her children and spouse after arriving home in a tired, distracted state negotiated a ten-minute quiet time. During that interval she relaxed and tried to separate the issues and stresses of work from those in her home environment. Another individual who suffered from chronic arthritic pain learned to take a relaxation period prior to discussing with his spouse any potentially stressful issues.

Enduring Pre-Anger Conditions

Anger is also influenced by relatively enduring psychological characteristics. One of these is a person's habitual way of construing, processing, and making meaning out of the world. Included in this area are the person's values, his or her expectations, their moral codes and personal rules for living, the things they believe should and should not happen, important tasks to be pursued and achieved, and so on. These are the kinds of things which Beck (1976) refers as the "personal domain" and Lazarus (1991) as the person's "ego identify." Trespasses upon the personal domain, blameful attacks on ego identify, violations of expectations and personal rules of living, and the blocking of important goals often lead to anger. Problematic anger increases when boundaries of the personal domain or ego identity become rigid and inflexible, when values are no longer personal guidelines for living but become dogma and dictates, when personally defined freedoms and rights become absolute, and when important goal-directed behavior becomes imperative. Beliefs such as these can shape the presence, intensity, and expression of anger and are often important targets of assessment and intervention.

Another factor in the pre-anger state that mediates anger is the person's set of cultural rules regarding anger. Every culture has norms regarding the experience of anger, including things one should and should not be angry about and appropriate and inappropriate targets of anger and forms of expressing it. Some cultural and sub-cultural groups may allow, even encourage, rather loud, animated arguing at close physical range, whereas another cultural group would label such behavior as offensive. Certain examples of problematic anger result from a kind of cultural mismatch. The individual may respond using scripts from his or her heritage, but those same experiential and display rules are inappropriate in the current cultural context. In other cases, the person may experience conflict between different social groups. For example, an adolescent is encouraged to be very angry and aggressive in his or her peer group, but finds that this expression is in conflict with other socialization forces such as the school or the family. Cultural norms are an extremely important (though sometimes overlooked) factor in understanding and assessing the potential contributing sources to dysfunctional anger.

Appraisal Processes

Triggers of anger and pre-anger conditions converge during primary and secondary appraisal process (Lazarus 1991). *Primary appraisal* describes the person's evaluation of the source or sources of anger in light of his or her enduring and momentary state. Most often, anger grows from an encroachment upon the personal domain, an insult or injury to the ego identity, a violation of values and rules for living, promises and expectations being unmet or unfulfilled, and/or obstacles to a valued goal. In essence, something has happened that the person judges "should not" happen, sometimes leading anger to be termed the "moral" emotion. The more inflexible and absolute a person's values, the more likely a violation will trigger intense anger.

The level of anger is also intensified by at least four other primary appraisal and attribution processes:

- Anger is more likely if the precipitant is deemed unjustified. That is, if a person sees the event as unwarranted or undeserved, anger is more likely because the precipitant has violated his or her sense of justice and fairness. Anger is less likely if the event is judged as fair and reasonable.

- Anger is also more likely if an event is judged as controllable or preventable. The implication is that if an event could have been prevented, then it should have been prevented, and the person should not have suffered because of it. Anger escalates from this sense that the event *should* have been prevented. Anger is less likely if a person attributes the event to less controllable sources such as chance, an unfortunate oversight, a misunderstanding, emotional distress in other people, a natural human error, and the like.

- Anger also is likely to increase if the person perceives events as intentional. If the individual senses that others perpetrated the event on purpose, then he or she is more likely to be on guard and respond with anger. Anger is less likely if the events are not personalized and deemed as intentional and their causes attributed to more benign causes.

- Finally, anger is more likely if the person sees the precipitant as solely responsible, blameworthy, or punishable. This kind of attribution totally externalizes the source of anger. It eliminates the individual's responsibility for the level of anger and type of response, and often justifies aggression and retaliation. The probability and intensity of anger is reduced if the person sees events as multiply determined, and if he or she accepts some responsibility for the response, and tries to limit the sense of blame and punishment.

Whereas primary appraisal involves judgments about the triggering or precipitating events, *secondary appraisal* involves an evaluation of the individual's coping resources. Anger is more likely if the person feels overwhelmed, exhausted, out of control, or unable to cope. People will often express this type of appraisal in statements like, "I was at my wit's end"; or "I just couldn't handle it. I was in way over my head and couldn't see anyway out"; or "I was totally out of control and didn't have a clue about what to do."

Another type of secondary appraisal has particular relevance to anger. This type is characterized by the person believing that he or she simply should not have to experience or deal with the triggering events. In other words, the individual invokes a narcissistic rule that he or she should not be subject to frustration, disappointment, inconvenience, rejection, or other negative events—a condition rational-emotive therapists describe as "low frustration tolerance" (Dryden 1990; Ellis 1977). Anger results, in part, because the person is experiencing something that should not have to be endured. Angry individuals often express this kind of appraisal process in statements like, "I just shouldn't have to put up with this"; or "Nobody should have to put up with this kind of crap."

A third kind of anger-engendering secondary appraisal is coding anger and/or aggression as appropriate responses to the situation. If anger and aggression are viewed as normal and expected responses to a situation, then they are more likely to be prompted. From the angry person's point of view, they are natural, reasonable reactions, not inappropriate or unwarranted. Such appraisals may be reflected in statements like, "I ought to be angry with them for doing that. Anyone would be"; or "I don't take crap from anyone, I just get right in their face and tell them exactly what I think." Anger is likely to be intensified and the probability of aggression increased if the person expects positive outcomes from aggression as well (Lazarus 1991).

What Is Anger?

Triggers, the pre-anger state, and appraisals interact and elicit anger. Anger is an experiential state composed of emotional, physiological, and cognitive processes (see next chapter for more detail on each element). They are experienced nearly simultaneously and are labeled by the person as anger.

Forms of Anger Expression and Anger-Related Behavior

Two people may be equally angry but respond to the same anger-inducing situation in dramatically different ways. Moreover, a person may respond to the same situation in different ways on different occasions, demonstrating that anger can be conceptually separated from the ways in which it is expressed, even though the individual is likely to experience anger and its expression as a simultaneous event.

Research has outlined a number of styles or ways through which people express their anger (e.g., Deffenbacher, Oetting, Lynch, and Morris 1996; Morris, Deffenbacher, Lynch, and Oetting 1996). Some modes of expression are adaptive and prosocial. For example, certain people attempt to engage in *reciprocal communication*, in which they express their feelings but also try to listen to and take into account the feelings and preferences of others. They try to problem solve and find solutions acceptable to all. Others become more cognitively reflective and *think before responding;* that is, they delay responding at least momentarily and attempt to consider possible behaviors and consequences. Another form of expression is taking a *time-out*, through which the person appropriately distances him or herself from the provocation in order to lower anger and generate more effective behavior. Finally, other individuals attempt to *control* or lower anger arousal and limit negative responding. Recent work by Spielberger (1999) suggests that control consists of two related elements: self-soothing efforts such as taking deep breaths to relax and calm down, and more behavioral efforts to limit or curb the dysfunctional responding.

So far we've looked at positive forms of anger response, but there are clearly more negative and maladaptive types of anger expression. For example, some individuals engage in *physical assault on people*, either threatening to or actually hitting, slapping, punching, or kicking others. Not all physical assault is directed toward people, however. Another form of anger expression is *physical assault on objects* (e.g., kicking, throwing, slamming, and pounding on things). Physical aggression is still involved, but the object of the aggression is the physical rather than the social environment. People may also express their anger through verbal aggression. One form of expression is *noisy arguing*, in which the person becomes loud and vituperative. It's as if turning up the volume is designed to make the person's point more forceful. Individuals also engage in *verbal assault*, which involves things such as putting the other person down, being cutting and sarcastic, name calling, and the like. Some other negative forms of anger expression depend on nonverbal messages. One involves *dirty looks*, in which the person expresses his or her anger through icy stares, glares, rolling one's eyes, and so on. Another nonverbal expression involves *negative body language* such as poignant sighs, crossed arms, hands on hips, etc.

A final form of anger expression is *anger-in*. The person experiences anger, but suppresses or holds it in. There is a tendency to be cognitively quite critical, perhaps harboring grudges and thinking other hostile and retaliatory thoughts. But rarely is there any overt action on angry feelings or cognitions. Thus, anger-in involves the experiences of anger, which can be intense, but also a reluctance toward any overt expression of that anger.

People who are frequently angry may report using only a few forms of anger expression. On the other hand, some people with anger problems report a wide range in the forms of anger expression, both positive and negative (Deffenbacher, Oetting, Thwaites, et al. 1996; Deffenbacher and Sabadell 1992). Their reports are likely to be accurate. Because they become angry frequently, they may express anger in effective, prosocial ways on some occasions, in aggressive ways on other occasions, and at other times may suppress anger altogether. Clinically, it's most important to map which forms of expression are used under what conditions and to see if positive forms of expression can't be adapted to situations where dysfunctional or aggressive forms of anger expression are being used.

In general, the experience of anger is not synonymous with any specific form of expression. Especially when anger is mild to moderate in intensity, people are more likely to use positive behaviors such as assertive communication, negotiation, problem solving, and the like. Negative and dysfunctional behavior can occur at any level of arousal, but as anger increases, the probability of maladaptive forms of expression increases.

Anger Consequences

Not all anger leads to negative outcomes. Anger, especially at mild levels, may prompt behavior that leads to redressing interpersonal concerns, solving problems, and standing up for one's self. However, as anger escalates, the probability of negative consequences increases. For example, one's anger can trigger anger and counteraggression in others, often fueling further aggression and potential violence. Anger can have a negative influence on one's health. At an obvious level, aggressive expression can lead to physical damage and injury (e.g., punching a door and breaking or cutting one's hand). Elevated anger has also been associated with increased incidence of coronary artery disease, essential hypertension, dental problems such as bruxism and damage to teeth, and the like. Anger can also cause significant damage to close interpersonal relationships and lead to a variety of problems in the workplace or in educational pursuits. Anger often contributes to a variety of legal (e.g., arrests and citations) and quasi-legal (e.g., being written up at work or being suspended from school) consequences. Anger may also lead to other negative behaviors such as reckless driving or becoming intoxicated, which, in turn, may trigger further negative outcomes. Finally, there is the issue of self-esteem. Being highly angry and expressing it poorly often leads individuals to feel badly about themselves (guilty, ashamed, and the like), resulting in lowered self-efficacy and self-esteem.

Problematic or Dysfunctional Anger

What constitutes dysfunctional anger and healthy anger expression? Like may clinical issues, this is a judgment call. While there are few absolute standards for judging anger, clinicians may look to the following dimensions in making their judgments.

Response Frequency

Infrequent anger, assuming that it is not intense or associated with negative consequences, is likely to be of little importance. The more frequent anger is, the more likely it is to result in both negative expression and consequences. Moreover, frequent anger taxes the person's overall coping resources and increases the probability that the person will live with a higher baseline of anger arousal and stress.

Response Intensity

Intense anger is very likely to be problematic. As anger escalates in intensity, it's not only more likely to generate negative feelings and health consequences, but also to prompt an uncomfortable sense of being out of control and aggressive.

Response Duration

Brief, low-level anger is not likely to be of much consequence. However, some individuals stay angry for long periods of time, with 25 percent caught up in anger for as much as a day or so (Averill 1982). The quality of one's life and coping are likely to suffer under such prolonged anger. Anger-related health consequences are more likely and the person is more likely to respond maladaptively to new provocations because of prolonged exposure.

Form of Expression and Consequences

Highly angry individuals are more likely to have injury to themselves and others, property damaged, compromised or destroyed interpersonal relationships, disruptions in work or school performance, greater alcohol involvement and alcohol consequences, and lowered self-esteem (Deffenbacher 1992; Deffenbacher, Oetting, Lynch, et al. 1996; Deffenbacher, Oetting, Thwaites, et al. 1996; Leibsohn, Oetting, and Deffenbacher 1994; Morris, Deffenbacher, Lynch, et al. 1996).

In general, anger is more likely to be problematic when it is more frequent, intense, or lengthy in duration and/or to the extent that it prompts dysfunctional behavior and more frequent and severe outcomes.

Diagnosis and Clinical Feature of Problematic Anger

Diagnostic systems such as the DSM-IV (American Psychiatric Association 1994) provide little assistance in conceptualizing and treatment planning for problematic anger. There are disorders in which anger is a secondary characteristic (i.e., the presence of anger helps rule in the disorder). For example, anger contributes to Axis I disorders such as posttraumatic stress disorder, dysthymia, major depression, some forms of schizophrenia and cognitive disorders, and intermittent explosive disorder. It also contributes to Axis II disorders such as paranoid, borderline, narcissistic, and antisocial personality disorders, and to some Axis III conditions such as coronary artery disease and essential hypertension. However, DSM-IV includes *no* disorders in which angry affect is a defining characteristic (i.e., anger must be present for a positive diagnosis).

This is in marked contrast to other disorders defined primarily by their affective qualities such as the anxiety and mood disorders. For example, if an individual suffers from chronic, unrealistic worry and moderate anxiety, then a diagnosis of generalized anxiety disorder may be warranted. However, there is no parallel diagnosis for an individual who suffers from chronic, moderate angry mood or frequent anger. Diagnostic categories exist for strong anxiety reactions and avoidance of specific situations (phobias). If people are afraid of and avoid situations where there is a possibility of being criticized and rejected, then they may be diagnosed as suffering from a social phobia. However, if they react with strong, dysfunctional anger to exactly the same situations, there is no parallel situational anger disorder.

Clinicians know problematic anger exists and clients suffer significant and, in some cases, tragic consequences because of their anger. The absence of specific anger disorders in our diagnostic systems, however, does not mean that people don't suffer anger-based emotional disorders and that anger is not worthy of diagnostic and clinical intervention efforts.

To assist therapists in conceptualizing, assessing, and treating problematic anger, five new diagnoses have been proposed (Deffenbacher 1994a; Eckhardt and Deffenbacher 1995). These are not presented as well-documented, reliable diagnostic categories because the research is not there to support such claims. They are proposed as working models or tentative diagnoses to assist clinicians in thinking about their client's anger.

These five working conceptualizations of anger problems are described by the convergence of three general dimensions: 1) indices of angry emotionality, physiological arousal, and cognition; 2) the nature of the triggering events; and 3) the presence or absence of aggressive behavior.

To make an anger-related diagnosis the clinician *must* see evidence that significant angry emotionality is present. That is, the individual must report strong feelings of anger, being furious, mad, pissed off, livid, enraged, and the like.

The client should also show several indices of anger-related physiological arousal and anger-related cognitions, although the specifics would vary from case to case. For example, in the physiological domain, one person might show elevated cardiovascular arousal, while another would report muscular tension. Nonetheless, elevated arousal is common to both. Physiological arousal is often reflected in the following ways:

- Elevated heart rate, heart palpitations, and/or elevated blood pressure

- Sweating or clammy hands

- Flushes, hot sensations, or reddening of the skin

- Increased muscle tension, which might be found in an overall feeling of being tense or in specific areas of tension such as clenched hands or jaws or tension across the shoulders

- Trembling or shaky feelings

- Restlessness, agitation, and/or pacing about

- Feeling very aroused, keyed up, or on edge

- Jumpiness and/or exaggerated startle reactions

- Rapid breathing

- Stomach upset, nausea, or other gastrointestinal upset

More indirect signs of physiological arousal could include tension or migraine headaches, bruxism or other dental problems, or flare-ups of such psychophysiological disorders.

For an anger-related diagnosis, clients should also evidence significant cognitive involvement such as the following:

- The person has a strong belief that he or she has been treated unfairly, violated, or trespassed upon.

- The person demands that self, others, and/or outside events be exactly as the person desires.

- The person believes that others have intentionally tried to hurt or harm him/her (i.e., an interpretation of malevolent intent on the part of others).

- The individual externalizes and blames others or outside events for the entire extent of angry feelings and other reactions.

- The client mentally labels people, things, events in highly negative, overgeneralized, and/or obscene ways (e.g., cursing, name calling, derogatory labeling, etc.).

- The person engages in thoughts or images of harm, revenge, retaliation, and/or derogation relative to the perceived source of anger.

- The person engages in periods of brooding or angry rumination about the perceived source of anger.

- The individual believes that anger and/or aggression are emotions and behaviors that are justified and appropriate to the situation.

- The person demands that he or she should not have to deal with or endure the frustrating or angering events.

- The person feels very guilty, sinful, wrong, and/or inadequate for having angry thoughts and feelings.

- The client experiences racing thoughts, difficulties in concentrating, and/or is unable to shifts his or her thoughts from the angering events.

The behaviors that people engage in when angry can also be critical for diagnosis. Some individuals may experience intense cognitive, emotional, and physiological arousal, but engage in minimal self-defeating or dysfunctional behavior. Others may show extreme aggression. Still others may not be highly aggressive, but may engage in other dysfunctional, risky, and/or self-defeating behavior (e.g., reckless driving, increased drug and alcohol involvement, or inappropriate isolation and withdrawal). Since aggressive behavior can have its own consequences and be meaningful in treatment planning, problematic anger is described for those cases that do and do not involve significant aggression (i.e., problematic anger without aggressive behavior and problematic anger with aggression).

Aggression might be reflected in the following kinds of behaviors:

- The person engages in loud verbal outbursts, yelling, or screaming.

- The client curses, becomes verbally threatening, insulting, intimidating, or argumentative.

- The person engages in repeated sarcasm, cutting or derogatory remarks, or hostile humor.

- The individual actively seeks out or provokes a verbally and/or physically aggressive confrontation.

- The individual makes obscene or other intimidating gestures.

- The person threatens physical harm or becomes physically intimidating (e.g., threatening to knock someone's head off or getting physically very close to others).

- The person assaults others physically (e.g., hits, slaps, kicks, punches, grabs, throws things at, etc.).

- The individual engages in physically assaultive behavior toward things, property, and the environment (e.g., throwing, slamming, or banging on things, pounding on or breaking things, etc.).

- The client engages in a belligerent or stubborn refusal to cooperate or be involved with reasonable requests in dealing with provocative events.

Though not exhaustive, this list outlines some of the most common ways in which people aggress. Repeated use of one or more forms of aggression, or the presence of several forms of aggression across situations and time, would support diagnosing an anger disorder with aggression. The absence of aggressive behavior or minimal, low levels of aggression would lead to a diagnosis of an anger disorder without aggression.

Finally, anger may also be defined by the kinds of events that trigger it. A strong anger reaction may appear after one or more psychosocial stressors. In other cases, anger appears primarily in response to specific situations (e.g., when driving or the recipient of an obscene gesture) or a series of situations tied together by a common psychological theme (such as being criticized or having one's integrity challenged). Such anger is situational or context bound. Still, other individuals experience anger as a frequent state, or in a wide range of situations that don't have a common theme.

Combining triggering events with problematic anger and with the presence or absence of aggression, provides the clinician with five patterns of problem anger. First is an *adjustment disorder with angry mood* (i.e., person has experienced one or more psychosocial stressors and is reacting with excessive or interfering anger). If the person reacts to the stressor(s) with dysfunctional anger and aggressive behavior, the current DSM-IV diagnosis of adjustment disorder with disturbance of mood and conduct would be appropriate. Second, if the person's anger is primarily in specific situations or contexts, he or she could be seen as suffering a *situational anger disorder with* or *without aggression*, depending on the presence or absence of aggression. Finally, if the individual experiences chronic, frequent anger across a wide range of situations and time, then the diagnosis of *generalized anger disorder with* or *without aggression*, may be appropriate. These working conceptualizations of problematic anger, along with clinical examples, are described further in appendix 3.

Prevalence, Consequences, and Correlates of Anger Problems

Given that there are no widely recognized anger-based disorders, prevalence rates are not available. In fact, this is one of the special difficulties in clinical anger research (Eckhardt and Deffenbacher 1995). There are no defined anger disorders from which to collect information on prevalence rates, other epidemiological information, and risk and protective factors.

Intermittent explosive disorder, a DSM-IV impulse-control disorder, may be the closest diagnostic category to anger-based problems. But this diagnosis hardly covers the full range of anger reactions. With intermittent explosive disorder, the focus is on expressive behavior, rather than angry emotion. Little information is available about the prevalence, onset, course, or outcomes of intermittent explosive disorder. "Reliable information is lacking, but Intermittent Explosive Disorder is apparently rare" (American Psychiatric Association 1994, p. 611). Thus, the Axis I disorder that might be most relevant to anger actually says little about anger and focuses primarily on infrequent, apparently unpredictable violent acts. Individuals with intense anger problems and the resulting impaired functioning would only meet the criteria for intermittent explosive disorder if they engaged in occasional acts of intense, impulsive aggression. Other conceptualizations are needed if problematic anger is to be adequately understood and categorized.

Although not meeting any DSM-IV criteria in their conceptualization, Fava, Anderson, and Rosenbaum (1990) described a group of patients who presented with "anger attacks." These individuals reported marked autonomic arousal (e.g., tachycardia and sweating) as well as intense anger, a desire to attack others, and feelings of being out of control. The authors initially likened the patients' experiences to panic attacks, but with anger as the dominant emotional feature (i.e., a rapid buildup of intense angry emotionality and physiological arousal). More recently, they (Fava, Rosenbaum, Pava, et al. 1993; Rosenbaum, Fava, Pava, et al. 1993) have de-emphasized the linkage between anger attacks and panic disorder and have suggested a greater link with depression. They reported that approximately 40 percent of individuals with major depression and 20 percent of general patient samples report anger attacks and that anger attacks respond favorably to antidepressant medications such as fluoxetine. Unfortunately, it is not clear from these studies what the general prevalence rates are; nor do they appear to capture the experience of problematic anger for many people.

There are certainly a number of clinical problems in which anger plays a significant role and for which interventions outlined in this manual may be a partial intervention plan. For example, uncontrolled anger and aggression play central roles in spousal/partner abuse and in the mistreatment of children. However, in DSM-IV these are general V code issues that have broad definitions and for which there is minimal prevalence data. Moreover, many other cases of relational and family problems involve high levels of dysfunctional anger, even if it doesn't reach the level of physical abuse. Again, good prevalence data are not available for those cases where anger is an essential element.

Averill's (1982, 1983) community and college samples provide some general information on anger. Participants in his studies reported an average of about one incident of anger per day and over three incidents of annoyance. Thus, at least at mild to moderate levels, anger is a frequent experience. The targets of anger were typically (75 percent) people who were well known and liked by the angry person, with another 8 percent of people who were known and not liked and 13 percent strangers. In Averill's study, the context of anger was usually interpersonal, which is consistent with other studies that suggest that approximately 80 percent of anger episodes involve other people, generally people who are well known to the individual (Deffenbacher 1993; Deffenbacher, Oetting, Thwaites, et al. 1996). Averill found that the ways in which people responded or expressed their anger were generally nonaggressive (Averill 1982, 1983). When aggression was involved, it was primarily verbal (49 percent) with only 10 percent of incidents involving physical aggression. Participants in Averill's studies reported that the outcomes of anger were generally positive; ratios of beneficial to harmful consequences were on the order of 2.5 to 3.0 to 1. Participants experienced positive outcomes such as realizing one's own faults, clarifying issues and relationships, and gaining respect for other people. Averill's studies suggest that anger is a frequent, interpersonal experience that doesn't necessarily result in negative outcomes. However, two things should be kept in mind regarding these findings. First, the sample was a general sample of college students and community members. While the information is interesting, it may not describe the experience, expression, and consequences for groups with problematic anger. Second, others have found somewhat different outcomes. For example, by employing a diary method with college students, Meltzer (1933) found that nearly two-thirds of students reported negative outcomes as a result of their anger and only about 15 percent reported improved feelings or outcomes.

Deffenbacher and colleagues studied clinical analogs of both situational and generalized anger disorders (i.e., people who experienced high levels of either situational or general anger that was problematic). High-anger drivers were studied as an example of situational anger problems (Deffenbacher 1999; Deffenbacher, Huff, Lynch, et al. in press; Deffenbacher, Lynch, Filetti, et al. 1999). Compared to low-anger drivers, high-anger drivers are angered by more things on the road and become more frequently and intensely angry when driving. They also express their anger in more hostile/aggressive ways (e.g., giving other drivers the finger and intimidating others with their car), eschewing more adaptive/constructive alternatives (e.g., paying close attention to safe driving). They engage in more risky behavior (e.g., drinking and driving or driving recklessly) and experience more accidents or accident-related outcomes (e.g., loss of concentration while driving or moving violations).

For over a decade, Deffenbacher and colleagues (Deffenbacher 1993; Deffenbacher, Demm, and Brandon 1986; Deffenbacher, Oetting, Thwaites, et al. 1996a; Deffenbacher and Sabadell 1992) have worked with a clinical analog of general anger. Their generally angry clients were college students who scored in the upper quartile on Spielberger's (1988) Trait Anger Scale, identified anger as a personal problem, and were interested in counseling for their anger problems. Compared to individuals low in general anger, they report that more things triggered their anger, that they experience more intense anger in a variety of situations, and that they have more anger-related physiological arousal and more frequent and intense anger in their daily lives. They tend to express their anger in outward, negative, less controlled ways, and are more likely to suppress their anger. They're also more likely to react to provocation with physical and verbal aggression. Moreover, they experience more frequent and, in some cases, more severe adverse anger consequences. That is, their anger is more likely to lead to things such as injury to self or others, property damage, damaged friendships and relationships, difficulties at school or in the workplace, financial costs or difficulties, increased alcohol and/or drug consumption, legal and quasi-legal difficulties, more fights with family members, and so on. They also are more likely to experience general anxiety, to drink and become intoxicated (as well as experience more adverse alcohol-related outcomes), to report lower self-esteem, and to cope less well with common sources of stress. They report more anger than college counseling-center clients generally or than a subgroup of counseling center clients who sought out counseling, at least in part, for anger problems. In summary, the high general-anger client analog describes a group of angry individuals who experience more frequent and intense anger, express it in more dysfunctional ways, and are at risk for frequent emotional, behavioral, and social consequences. They also represented a sizable group as well—4 percent to 7 percent of students.

Although there are no defined anger disorders with good prevalence and consequence data, there are a number of different lines of research and clinical inquiry suggesting that there is a significant number of individuals for whom anger is a serious personal problem and who need assistance.

Treatment Approach

Unlike other emotion-based disorders such as anxiety or depression, there are few recommended or gold standard approaches for anger reduction. Some pharmacological research has provided encouraging results using serotonin reuptake inhibitors with anger-involved individuals who have borderline personality disorder (Cocarro and Kavoussi 1997) and those suffering "anger attacks" (Fava, Rosenbaum, Pava, et al. 1993; Rosenbaum, Fava, Pava, et al. 1993). Three recent meta-analyses (Beck and Fernandez 1998; Edmondson and Conger 1996; Trafate 1995) provide general support for cognitive behavioral approaches to anger reduction. Another review suggested that although there was little evidence of superiority of any one approach, there was promising support for relaxation, cognitive, and social/communication skill building interventions, as well as the combination of these components (Deffenbacher, Oetting, and DiGuiseppe 1999). These findings suggest that there is a solid, initial base for adopting a cognitive behavioral approach to anger management, and cognitive-relaxation coping skills (CRCS) is anchored within that general model. CRCS provides alternative self-understanding and learning experiences and is based in several important clinical processes.

Key Issues in a CRCS-based Anger Treatment

The Importance of the Working Alliance

CRCS assumes a positive, quality working alliance. The working alliance is composed of three general elements: 1) a warm, empathic, accepting relationship in which the client feels safe to explore his or her issues and through which the therapist explores and clarifies the client's concerns; 2) client-therapist agreement on the goals of therapy; and 3) client-therapist agreement on the means of therapy or the therapeutic tasks to bring about the desired changes.

It is assumed that the clinician can form a positive relationship and rapport with his or her angry client, but anger is sometimes very hard to listen to. If the clinician doesn't feel comfortable with angry clients generally or with a specific client, it is suggested that he or she explore the issues internally or refer the client. If you can't deal with the discomfort, it's likely that the client will pick up on this dynamic and that therapeutic difficulties and impasses will develop. Building a positive relationship doesn't mean agreeing with, or supporting any or every thing that the client says. To the contrary, the client may report things with which you disagree, and which become the focus of intervention. What is important is that you are able to listen and empathize openly with the angry client, as you would do with any other client.

The client and therapist must also agree on the goals of therapy. With many other clinical problems, this is relatively easy. The client is suffering, and the therapist and client join to lower that suffering. However, this may not be as easy with angry clients. Some angry clients are not in therapy to lower anger—they are there to get some person or some system off their backs. For example, they may be there to get a lighter court sentence or even have therapy serve as an alternative sentence, but may not be really invested in changing their anger response. For example, a person might enter anger management in order to keep a spouse from leaving the relationship, but only be giving lip service to changing anger. For example, the person may acknowledge anger but totally blame others for it. The implicit goal of therapy for these clients is not personal anger reduction, but getting others to change their offending behavior. In all of these examples, the client's goal is not consistent with the goal of teaching anger-management skills. Anger-reduction interventions such as CRCS are based on the client owning, at least to a significant degree, that he or she has a personal problem with anger and wants help with that problem. If the therapist and client are not in common agreement on this goal for therapy, then difficulties and impasses are highly probable and the course of therapy should be modified or terminated and a referral made.

Even when the client and therapist agree that the goal of therapy is anger reduction, it's important that they also agree on the means of achieving that end. For example, if the client wishes to lower anger through medication or prayer, then CRCS may be of little relevance. Thus, it's important that the therapist and client not only agree that anger management is the appropriate goal of therapy, but also that CRCS procedures make general sense to the client as a way of approaching anger reduction.

To summarize, CRCS requires a strong working alliance in which: 1) the client feels understood and treated with respect; 2) the client owns anger as a personal problem and wants to reduce his or her anger as the goal of therapy; and 3) the client and therapist agree that cognitive and relaxation interventions are reasonable ways of approaching such anger reduction.

The Importance of Readiness Assessment

CRCS is an action- or change-oriented intervention. Yet, many angry individuals are not at an action stage of change. They neither own anger as a personal problem nor actively seek to change their anger. They are often at a precontemplative or, at best, contemplative stage of change. However, there is a large body of literature showing that interventions appropriate to one stage of readiness won't work for clients at a different stage. Only interventions and changes appropriate to a client's particular readiness stage will be effective (Prochaska, DiClemente, and Norcross 1992; Prochaska, Norcross, and DiClemente 1995). If frustrating exchanges, therapeutic impasses, and potentially premature terminations are to be minimized, the clinician should assess accurately the stage of readiness and do one of three things—adjust the therapeutic contract and procedures to the client's stage of readiness, refer the case, or terminate.

There are several reasons why clients may not be at an action stage of readiness and, therefore, are poor candidates for CRCS. These are listed below so you can assess these possibilities and rule out CRCS as an appropriate intervention, if necessary:

- Some angry individuals are very out of touch with their anger and how they express it. They don't see anger reduction as relevant, because they simply don't see the problem. They possess little understanding of their anger and until they develop greater self-awareness, they are not really in a position to address anger as a problem.

- Other angry clients may be aware that they're angry but have little sense of the consequences. They can't really see what harm is being done or why others react as they do. They often have difficulty empathizing with the point of view of people around them. Even though they may be somewhat dismayed and confused at the reactions of others, they don't own anger as a problem because they cannot vicariously experience the consequences of their anger for others.

- For some angry individuals, anger and perhaps aggression are fundamental aspects of their conceptions of themselves. Anger seems like a natural, expected experience because it's part of who they are. Such people may have developed an angry, tough persona, and anger is essential to playing this part. In some cases, anger may seem appropriate to a role the person occupies. For example, in being a supervisor, a parent, a teenager, or an athlete, the person may see anger as a central part of executing that part of themselves, even though they may have relatively low anger in other roles. Anger reduction for these individuals creates dissonance as it ostensibly undermines the person's identity. Lowering anger becomes so threatening to some individuals that anger-reduction efforts must be rejected.

- Many of the angry clients who aren't at an action stage of readiness for change are those who totally externalize the sources of their anger, blaming their anger on those sources. They don't experience anger as a personal problem because they see others or outside events as the cause of their anger. They have little or no need for personal anger reduction, because it is the sources of provocation that should change, not them. Such individuals may be referred or brought to therapy because of the impact of their anger on others. They are, however, poor candidates for action-oriented interventions like CRCS because the locus of change is outside of them.

- In some cases, anger may be part of another disorder. These clients may acknowledge anger as a personal problem and seek to reduce it, but anger may be best conceptualized as an element of another disorder (e.g., borderline personality disorder, posttraumatic stress disorder, or major depression) that should be the focus of intervention. However, CRCS may be a relevant intervention at some point in the overall treatment planning for this individual. The place of anger in the larger scope of things should be clarified, and the client's readiness for interventions appropriate for that disorder should be assessed.

- Anger may be embedded in highly violent situations. An individual may experience high levels of problematic anger but may also be highly violent or involved in a highly violent situation. Anger reduction may become a relevant treatment goal at some point in time; the superseding goal is initiating steps to reduce the violence and protect the welfare of those involved. CRCS is not appropriate until violence is under control.

Action-oriented anger interventions are not appropriate to the above kinds of clients. They are not at an action stage of readiness for anger reduction. Interventions, if they are to be successful at all, should be matched to the individual's stage of readiness in an attempt to move them to the next stage of readiness. Although such interventions are beyond the scope of this manual, they often require things such as: 1) enhancing the person's awareness of his or her anger and its impact on others; 2) helping the person assess whether anger is achieving all of the person's short- and long-term goals; 3) increasing dissonance in identity and role structures; and/or 4) increasing the person's range and flexibility of alternative scripts, roles, and identity constructs (Deffenbacher 1995; DiGiuseppe 1995). If these interventions are successful, they may provide the motivation for more action-oriented therapy. CRCS then becomes relevant as the person begins to own anger as a personal problem and seeks to change it.

The Importance of Collaboration

CRCS is based on the client and therapist working together to understand and intervene for anger reduction. Certainly, the therapist will have knowledge about tactics for change that the client will not. However, throughout therapy every attempt is made to forge a collaborative relationship in which client and therapist work jointly toward agreed-upon goals. Even when the therapist introduces interventions unfamiliar to the client (e.g., a self-assessment instrument or relaxation procedures), every effort is made to link these back to the client's issues and to frame them in the client's experience, language, and metaphors. For example, a self-assessment questionnaire might be introduced as a way of helping the client understand his or her anger, or relaxation presented as a way of helping the client calm down—both of which the client had mentioned as goals. Collaboration attempts to foster the working alliance, to minimize reactance to what might be felt as externally imposed tasks, and to facilitate compliance and involvement in therapy.

Relaxation and Cognitive-Change Processes in Anger Reduction

A person can't be both relaxed and angry at the same time. Relaxation directly affects emotional and physiological arousal components of the anger response. As the individual learns how to employ relaxation coping skills when angry, he or she can calm down. Indirectly, a calmer state may increase the probability of anger-lowering cognitive, problem-solving, and behavioral processes. The literature, as will be reviewed shortly, shows solid evidence of the effectiveness of relaxation interventions for anger reduction.

Angry individuals usually have learned a number of cognitive processes that are embedded in the enduring elements of the pre-anger state. These shape primary and secondary appraisals so they see higher levels of threat and anger than are really in the environment. The person responds to this distorted reality with elevated anger and dysfunctional behavior. Cognitive-change procedures address these cognitive processes and seek to replace them with anger-lowering, reality-based, problem-focused thoughts. Cognitive-change procedures, therefore, focus directly on enduring elements of the pre-anger state, primary and secondary appraisal processes, and cognitive elements of the anger response. There is also a reciprocal relationship between cognitive and relaxation interventions—one seems to enhance the other. The literature shows a solid base of empirical evidence supporting cognitive-change interventions for anger reduction and for the combination of cognitive changes and relaxation in CRCS.

The Importance of Practice

Knowing how to relax or how to think differently often is insufficient. Old anger habits are strong, and unless new relaxation and cognitive coping skills are rehearsed, it's unlikely that they'll override old patterns in the face of anger-provoking events. Therefore, CRCS requires clients to practice coping skills while they are angry. Rehearsal within the session is achieved by having the person visualize previous anger-provoking events, experience a significant elevation in state anger, and then practice relaxation and cognitive coping skills to reduce that anger. Over time the anger level of the visualized scenes is increased so the client learns to cope with higher levels of anger. Rehearsal within the session, however, is insufficient. The client must also practice the skills during contracted exposure to angering events and to naturally occurring events wherever they happen. These efforts are recorded in diaries, are reviewed within sessions, to be honed and shaped further for future rehearsal within and between sessions.

Maintenance and Relapse Prevention

Anger reduction is not achieved in ten sessions of therapy with the client never needing to use it again. Anger management is likely to be a lifelong process for at least two reasons. First, life is likely to continue providing old and new sources of aggravation for which cognitive and relaxation coping skills are appropriate. Second, humans are creatures of habit. Unused habits tend to fade and be replaced with older, stronger habits. As a consequence, clients are taught to expect future anger, slips, and setbacks, and to use these opportunities to continue employing what they have learned in therapy. Portions of the last sessions outline specific strategies to prepare the client for inevitable slips and future corrective action (see the section on maintenance and relapse on page 32–33 for specific suggestions).

Research

When the cognitive-relaxation coping skills approach outlined in this protocol was first being developed in the early 1980s, the literature contained few empirical studies of anger reduction. The single best study at that time was Novaco's (1975) pioneering component analysis of stress-inoculation training. A combination of cognitive and relaxation interventions were compared to cognitive and relaxation components alone as well as to an attention control. The combined condition proved to be most effective, but the cognitive component was nearly as effective. Effects for the relaxation condition, however, were much more limited, leading Novaco to the conclusion that the cognitive component was the central effective ingredient in the combined condition and that relaxation was less efficacious than cognitive interventions.

Novaco's findings for the relaxation condition were somewhat perplexing. Relaxation interventions had an established record with other high arousal states such as anxiety. Additionally, a contemporary study from our research group (Cragan and Deffenbacher 1984) had shown two self-managed relaxation interventions—anxiety-management training and relaxation as self-control—not only lowered anxiety and stress, but also lowered anger, as well. So, if relaxation led to lowered anger in anxious/stressed individuals, then why shouldn't it lower anger in angry individuals? In attempting to answer this question, Novaco's relaxation procedures were reviewed carefully. That review suggested that intervention effects for the relaxation intervention may have been compromised by issues of intervention design. For example, few relaxation coping-skills were explicitly trained, rehearsed at home, or applied in vivo. The time frame was very short, making it difficult to learn and apply relaxation. Thus, clients may not have developed a repertoire of relaxation skills and failed to employ them to a sufficient degree to help with anger control.

This led our research group to address these issues in intervention design and see if relaxation effects might be improved. In the first study (Deffenbacher, Demm, and Brandon 1986) anxiety-management training (Suinn 1990; Suinn and Deffenbacher 1988) was adapted to anger. This is a self-managed relaxation intervention with consistent rationales and training methodologies, training and rehearsal of specific relaxation coping skills, and in-session and between-session application of relaxation coping skills. Compared to an untreated control of generally angry individuals, this relaxation coping skills intervention lowered numerous indices of anger, and the effects appeared significantly stronger than those of Novaco's study. Anger-reduction effects were maintained at one year follow-up, suggesting long-term maintenance of anger reduction as well.

These findings led to the question of how the apparently more effective relaxation intervention would compare to a cognitive intervention. A second study (Hazaleus and Deffenbacher 1986) compared the relaxation coping-skills intervention to a cognitive coping-skills intervention and a no-treatment control. The relaxation intervention was again effective compared to the control and equal in effects to the cognitive intervention. This was very different from Novaco's finding of greater effects for the cognitive intervention, and the relaxation intervention thus appeared very promising. Three subsequent studies, one with general anger, (Deffenbacher and Stark 1992) and two with driving anger (Deffenbacher, Huff, Lynch, et al. in press; Deffenbacher, Lynch, Filetti, et al. 1999), have shown the relaxation coping-skills intervention effective for anger reduction. Moreover, other studies with similar relaxation interventions have also reported positive effects for relaxation interventions (Dua and Swinden 1992; Schlichter and Horan 1981). It now appears that relaxation, when conducted with enough time and training, can be effective for anger reduction.

This conclusion raised a new question of efficacy. If relaxation alone was effective, could it interact synergistically with cognitive interventions and lead to increased effectiveness for combined cognitive and relaxation coping skills (CRCS)? The first study investing this question (Deffenbacher, Story, Brandon, et al. 1988) compared the combined CRCS intervention to a cognitive-alone condition and to a no-treatment control. The cognitive condition was effective compared to the control, and anger-reduction effects were maintained at a fifteen-month follow-up, replicating the earlier findings by Hazaleus and Deffenbacher (1986). Similar results were also found by others using slightly different cognitive interventions (Achmon, Granek, Golomb, and Hart 1989; Moon and Eisler 1983; Novaco 1975). Evidence of added effectiveness for the combination of cognitive and relaxation skills, however, was not found. CRCS and the cognitive coping-skills-only condition were equally effective for anger reduction, and anger reduction effects for the two were maintained at one-month and fifteen-month follow-ups. Additionally, three subsequent studies (Deffenbacher and Stark 1992; Deffenbacher, Huff, Lynch, et al. in press; Deffenbacher, Lynch, Filetti, et al. 1999), have shown similar effects in the comparison of CRCS to a relaxation-alone condition—CRCS and relaxation were equally effective. Equal effects for combined cognitive-relaxation and relaxation conditions have also been reported for angry college students (Dua and Swinden 1992) and angry delinquents (Schlichter and Horan 1981).

Other studies from our research group have shown CRCS to be effective in reducing anger (Deffenbacher, Lynch, Oetting, and Kemper 1996; Deffenbacher, McNamara, Stark, and Sabadell 1990a; Deffenbacher, Story, Stark, Hogg, and Brandon 1987; Deffenbacher, Oetting, Huff, Cornell, and Dallager 1996; Deffenbacher, Thwaites, Wallace, and Oetting 1994). Moreover, anger reduction for CRCS was maintained at twelve to fifteen month follow-ups (Deffenbacher 1988; Deffenbacher et al. 1990; Deffenbacher, Oetting, Huff, et al. 1996; Deffenbacher, Oetting, Huff, and Thwaites 1995). Additionally, CRCS was as effective as anger-focused, process-oriented group therapy (Deffenbacher, McNamara, Stark, et al. 1990a), as well as structured and unstructured social/communication-skills programs (Deffenbacher, Stony, Stark, et al. 1987; Deffenbacher, Lynch, Oetting, et al. 1996; Deffenbacher, Oetting, Huff, et al. 1996; Deffenbacher, Thwaites, Wallace, et al. 1994). Other researchers (Dua and Swinden 1992; Gerina and Drummond in press; Novaco 1975) have also reported positive effects for CRCS-like interventions.

Although there is minimal data to suggest that CRCS is significantly more effective than other interventions, there are good empirical and clinical reasons for suggesting that it be considered as a basic intervention of choice for many anger problems. First, it is the most empirically supported anger-reduction intervention to date (Deffenbacher, Oetting, and DiGuiseppe 1999) and has been evaluated with a wide range of angry clients, including generally angry college students, angry drivers, angry police officers, angry delinquents, and angry community samples. Second, long-term follow-up studies support maintenance of anger reduction over periods of twelve to fifteen months. Third, there is evidence that effects generalize to other sources of emotional distress such as anxiety (Deffenbacher and Lynch 1998). Fourth, it appears to readily address an important clinical issue in the literature: the finding that cognitive-only interventions were initially resisted by clients and therapists alike (Deffenbacher, Story, Brandon, et al. 1988; Hazaleus and Deffenbacher 1986). Clients felt they were being told that they and their thinking were wrong and reacted with anger in the first two or three sessions. Therapists reported feeling "verbally beat up." Such initial resistance and reactance might lead to breeches of the therapeutic relationship and premature termination in some settings. However, no such problems were reported when cognitive interventions were preceded by two sessions of relaxation in CRCS. The final reason CRCS might be considered the treatment of choice is that it can address anger that is outside an interpersonal context. While 75 to 80 percent of anger happens in an interpersonal context (Averill 1983; Deffenbacher, Oetting, Thwaites, et al. 1996), suggesting that social communication and conflict-management skills would be most appropriate, 20 to 25 percent of anger doesn't occur in connection with other people. CRCS is applicable to both interpersonal and noninterpersonal sources of anger, whereas social-skills interventions are limited to interpersonal sources of anger. In summary, CRCS is strongly supported in the literature, is flexible for a wide range of anger triggers, and appears to lower initial resistance to therapy. It is therefore recommended as a base intervention for both situational and general anger problems, or conditions in which anger management is a significant element of the overall clinical picture.

Duration of Treatment

CRCS typically takes place in one-hour outpatient sessions, once a week for nine to twelve weeks. Depending on the nature of the client's anger problems, the anger consequences, and the involvement of others in the course of treatment (e.g., courts, employers, schools, etc.), assessment will typically take from one to three sessions. Cognitive and relaxation coping skills training typically takes seven to nine sessions after the assessment. The first two intervention sessions are focused on progressive relaxation training and the development of basic relaxation coping skills (e.g., relaxation without tension, breathing-cued relaxation, cue-controlled relaxation, and relaxation imagery). The next session typically introduces cognitive restructuring, brief rehearsal of relaxation, and the first in-session application of cognitive and relaxation coping skills for anger reduction. Subsequent sessions begin with a brief review of homework, twenty to thirty minutes of cognitive restructuring relative to the sources of provocation for that session, twenty to thirty minutes of cognitive and relaxation coping skill rehearsal involving anger-engendering imagery, and a few minutes to review the session and negotiate homework assignments. The interval between the last sessions may be lengthened in order to provide more time to practice and consolidate skills. Occasional follow-up sessions may be needed to troubleshoot issues and deal with maintenance and relapse prevention. Such sessions are not necessary in many cases, but occur frequently enough that you should be prepared for them and mention the possibility while addressing maintenance and relapse prevention.

The duration of therapy may also be extended if, after successful anger management through CRCS, additional skill deficits (e.g., low assertiveness, minimal reciprocal communication skills, or poor parenting skills) or other issues remain. Moreover, if CRCS is being employed as part of a more extensive treatment plan, then the length of therapy will be dictated by the nature of the overarching treatment plan. Nonetheless, basic elements of CRCS should be deliverable in no more than twelve sessions, either as a stand-alone intervention or as part of a more comprehensive treatment plan.

The course of CRCS will vary somewhat from client to client, but potential application with the five anger disorders touched on previously (adjustment disorder with angry mood, etc.) will be briefly described to provide you with some general ways of thinking about the course of CRCS with each type of anger problem.

Adjustment Disorder with Anger

The clinician working with an adjustment disorder with anger will want to begin with an emotionally focused interview in which the nature of the stresses and the reactions are explored. In many cases, the clinician will want to support a degree of anger to the extent that the client has been treated unfairly, unjustly, or inappropriately. As with all angry clients, the clinician will want to empathize with and clarify those angry feelings and reactions. These activities alone will often help clients suffering from adjustment disorders achieve some benefit and emotional resolution. However, the principles and interventions described in this protocol would be an appropriate addition if anger control was identified as an important treatment goal. Typical procedures of CRCS may be appropriate, but the therapist might also use several of the strategies in a less formal way to address issues related to coping with the stressor (e.g., briefer versions of applied relaxation or cognitive restructuring in exploring the individual's reaction to the stressor). Procedures may not be extended as fully as they are described in later sessions. That is, the nature of anger reactions in adjustment disorder with anger may not be as deeply established or need as much rehearsal as in some other cases involving anger.

Situational Anger Disorders

CRCS is highly appropriate for situational anger disorders without aggression (e.g., Deffenbacher, Huff, Lynch, et al. in press; Deffenbacher, Lynch, Filetti, et al. 1999). Cognitive and relaxation coping skills are targeted to the elevated anger in specific contexts, and anger scenes employed within the sessions can be developed around the situational anger theme (e.g., driving, arguing with a spouse about money, or dealing with performance appraisals at work). If situational themes can be role played or otherwise enacted within the session, some rehearsal of cognitive and relaxation skills may take place during these role playing activities. Rehearsal using anger-arousing imagery may therefore get less emphasis. Contracted assignments can be developed in which the client agrees to apply coping skills in real life situations similar to those rehearsed within the session. If skill deficits or dysfunctional means of anger expression need clinical attention, these issues can be addressed when the anger has been lowered by CRCS. For example, the person might benefit from assertive communication skills (e.g., Deffenbacher, Story, Stark, et al. 1987; Deffenbacher, Oetting, Huff et al. 1996). Moreover, the experience with rehearsing cognitive and relaxation skills often provides a good model for training new behavioral skills (e.g., covert rehearsal of behavior in response to anger-arousing imagery and homework to transfer to real life environments).

CRCS may also be valuable for clients with situational anger reactions that include aggressive behavior. Anger-management strategies are targeted to the specific situational contexts in which anger is aroused and aggression is expressed. These anger-reduction efforts should either precede or run concurrent with interventions to change the aggressive styles of anger expression. Often as the individual is able to lower anger through CRCS, he or she will be able to access other coping or problem-solving skills. That is, many people have coping skills appropriate to a situation, but these competencies go unused because anger disrupts their access and prompts aggressive behavior. When clients can lower their anger, they are able to access these skills and begin to deploy them. However, skills deficits still may be present despite CRCS interventions. Such issues should be addressed, but progress may be easier because successful anger reduction permits the client to develop, practice, and implement new skills and strategies. Once trained, these skills can be integrated with cognitive and relaxation coping skills (i.e., relax, rethink the situation, and deploy more appropriate behavior).

Generalized Anger Disorders

CRCS is appropriate for individuals with generalized anger problems, but the focus may need to be shifted. Since the anger reactions are not situational, training should emphasize a number of heterogeneous situations. That is, anger-engendering imagery employed within sessions should represent a wide range of provocations. This should maximize transfer to real life conditions and decrease the probability of relapse. The application of cognitive and relaxation skills to internal states and conditions (e.g., anxious or hurt feelings, general negative mood, physical pain of a tension headache, or ruminating about prior mistreatment) may take on even greater relevance with these types of clients. Since the anger is so pervasively experienced, external cues alone won't be sufficient to trigger the application of cognitive and relaxation coping skills. Attention to the internal states that trigger anger may be even more important for these individuals. For these reasons, it sometimes takes a few more sessions to work with the generalized anger disordered individual, and additional sessions to address maintenance and relapse may also be necessary.

Employment of CRCS for individuals with generalized anger disorder with aggression would follow the general guidelines for generalized anger disorder without aggression. However, as the individual is able to lower his or her anger, then residual aggressive behavior should also be addressed. It is suggested that the cognitive and relaxation coping skills training precede other interventions. This will lower anger and may lead to the relatively natural access and utilization of previously unused skills.

Patient Self-Rating Scales

Three self-report questionnaires are frequently used in CRCS—the State-Trait Anger Expression Inventory (STAXI) (Spielberger 1988, 1999), the Anger Situation, and the Anger Symptom (Deffenbacher, Demm, and Brandon 1986). These may be supplemented by other self-report measures as the clinician deems appropriate (see appendix 1 for a brief review and examples of other scales).

The most recent version of the STAXI contains fifty-seven items on the front and back of a single page and is accessible at relatively low cost from Psychological Assessment Resources, Inc. The STAXI provides three different types of information on anger.

1. The ten-item Trait Anger Scale (items 16-25) provides a general index of the individual's propensity to become angry across a wide range of situations and, therefore, is a quick, reliable index of general anger. The Trait Anger Scale may not adequately assess anger in specific situational contexts (e.g., anger while driving or anger in discussions with spouse), but does provide a quick general screen of general anger or the tendency to experience anger a good deal of the time and across many different situations. Elevations suggest the kind of anger described earlier in the introduction for generalized anger disorders with and without aggression.

2. The fifteen-item State Anger Scale (items 1-15) measures how angry one is and how one feels like reacting to that anger at a specific moment in time. Five items measure angry feelings (e.g., feeling angry), another five the urge to respond with verbal aggression (e.g., feeling like yelling), and a final five the urge to respond with physical aggression (e.g., feeling like hitting someone). The latter two subscales measure state tendencies toward verbal and physical aggression, whereas the former assesses angry feelings of the moment. If the State Anger Scale is elevated, it suggests that the individual was angry at the time the scale was administered. The clinician may wish to follow up on this and inquire what was angering the person at the time and why. The clinician may also have the client complete the State Anger Scale every time a certain situation is encountered or at the same time of day for several days in a row. If the scale is consistently elevated, this suggests anger at those times or in those situations. It can be usefully employed to assess one's feelings and reaction tendencies in response to role plays, simulations, and visualizations. Depending on how and when it is administered (e.g., in the clinician's office after a positive first session), the State Anger Scale may not be elevated. The clinician should not take this as an indication that there are no anger problems, but only that the client was not experiencing anger at the time the scale was completed.

3. The thirty-two-item Anger Expression Inventory (items 26-57) provides four eight-item indices of reported tendencies to express anger through: 1) suppressing anger and harboring grudges (e.g., keeping things in when angry), 2) outward, negative expression (e.g., striking out at whatever infuriates the person), 3) instrumental efforts to control and reduce anger (e.g., being pa-

tient with others), and 4) emotion-focused efforts to control anger (e.g., trying to relax). Many generally angry clients paradoxically indicate that they use all four forms of anger reaction fairly frequently. The clinician may wonder how they can use such different forms of anger reaction and the answer seems to lie in the frequency with which they become angry. Since they often become angry many times a day, they have the opportunity to experience many different forms of anger reaction. They suppress on some occasions, blow up on others, and control their anger on still others. The clinician can ask what makes the difference regarding which anger reaction strategy is chosen and perhaps identify situations that are related to specific forms of reaction and assist the person in identifying strengths and resources that are not applied in some situations.

The Anger Situation measure (Deffenbacher, Demm, and Brandon, 1986) was designed to address situational anger and aspects of anger specific to the individual. It has the person identify the most problematic, ongoing source of anger in his or her life (see copy at end of session 1). It asks the individual to describe, in detail, the ongoing situation that creates the greatest feelings of anger for them. By doing so, it attempts to be a sensitive person-specific instrument assessing the unique provocations in the person's life. After describing the situation, the person rates the intensity of his or her anger on a 0-100 scale. The Anger Situation may also include ratings of the frequency, duration, and life interference of the anger. The last rating involving interference is a general consequence index, but in going over the Anger Situation, the clinician can inquire about specific types of consequences that occur in this situation and note them on the questionnaire. If the clinician desires a second assessment of the anger in the individual's life, he or she can have the client repeat the Anger Situation again, but describing his or her second most angering, ongoing situation.

The Anger Symptom is an analogous measure (see copy at end of session 1), but inquires about physiological reactivity. It asks the person to identify the physiological symptom of anger experienced most frequently. Once described, the person rates the severity of the symptom on a 0-100 scale. The Anger Symptom index may also include ratings of frequency, duration, and interference. A second Anger Symptom may also be assessed, providing additional data on anger-related physiological reactivity.

Specific Goals of Treatment and Limitations

Over the course of CRCS, the client should achieve the following goals: 1) become more aware of the situations triggering anger, of the appraisals of those situations, of the emotional, physical, cognitive, and behavioral responses to those situations, and of the consequences; 2) develop one or more effective relaxation coping skills and be able to deploy relaxation to calm down when becoming angry or encountering angering situations; 3) develop a series of anger-lowering cognitive strategies and employ them to reduce anger when encountering provocations; 4) receive sufficient practice within and between sessions to become reasonably confident in the cognitive and relaxation skills; 5) rehearse for future problems so there are sound strategies to handle them. The client should also know how to access the therapist for future support, consultation, and/or remedial sessions should these prove necessary.

CRCS often leads to improved behavioral functioning. When the person is less angry, he or she is able to think things through in a more calm, reflective manner and to access other behavioral coping resources associated with calmer states (Berkowitz 1994). If behavioral expressive problems still exist, CRCS should make addressing these issues easier.

As noted earlier, not every individual is a good candidate for CRCS. Many clients are not at an action-oriented stage of readiness, do not conceptualize anger reduction as relevant to them, do not value the goals or means of CRCS, and/or display anger that is embedded in other psychological problems or in highly toxic or violent situations requiring other interventions (see earlier sections for description and discussion of problems which would suggest that clients be excluded from CRCS).

Agenda Setting

Any empirically supported protocol poses a potential conflict between two important therapeutic elements. On the one hand, the clinician wants to be sensitive and responsive to the individual needs and characteristics of the client. On the other hand, the protocol has an inherent structure, time line, and set of procedures. The client is likely to benefit significantly if the general scope and parameters of the intervention are followed. This can set up a kind of dynamic tension for the clinician, one of paying attention to the client and at the same time paying attention to the protocol

Persons' (1989) book, *Cognitive Therapy in Practice: A Case Formulation Approach*, provides some good suggestions for addressing this issue, but it is the stance of the authors of this protocol that the tension between attending to the client and to the therapeutic tasks is good. The therapist should pay close attention to both individual client needs and the structured tasks described in the protocol. If there are truly important issues and intercurrent life events (e.g., a serious act of aggression, a job termination, a divorce, etc.) that need attention and outweigh following the protocol, then, of course, they deserve focus. However, under most circumstances, the therapist should collaborate with the client to stay on track and follow the protocol.

One of the best ways of achieving this is to use the first five or ten minutes to review intercurrent life events and homework from the prior session. Then outline the agenda and activities of the current session in light of the homework and recent experience. This provides a good place for the interface of the individual's experience and the protocol. Keeping track of the client's experience leads to a flexible implementation of the protocol. At the same time, the protocol provides the general structure to promote change. It is the canvas upon which to paint the details of the session. In these endeavors, the clinician should listen carefully to the client but resist the temptation to be sidetracked into general discussions and particularly into blaming and "yes but" types of discussion. When these are encountered, the therapist should gently but firmly redirect the focus back to the tasks of the session, toward an action response to the problematic situation. In summary, clarification of experience since the last session and linking it to the protocol by clear agenda setting are very powerful tools for keeping the client and clinician on the tasks at hand.

Homework

Assignments between sessions are vitally important in CRCS. Homework provides critical information for assessment, whether this is for establishing an understanding of the presenting problems or the effectiveness of intervention. Additionally, homework plays a crucial role in transferring change from the session to real life. Training within the session provides initial experience in anger reduction, but it's the real life application that tell the client and clinician whether the interventions are working.

As much as possible, homework assignments should follow the following general guidelines.

- Make every attempt to establish the assignments collaboratively. Ask the client how he or she thinks a certain kind of task can be achieved. Follow up on client suggestions and shape them into an achievable homework assignment.

- Take the time to clarify and check the client's understanding of the homework. Ask the client what his or her understanding is of the homework assignment. One of the most common reasons for failure of assignments is because they were not clear and concrete, and the client didn't understand specifically what had to be done.

- Use written aids or other supports to concretize the assignment. Write it down. You could even send it via e-mail to the client. Also, consider having the client post reminders of assignments where they are easily visible to prompt attention to follow-through. Whatever the methodology, if possible, provide prompts for the client to do and use the homework.

- Make reference to the homework. A common mistake is to have the client complete homework and then fail to refer back to it. This undermines the value of the specific assignment, but also may undermine the general value of homework. The client may pick up the countertherapeutic message that homework is not important and, therefore, need not be done. Whenever possible, the client should drop the assignment off the day before so the clinician can review it prior to the session. Then, early in the next session the therapist should make reference to the homework and to observations taken from it. This not only provides for an efficient use of session time, but also underscores the larger message of the value of homework (i.e., the client is to do his or her homework, and so will the therapist).

- Consider activity contingent rather than purely time-contingent scheduling. Therapists usually schedule sessions based on a specific time interval, whether or not the client has completed the assignment. An alternative is making the next session contingent upon a certain number of opportunities to practice the anger-management strategies. For example, the client might contract to employ anger-management skills four times in dealing with a spouse or adolescent offspring. After completing the fourth time, he or she would call and make an appointment.

This protocol has handouts in each session which you can duplicate and give to clients as homework guides or worksheets. A client manual has also been published to be used with this protocol (same title and authors) containing all necessary didactic and homework materials. If you prefer, or if the client manual isn't available, there are several trade workbooks that clients may purchase in bookstores that can provide supplemental material (McKay and Rogers, 2000; McKay, Rogers, and McKay 1989). There is also a trade book available offering a cognitive behavioral self-help program for angry parents (McKay, Fanning, Paleg, and Landis 1996).

Concurrent Pharmacological Treatment

Some pharmacological trials have suggested that certain serotonin reuptake inhibitors are effective with some angry individuals. Beta-blockers and some of the newer anticonvulsant drugs, too, have shown a degree of promise. The therapist can work with a psychiatrist who can help evaluate the emerging literature and who will work closely with the therapist in evaluating, monitoring, and prescribing if pharmacotherapy seems warranted.

Common Problems

As with any therapeutic enterprise, problems can develop in the implementation of CRCS. Six of the more common are listed below along with suggestions for addressing them.

- A fairly common issue in initial relaxation training is whether to use relaxation tapes or not. Often, clients will report that they can relax better in response to the therapist's voice and instruction than on their own. This would suggest that taping the session and having the client use the tape would be beneficial. While potentially helpful, this can also create a problem. The underlying model is one of self-management (i.e., the client learns to pay attention to the triggers and experience of anger and to apply relaxation when anger-arousing conditions are encountered). It follows that clients should learn to relax to their own self-instruction, not the therapist's. Clients may have trouble weaning themselves off the external instruction and developing effective internal cueing of relaxation. Therefore, it's preferable that relaxation tapes not be used, but that the clinician have a detailed written handout (such as the one provided at the end of session 2) that tells the client how to engage in home practice of relaxation. Homework is then aimed only at self-directed relaxation practice. If the client insists on a tape, then the clinician should help the client develop his or her own taped instructions.

- A second problem with relaxation is the failure to practice relaxation sufficiently at home. One reason for this is that the client expects to practice relaxation only when angry or stressed. Then, when this is the case, only minimal practice occurs, because he or she may never have felt sufficiently upset. This problem can be addressed by a review of why it's important to practice relaxation five days a week. A second reason for failure to practice relaxation is not allocating enough time to it. Clients often report that they were too busy or that other things got in the way of practicing. Reviewing the reasons for relaxation practice and developing plans to circumvent the previously identified problems of commitment may be sufficient. However, it may also be helpful to make scheduling of sessions activity contingent, rather than time contingent. That is, the next session is scheduled when the client has practiced relaxation for a given number of practice sessions.

- Other homework assignments may not receive attention and follow-through, even though they are important to success. The first suggestion is that the clinician look at how homework assignments are being developed. If they have the tone of mandated assignments rather than collaboratively developed extensions of what is going on in therapy, then it's suggested that the therapist work to strengthen the spirit of collaboration. This, however, may not be the source of the problem. In that case, the clinician and client should openly discuss the nature of the noncompliance and develop specific plans to overcome it.

- Many clients find it easy to externalize, blame, and not take responsibility for their part in anger mismanagement. In this case, the therapist should gently but firmly refocus the discussion back on what the *client* can do to change an anger response. Clients will often get frustrated, because they feel that the therapist doesn't understand how they've been victimized. The clinician should listen empathetically and communicate an understanding of the client's perspective, but nonetheless refocus upon what the client can do. Sometimes, the distinction between the elegant and practical solution can be helpful in making this shift. The elegant solution is that others would do things the way that the client wants and anger would never again be provoked. However, the practical solution accepts that the client may not get what he or she wants, but can do a great deal about how to respond and cope with the situation. The practical solution is often the only one available to the client and is the one upon which the therapist refocuses therapy.

- Another common trap, especially in the cognitive therapy portions of CRCS, is when the client maneuvers the clinician into trying to disprove the client's position. The client may attempt to state things as if they are givens and essentially invite the therapist to disprove that claim. At best, this is a very difficult task; at worst, it shifts the focus from the client onto frustrating, fruitless discussions in which the client almost always can find an exception to the clinician's logic and provide a "yes, but." To meet this problem, the clinician can work to keep the focus on the client having to prove his or her points, not on the therapist having to disprove them. For example, the clinician might respond to a demand that things be a certain way by saying, "I understand why that is frustrating, but why shouldn't you have to live with frustration like that?"

- Another common issue in the cognitive portions of CRCS is the tendency for a client to want the therapist to agree with his or her shoulds or demands. As the clinician explores these via Socratic questions and other strategies, the client may accuse the therapist of lacking a sense of values. This should be addressed head on. The therapist should indicate quite clearly that he or she believes in the importance of values and valued things and that it is healthy to want them, care about them, invest time, money, and energy in pursuing them. What is being questioned is the tendency to elevate these to absolute rules by which the client or others must live, and then to become enraged when they are not met. Wanting things is perfectly healthy. Frustration, disappointment, and other mild to moderate negative emotions are quite natural outcomes of not getting what one wants. What is unhealthy is the high level of anger and dysfunctional behavior associated with demanding that one get what one wants.

Closure and Follow-up

Termination of treatment should be performance based. The client is ready to terminate when he or she can manage anger reasonably well. This decision should be made collaboratively by the client and the therapist, based on anger control efforts within and especially between sessions. As noted earlier, the length of time between some of the latter sessions may be lengthened in order to provide sufficient time to practice, consolidate, and ensure quality application of skills in vivo. Thus, quality homework records and self-reports from the client, and, in some cases, reports from others provide the information for making this collaborative decision.

Maintenance and relapse prevention are addressed in the latter sessions of CRCS. Although no single client is likely to need all of the following, interventions such as these improve the likelihood of maintenance over time.

- Clients should be alerted to the likelihood of relapse and any problems in maintaining anger control. This should be openly discussed and normalized as part of ongoing anger management. You might make an analogy to weight loss. Losing the weight of anger is hard work, but when a person has increased exercise (cognitive and relaxation coping skills) and lowered calorie intake (cognitive interpretations which fuel anger), they can reduce this "weight." However, even when anger is generally lower, only half the battle is won. One still has to work at keeping the weight of anger off. A person is likely to overeat on occasion, by analogy becoming overly angry. But any given slip in diet or exercise isn't likely to be all that critical. What is critical is understandnig what went wrong and recommitting to dietary and exercise activities (skills learned in therapy) which maintain weight loss (lower anger). Thus, like the client who has lost weight, the clinician and the client should plan for slips and relapses and for how the client can refocus again on anger management.

- Having the client simulate relapse and practice the coping strategies can be very useful in consolidating relapse plans and increasing the client's self-efficacy in implementing those plans. For example, the client might contract with a spouse to become overly angry on purpose and then initiate coping skills for relapse recovery. Also, difficulties in the latter stages of therapy can be used as examples of relapse, and the therapist and client can discuss them as examples of what would need to be done. They, too, might be rehearsed in imagery or role playing as examples of coping with a relapse.

- The client should plan for continued self-monitoring and anger management efforts and to schedule specific times for self-review and maintenance planning. Once a week is good in the beginning, with an increase in the time frame as time and success go on. However, most clients find that a self-review of coping efforts at least once per month is useful in keeping the focus on ongoing anger reduction. It's also important for the client to consider self-reinforcement of these activities to continue such behaviors. That is, the client can find a way to connect self-review to an event or experience that they find rewarding.

- As noted previously, the time interval between the last sessions can be lengthened in order to provide more opportunities for coping and for potential relapse to be reviewed and addressed. This principle can be built into scheduled booster sessions. For example, a session might be scheduled at one-month intervals for the first two months after termination with an additional follow-up session in six months.

- The clinician and client can develop a variety of ways that the client can have continued but minimal contact with the therapist in order to report on ongoing coping and relapse efforts. For example, specific behavioral contracts for maintenance and relapse might be developed and signed by both parties. The client might call in for a brief phone interview every two weeks, during which coping and relapse efforts would be discussed and revised. The client might mail in his or her self-monitoring logs with brief written or phone feedback from the clinician.

Whatever the format, all of these interventions have two things in common. They create an expectation for ongoing anger-reduction efforts, and they provide clients with the opportunity to keep focusing on anger management. Many clients report that just knowing they are going to communicate again with the therapist serves a valuable function of keeping their attention on sustained anger coping. Although they aren't always needed, some clients may require a few additional sessions to refresh anger-reduction skills. The therapist should take care to indicate that this is not expected, but that it is perfectly normal and acceptable to do so if the need arises.

Dealing with Managed Care

The current era of managed care can pose restrictions on any psychotherapeutic care. These issues should be discussed openly, and the client and clinician should investigate the nature and scope of coverage very early, perhaps even prior to the initial session. This information should be openly discussed and contracted.

Anger-management counseling may pose particular problems for insurance and managed care. First, as noted previously, there are no DSM-IV diagnoses that are likely to capture the nature and scope of the client's anger problems. This poses a practical and ethical problem for the clinician. How can he or she adequately describe and diagnose the client's problems and communicate this to managed-care reviewers? This is further compounded by the fact that there are few, if any, established guidelines for the treatment of anger. Moreover, depending on the nature and context of the individual's anger (e.g., marital conflict or anger as part of a personality disorder), managed-care guidelines may be even more exclusionary. A final potential issue is the extent and nature of other people's involvement in the client's care. For example, if a court, school system, or employer is involved, how will the clinician's time for reports, phone contacts, etc., to such systems be compensated. It is nearly always a good suggestion that the clinician clarify and address these issues forthrightly and early. The nature and extent of client coverage should be explored early to prevent problems and misunderstandings later.

Initial Contact, Assessment, and Treatment Planning

The assessment phase includes many different tasks and decisions, and achieving its goals sometimes takes more than a single, one-hour session. During the initial assessment phase, the clinician should attempt to address the following tasks: 1) build a positive working alliance rich in respect, rapport, and empathy; 2) clarify the client's goals for therapy; 3) conduct a thorough assessment of anger; 4) assess collateral issues such as the potential for violence and suicide, comorbid problems, psychiatric history, and readiness for action-oriented interventions; 5) make a decision with the client about the nature of treatment, and provide a treatment rationale for CRCS if it is selected; and 6) clarify other issues such as insurance coverage and what people or systems (such as schools, employers, and courts) may have a stake in the client's treatment.

Building a Positive Working Alliance

A positive working alliance has three elements: 1) a relationship rich in empathy, respect, and warmth; 2) mutual agreement upon the goals of therapy; and 3) mutual agreement on the means or approach to therapy. Hopefully by this session's end the clinician and client have reached a general agreement on the goals and means of therapy. However, the first goal is to develop a positive relationship. The clinician should listen openly and with empathy, communicating warmth, acceptance, and respect for the angry individual and his or her perceptions, interpretations, and concerns. The clinician should communicate an understanding of the client's perspective and sense of being harmed, wronged, or treated unjustly (DiGiuseppe 1995). The therapist need not agree with the client's perspective (e.g., yelling and cursing at a child for misbehavior or threatening to punch a supervisor because of a negative comment), but should listen carefully and openly, communicating an understanding of the client's pain. Joining the person to appreciate their feelings of enormous hurt, loss, or helplessness builds a positive working alliance because you're letting the client know that their pain and distress matter to you. In this type of empathic relationship the client is likely to feel respected and cared about and to be more open and willing to explore issues.

Clients with anger problems may bring three characteristics to the interview that may make it difficult for the clinician to respond positively. First, angry clients are often very sensitive to being blamed. Rightly or wrongly, they often feel like they're being told that everything is their fault. They are usually very tired of it, vulnerable to perceiving themselves as being blamed, accused, or criticized, and often react defensively. So when you inquire about anger and its context, some angry clients may feel attacked and misunderstood. You should clarify and empathize with their sense of being accused and blamed, but suggest that what you're trying to do is to understand what the client is feeling and what is going on at the time he or she is angry. It's best not to spend too much time clarifying what you're attempting to do, but get back to clarifying the content with empathy and communicated understanding.

The second difficulty with angry clients is that they may react with anger in the session, or they may talk about things that put you off or make you anxious (e.g., child or spouse/partner abuse). If a therapist is anxious or put off, he or she may avoid these topics. Clients with anger problems are likely to be sensitive to a therapist's negative reactions and avoid with the therapist, minimize problems, and/or use it to manipulate. Whatever the response, they will likely disrespect and minimize the therapist, and important issues are not likely to be addressed. You should explore your own issues (countertransference) so they don't interfere with your listening to and exploring the client's world. A special case of this is when the clinician finds him or herself being judgmental. Certainly, you are free to hold values and preferences in life, but when you find it necessary to judge the client and label the person as opposed to behavior, this is a key sign of trouble in the client/therapist relationship. The client is very likely to pick up on the implicit or explicit labeling, to feel discounted and disrespected, and either withdraw or become angry and counterattack in some way.

The third problem with angry clients is that they often bring some of their interpersonal style to the interview. They may express themselves in ways that grate on the clinician (e.g., loud, intimidating, abrasive manner or indirect, sarcastic, passive-aggressive ways). That is, the client may deal with the clinician in the same way he or she does with the rest of the world. It's important for the clinician not to be put off by these characteristics and distance him or herself from the client. You need not like the characteristics and may need to set limits at some point, but early in the therapeutic relationship it's important to try to genuinely like and respect the angry person, even if some of their behavior is frustrating. It may also be helpful to view some of the angry individual's characteristics as assests or strengths that can be turned around and used positively in therapy. For example, a client's direct, confrontational approach to external problems can often be refocused on his or her own anger and the problems it creates, as in the exchange below.

Therapist:	(Referring to angry interaction between a client and his supervisor at work) So, you walked right up to him and asked him just what the hell he thought he was doing?
Client:	Yeah. I don't take crap from anybody.
Therapist:	What do you think would happen if you used the same approach on yourself? I mean walk right up to yourself and ask yourself what the hell you thought you were doing responding that way.
Client:	Huh? What are you talking about?
Therapist:	Well, in some ways you can respond to yourself like you do to others. One of your strengths is in being able to directly approach things, taking them head on. You can go right up to yourself and ask yourself if you're giving yourself crap and ask yourself if you are making sense. You can talk to yourself like you talk to others and see if you make sense to yourself.
Client:	Never thought about it like that. I never really take myself on like I do other people, even if I am giving myself crap.
Therapist:	Want to try doing it right now?
Client:	How?
Therapist:	Why don't you take the situation where you blew up at your supervisor last week. You know, the time when you thought he was putting you down when you and the other guys were loading the trucks—the one where you yelled at him. I want you to think about it out loud, but this time I want you to walk right up to yourself and ask yourself if you're making any sense. Okay?
Client:	Okay. So Jim, what the hell is going on here? Sure, Chuck is being a pain in the butt, but what's the big deal? You're being a bigger jerk than he is. Yelling at him sure as hell isn't going to help. Like that's going to make him like you. He's just going to get pissed and write you up for being a smart ass. Get your head together and help the guys get the trucks loaded. Talk to Chuck later if you need to, but this stuff has to get on the truck and get shipped or the management is going to land on all of us. (Pause) You know I never thought about it like that before. I just go off and get right in people faces, but never get in my own face to see if I make any sense.
Therapist:	It may be useful for you to do that, you know. Get right in your own face and make sure that you're not giving yourself crap and that you're making sense in how you handle the situation. Your direct approach can be a real asset in dealing with your anger.

In summary, some angry clients are not the easiest people to work with. Some of their characteristics can be frustrating and difficult for the therapist. However, it's important for the clinician to like and respect the individual, to try to understand the client's perspective and actively and empathetically communicate an understanding and appreciation of that perspective. It's important for you not to take elements of the client's behavior personally or react defensively or avoidantly. See the individual as a person struggling with life, albeit in an angry, self-defeating way at times, and look for assets as well as liabilities.

Client Goals

Agreement on the goals of therapy is a second critical element of a successful therapeutic experience. CRCS is focused upon working with the client to reduce his or her anger. This requires a client who owns anger as a personal problem and wants to reduce it. However, not all angry clients own their problems; it's important to understand clearly the client's goals and see if a person-focused anger-reduction program fits with the outcomes they want. Otherwise, the lack of congruence between the client's goals and the actual interventions is likely to lead to therapeutic problems and impasses.

Sometimes goal setting happens early in the session when the client is describing why he or she is there and sets the tone for assessment activities. However, at other times, goal setting may happen more toward the end of the session after much assessment of the nature and experience of anger. Also, goals sometimes grow directly out of initial inquiries about anger issues and what can be done about them. In this case, goals can often be clarified by simple summaries and perception checking. For example, "So, you and your doctor suspect that all the anger you've felt since your divorce and your tendency to brood about it have contributed to your very high blood pressure. Both of you are concerned about the effects of the anger on your blood pressure, and you're here to see if you can learn some ways to lower it. Is that about right?" In other cases, goals may not be so clear, and the clinician should follow up with direct requests for therapy goals. Sample inquiries are provided below.

- "You say that you would like to be less hassled and angry. But, if counseling were successful, what specifically would you like to feel or do differently?"

- "Of the different aspects of your life that we've been discussing, what are the top two or three things that you want to focus on in therapy?"

- "I think I'm getting a sense of what you want to work on in therapy, but I'd like to make sure. Would you please list the goals you have for therapy and be as specific as you can?"

- "You've been describing a number of different problems over the last hour. I was wondering what priorities you have among them. That is, if our therapy worked out the way you would like, what would you like to have achieved?"

- "Therapy is like taking a trip. It goes better if you have a good map and know where you're going. I would appreciate it if you would put in your own words exactly where you would like to go in therapy. Draw out a kind of map for me of where you would like to go, what you'd like to get done."

- "People tend to reach their goals better if they know what they are and can specify them clearly. As best you can, would you please outline your goals for therapy?"

Specific, concrete, personal goals tend to facilitate therapeutic change. Three examples are listed below.

- "I would like to keep my anger under a 3 or 4 on a 10-point scale when I'm driving. No matter what is happening on the road, I want to keep it at that level or under."

- "I want to stay calm and not talk much outside my normal tone when speaking with my son, even if I think he's unreasonable."

- "I want four things from counseling. First, I want to stay calm and focused in talking with my wife, especially about money and the kids. Second, even when I'm frustrated, I want to be able to listen to what she has to say without interrupting and cutting her off. Third, I want some ways I can ask her to listen to my point of view if I feel like she's not listening. Fourth, if I start to get pissed, I want to be able to walk away and get my head together instead of starting to put her down and call her names."

When goals are concrete and in the first person, they help structure therapy. There tends to be more client-therapist agreement on the therapeutic tasks. But client goals are rarely specific and clear, especially in the first session. Even when they're personal, they may be much more general and on the order of "get a handle on my anger," "not be so pissed off all the time," or "be less angry." The therapist and client should endeavor over time to become more precise in the meaning of such statements (e.g., contexts in which anger occurs, which elements of anger are most salient and in need of attention, and what kinds of skills seem most applicable).

Clients with broad, general goals can still be treated with CRCS. First, anger may in fact be fairly generalized, and the general goal may capture the situation well. Second, enhanced awareness of the situational, experiential, and consequential aspects of anger often emerge over the initial sessions of CRCS. The goals or treatment targets of cognitive and relaxation coping skills may become more clear over time. If initial goals are general, then it's best if the initial treatment contract be focused on increasing clarity of therapeutic goals and devloping a better understanding of anger, and be a bit more tentative in nature (i.e., the therapist and client will try out several things and see if they help the client reduce anger).

It's also important that goals be personally focused and framed in personal terms. That is, they should not only be what the person wants to achieve, but also what he or she can reasonably do and what he or she is motivated to attain. This is another aspect of the therapeutic alliance that takes on additional importance for those dealing with angry clients. Individuals often externalize anger and blame their anger and responses on others. The implicit means of therapy lies in changing external sources of provocation, not on changing something about the individual.

However, CRCS is an individually focused intervention. It provides clients new anger-management skills. Deployment of those skills may free resources to deal differently with and negotiate change in the external environment, but it achieves this through individual anger reduction, not through a direct alteration of the environment and/or the behavior of others. Thus, it's very important to clarify the individual's goals and make sure that the goal is for *personal* change before CRCS is introduced.

Sometimes it is clear from the beginning that the individual seeks to change his or her anger. For example, one client stated as follows: "I'm so tired of being angry all the time. I don't care what others do. I want to be free of that kind of tension." In other cases, it's not nearly so clear. For example, a client may talk about being angry, but attribute most of it to others. In such cases, it's not clear whether the focus of intervention should be on them or others. As part of goal setting, you should clarify and specify this issue (see examples below). If this isn't done, the client and therapist may not agree on the means of therapy and may find themselves working at cross-purposes, with the client wanting the clinician to help him/her to change others and the therapist focusing on individual change.

As an example, consider Bill, a single parent who was yelling at his eleven-year-old son, Dan, when Dan didn't do his chores or follow through on verbal agreements with his dad.

Therapist: Bill, you've been describing how angry you get at Dan when he doesn't do his chores or follow through on agreements. Things such as him not cleaning up his room after returning from a friend's house, as he promised. But it's not clear to me which one of these things you want to change—your anger or Dan's lack of follow-through.

Client: Damn, do I have to convince you, too? He ought to be responsible and do what he agrees to.

Therapist: (I'll ignore his anger at me for now and focus on clarifying goals.) Bill, I certainly appreciate the frustration he creates when he doesn't follow through. That's a real hassle, but it's not clear to me whether you want to focus on reducing the amount of anger you feel and the yelling that follows or whether you think we should focus on his behavior.

Client: Both, I hope. If he'd get his act together, I wouldn't be so pissed so much of the time.

Therapist: (It's still nor clear what the goal or focus should be. I'll push this a little further.) Ideally, both of you would change. You wouldn't get so angry, and he wouldn't provide you with so many opportunities. But it seems to me like we have two general directions to go. We can focus on changing how the two of you negotiate things that frustrate you, or we can work on helping you lower your anger and see if that helps you feel better and deal with him differently.

Client: You know, I deal pretty well with him when I'm not so pissed. I don't like feeling so mad and out of control. I don't like yelling at him, either. Makes me feel stupid.

Therapist:	So you have more resources to deal with him when you're not so mad and want to work on lowering your anger. Is that it?
Client:	Yeah. I don't want to be so pissed at him and feel like that. I don't like feeling angry at work, either. It's worse with Dan, but I'd like to learn how to deal with anger at work, too.
Therapist:	(I'll just push this one more time to make sure.) Sounds like we're agreeing to focus on your anger first and keep an eye on how you and Dan deal with each other and how any changes carry over to work, as well. But, let me put things just a little differently and see what you think. Suppose I had a crystal ball and could see clearly into the future and could tell you with great certainty that Dan will change very slowly. It'll take years. If you knew that for sure, would you still want to work on your side of the equation, your anger, anyway?
Client:	Yeah. Win or lose with him, I want to get a grip on my anger. I don't like how it makes me feel and what I do when I feel like that. Yelling at him is no good. I don't want him feeling like I did when I was a kid and Mom would unload on me.

The latter part of the dialogue above provides a contrast that can be useful in clarifying whether the goal is personal anger reduction or not. It poses a relatively unchanging environment and asks the client whether he or she would choose personal anger reduction regardless. If clients continue to focus on external change exclusively under this condition, then the clinician should do two things. First, you should consider that the client might be right, and environmentally focused interventions are appropriate. If you reach that conclusion, then focus interventions accordingly. The therapist, however, needs to agree that this is an appropriate target. If you don't agree that environmental change is paramount, you should probably undertake a different discussion of the reasons for your dissent, and potentially refer or terminate. Second, the clinician should *not* undertake anger reduction with CRCS at this time. To do so would undermine the working alliance, as the client and therapist would not be agreeing on the means and perhaps the goals of therapy.

Assessment

Assessment of anger is not limited to the first session or two, never to be reconsidered. On the contrary, it's an ongoing process in which the client and clinician continually collect new data and understanding, potentially leading to revisions in strategy and approach. Assessment is more like filling in the pieces of a puzzle or mosaic, except even more dynamic in that the addition of some pieces may actually change the shape of other pieces. It is a collaborative process, with the client and therapist adding and updating the picture throughout the therapy.

Before exploring the content and methodologies of assessment, some general issues and approaches will be considered.

Attention to the working alliance is critical in the first session generally, but it is especially important in assessment. For example, some individuals with anger problems are easily angered when they feel others are controlling or manipulating them. If they interpret assessment activities in these ways, they may resist the clinician. This may be compounded if the client feels coerced or mandated into treatment. He or she may be resentful and resist assessment as a way of getting back at others and not letting others have their way. You should be aware of these possible dynamics and see assessment not as a unique activity but as an extension of the working alliance, a way to foster collaboration. You may wish to decrease your role as an authority figure, a source of resistance for some angry individuals, and move into assessment simply as part of trying to understand the person and his or her anger. This can be done with open-ended inquiries into the nature of the individual's concerns and focusing on anger as it comes up naturally. The clinician may also use a collaborative, reduced authority role in addressing other assessment strategies. For example, the client is not likely to be aware of or suggest using various self-report scales or inventories. The clinician should make every effort to link these back to the individual's concerns (e.g., completing the instrument is only the individual reporting on what he or she does or feels, and this information can be used to help understand the patterns in responding). The clinician can try to connect self-monitoring to client goals such as following up on the client's statement that "I really need to get a handle on what pisses me off." The clinician might inquire as to how the client could do this and follow up by constructing a self-monitoring form. In summary, the small amount of time needed for framing assessment activities in this way pays large dividends in terms of the working alliance, cooperation, and compliance.

Assessment should always focus on collaboration. Assessment is not something administered to the client by the clinician. It's a cooperative endeavor, much like two detectives trying together to solve a mystery. As the mystery becomes partially solved, the therapist and client develop a jointly shared understanding of anger and design an appropriate intervention plan. Since the client participated in the plan from the start, resistance is minimized, and commitment and follow-through are maximized.

Individuals with anger problems often don't have a clear sense of their anger, its triggers, processes, and outcomes. Anger has become an automatic response and just seems to happen to them. Thus, as much as possible, the clinician should structure assessment to facilitate client self-awareness, as well as to provide additional data to the clinician. For example, when self-report inventories are used, they may not only be analyzed compared to norm groups, but may also be compared with the client's own past reports to illuminate any patterns or improvements and to further illustrate the client's particular relationship with anger. Increased self-awareness may be beneficial in its own right. As the client becomes more aware of the patterns of triggers and responding, he or she may be able to interrupt the automatic response and employ new coping skills. Moreover, increased awareness is a critical part of later therapy as it provides the internal and external cues from which to initiate cognitive and relaxation coping skills.

The content of the assessment is essentially filling in the skeleton of the working model of anger (see overview). You won't get all the information in the first session; some will emerge over the course of the treatment. Nonetheless, you should attempt to fill in as much of the picture as possible in order to facilitate treatment planning. That means developing an initial picture of the individual's anger problems, including the triggers of anger, the pre-anger state, appraisal processes, the cognitive-emotional-physiological experience of anger, behavioral expression of anger, and the consequences of anger. You should also get some sense of the frequency, intensity, and duration of anger episodes and whatever life complications arise from anger. Below are listed the general areas to be assessed and a series of questions that are often helpful to have answered. These questions are, however, best answered collaboratively and inductively from the interview and other sources of data, rather than as a series of clinician-directed queries.

Triggers of Anger

You need to understand the sources or triggers of client anger in order to target interventions appropriately.

1. *External triggers.* Are there patterns in the antecedents—where, when, with whom, and how often does the anger takes place? Is anger triggered primarily by external events? Does the client tend to say things like "X makes me mad"? If so, what are these things (e.g., specific situations or objects, behavior of the individual or others, specific characteristics of self or others, or impersonal events)?

2. *Memories.* Is anger triggered somewhat by external events but appear to involve significant memory components as well? If so, what are the memories and/or imagery involved? Specify as much as possible. The clinician should also assess if anger is embedded in a full-fledged case of posttraumatic stress disorder.

3. *Internal triggers.* Does anger primarily arise from internal experiences? If so, is anger secondary to or following other feelings (e.g., anxiety, stress, depression, guilt, shame, embarrassment, feeling out of control, etc.)? Alternatively, does anger seem to follow periods of worry, brooding, and/or rumination? If so, what kinds of things is the individual worrying or brooding about? Specify the content as much as possible. Does anger seem to be a kind of general mood state? Is the individual angry a great deal of the time? Has the person been like this for a long time or did it seem to start following a precipitating event or condition (e.g., lost job, divorce, medical condition, etc.)? If the latter, specify and try to understand the linkages between the event or condition and the current level of anger.

Pre-Anger State of the Individual

Anger may be influenced by both momentary and enduring characteristics of the individual.

1. *Momentary state.* Is the anger threshold or degree of anger influenced by the individual being angry about other things? If so, can the client describe and

predict when/where he or she will be angry and how this influences subsequent anger and behavior? Get answers as specific as possible. Is anger influenced by the presence of other aversive non-anger emotional or physiological conditions (e.g., illness, fatigue, stress, chronic pain, hunger, jet lag, etc.)? If so, specify and clarify the linkages to anger. Also, can the client predict the occurrence of some of these conditions or are the problems hard to anticipate?

2. *Enduring attitudes, beliefs, and values.* Does the individual rigidly hold any values, attitudes, or beliefs that predispose him or her to anger? If so, what are they? Does the client habitually tend to code events in ways that predispose him or her to anger (e.g., believing others are out to take advantage of or harm the client)? If so, what are they? Does the individual believe that getting angry is a good thing and that blowing off steam is good? Does the individual believe that anger and aggression are desirable or acceptable ways to express negative feelings toward others or get one's way with others?

3. *Cultural and familial norms for anger and aggression.* What is the individual's cultural and familial background relative to anger? How much anger is acceptable? To whom may or may not anger be expressed? In what ways may it be expressed and what ways are prohibited? Has the individual experienced physical, psychological or sexual abuse as a child? If so, explore. Is one or more members of the client's family prone to anger or aggression? If so, clarify who the individuals are, how they express anger, and their relationship to the individual.

Appraisal Processes

Anger is significantly influenced by the ways the individual codes or interprets events and his or her coping capacities.

1. *Primary appraisal.* What are the sources of harm or sense of violation that trigger anger for the individual? Does the client have certain rules for living that lead to significant anger when violated? Does the individual become angry when the expectations or promises are broken? If so, what are these and by whom? Does anger eventuate from frustration and blocked goals? If so, which goals and what kinds of impediments lead to anger?

2. *Secondary appraisal.* Does the individual become angry when he or she feels overwhelmed or out of control? Is anger secondary to simply not knowing how to deal with stressful events? If so, what skills or competencies would the client need to address the situation and how might these be learned? Does the individual believe that he or she shouldn't have to experience negative conditions or have to cope with frustration? If so, how is this expressed?

3. *Other anger-engendering appraisals.* Anger tends to escalate if the individual momentarily or habitually codes events in the following kinds of ways. Does the person often think that others did things intentionally or on pur-

pose to him or her? If so, check for possible validity but be aware that intentionality it is often over-attributed by angry individuals. Does the client think that events were controllable or preventable and should have been controlled or prevented? Does the person believe that the event was justified and deserved or unjustified and undeserved? Does the person look for someone or something to blame or scapegoat? Does the individual hold positive expectations for the success and legitimacy of anger and/or aggression? If so, find out how anger is expected to bring about desired goals.

The Experience of Anger

Anger is an experiential state with emotional, physiological, and cognitive components. Although each is separated below, they tend to coexist and to rapidly recycle and influence each other.

1. *Physiological arousal.* How does anger manifest itself physiologically (e.g., muscle tension, racing heart, sweating, etc.)? Does anger show up in other physical conditions such as high blood pressure, bruxism, upset stomachs, headaches, and the like? Although the latter issues might be considered outcomes or consequences of anger, they are sometimes described by clients as part of how they respond physiologically.

2. *Emotional arousal.* Does the individual report being "angry," "pissed off," "furious," "mad," or the like? Clarify any pet words or phrases the individual uses to describe anger.

3. *Cognitive involvement.* How is the person thinking and processing information when angry? Does the client, for example, curse or label others negatively? Does he or she engage in global, overgeneralized conclusions about events? Does the client jump to egocentric, unverifiable, or unlikely conclusions? Is the individual demanding? If so, clarify the nature of the demands (e.g., personal or social perfectionism, people needing to love, like, and approve of the person, etc.). Does he or she have tunnel vision and seem incapable of seeing any other interpretations or alternative ways of thinking about the situation? What kinds of attributions is the person making? Specify concretely. Does the person think in terms of hostile, angry imagery? If so, clarify and specify these types of thinking processes.

Behavioral Expression of Anger

Although the manner in which anger is expressed often happens nearly simultaneous with cognitive, emotional, and physiological arousal, anger is not synonymous with how it is expressed. At least for diagnostic and treatment planning purposes, anger should be separated from how it's expressed behaviorally. Anger can be expressed in many different ways, including positive and prosocial ones when anger is mild to moderate. Thus the nature of anger expression should be carefully mapped and related to the conditions that give rise to one form of expression or another.

How does the person express anger? Does he or she respond appropriately? If so, specify the nature of the behavior. Does the client behave aggressively? If so, what are the primary forms of expression (e.g., loud verbal aggression, sarcasm, put-downs, physical assault or threat of assault on others or on property)? Specify behavior clearly. Does the individual suppress expression? If so, how is this done? Does the individual respond with passive-aggressive behavior? If so, specify the nature of the behavior. Does he or she respond with non-aggressive, but otherwise dysfunctional behavior (e.g., becoming intoxicated or drug involved, engaging in reckless driving, becoming depressed, etc.)? If so, specify what kind of behavior? Throughout this process, try not only to map the form of anger expression but also determine why one behavior is chosen over another. Important strengths and positive coping capacities may be unearthed as you explore benign and positive forms of expression.

Anger Consequences

Anger may lead to many different outcomes. Some may be positive and constructive, others minimal and neutral, and still others negative and problematic. The clinician should map the nature of these outcomes and the contexts in which they occur.

What happens when the person expresses anger in certain ways? How does he or she feel? How do others respond? Are there problems in terms of interpersonal relationships, educational or vocational pursuits, or health? Did anger expression damage self, others, or property physically? Have there been legal problems? Try to get concrete answers to these questions.

Other Assessment Priorities

So far the focus has been on the content parameters of assessment, but other quantitative and qualitative dimensions should be assessed. For example, it's important to assess frequency (how often anger and forms of anger expression occur), intensity/severity (how strong anger and forms of anger expression are), and duration (how long anger and forms of anger expression last). Sometimes latency of responding can also be important. For example, does the person respond immediately and impulsively or take some time to respond reflectively? The quality of the experience and outcomes are also important. Relatively transient and minor expressions are not likely to be problematic. Other outcomes can be quite severe (e.g., feeling out of control and greatly embarrassed, becoming physically assaultive and being arrested, or losing a marriage or important relationship because of habitual verbal aggression). Anger is more likely to be perceived as dysfunctional or problematic to the degree it is reflected in: 1) greater frequency; 2) greater intensity; 3) longer duration; and/or 4) leads to more frequent and/or more adverse consequences.

Best Coping Strategies

Another area that you should assess is the person's past efforts at coping with or reducing anger. The clinician should inquire in at least two areas, how the person copes with problem anger and how the person at times keeps from becoming angry. Regarding the latter, people often have anger-reducing strategies that they use in life, but which they do not adapt to and use in problem areas. It is not only important to identify strengths and resources, but surveying them may provide the clinician with suggestions of more adaptive coping strategies that can be strengthened and transferred to problem areas. For example, the person may describe attitudes or ways of thinking that prevent anger or may talk of walking away from the situation. These provide natural linkages to cognitive restructuring or time-out strategies.

Here are helpful questions for uncovering best coping strategies. How have you attempted to cope with the angry situations that arise? What has worked the best for you? What are the most successful things you have tried? Have you ever kept yourself from becoming really angry? If so, how did you do that? If your life depended on it or someone made you a large bet, could you keep yourself from becoming angry in that situation? If yes, what would you do? Are there some situations that other people become angry in, but in which you do not? Have the client describe one or two briefly. Why don't you become angry there? What do you think or do that keeps you from becoming angry like other people?

Interview-based Assessment Choices

The clinical interview is perhaps the most widely used assessment strategy. It is flexible and can build rapport and the working alliance at the same time. The clinician will want to start by phrasing questions in as open-ended a fashion as possible (e.g., "Describe for me the kind of anger you experience") and continue open-ended questions even when the focus becomes more narrow (e.g., "And when you are feeling so angry with your daughter, what are you thinking about her?"). Open-ended inquiries can be followed by summaries and perception checks as a way of confirming and integrating the developing picture of anger. Though it is a versatile assessment strategy, the interview is open to bias and potential falsification as the client may withhold or distort key information. The interview is also open to memory fallibility and distortion that is not conscious.

One option in mitigating these potential problems is to extend the interview to collateral informants. The clinician may wish to employ the same style of interviewing with parents, spouses/partners, coworkers, supervisors, friends, and the like. While their input is shaped by their biases, interpretations, and agendas, others who know the client can be rich sources of information that may extend, clarify, or even contradict the client's description of anger. Collateral-informant input should not be taken as the truth either, but can be a rich source of information and should be considered after garnering the client's written release.

The interview can also be supplemented by imagery recall and simulation procedures which attempt to recreate "hot" emotions and cognitions. This is important because there is evidence (e.g., Persons and Miranda 1991) that automatic thoughts and impulses are somewhat state dependent. Accurate assessment may be improved by creating "hotter" states and sampling the feelings, cognitions, and impulses within that context. These procedures involve having the client engage in role plays or simulations, or visualize a provocative event and attempt to experience anger. At different points in the visualization or simulation, the client may be asked what he or she is feeling, thinking, and wanting to do. Simulations and role plays can be extended by audio or video recording. Tapes can be stopped at various places, and the client interviewed as to what is being experienced. While enactment and imagery recall procedures are often closer to the real experience, they too are open to distortion because the client may not get sufficiently invested to have authentic reactions.

Self-Monitoring and Self-Report

Self-Monitoring

Having the client make observations and records of anger in vivo is an excellent strategy. It often enhances the client's self-awareness of different aspects of anger, while at the same time providing a current, contextually rich source of information. Self-monitoring reports should be made as close to the anger experience as possible, thereby providing a hotter record of the actual experience. Self-monitoring is an unusual behavior so should be developed collaboratively with the client. Start simply and evolve to more complexity over time. For example, initially the client might only record the time of the event, the situation, and his or her reactions. Later you can ask the client to differentiate between cognitive, emotional, physiological, behavioral, and consequential aspects of anger in their reporting. Finally, as the client begins to make changes you might add coping efforts and their consequences to the self-monitoring.

Logs and journals are excellent, but the form of self-monitoring should be tailored to the client and the nature of his or her anger issues (e.g., a simple frequency tally for the urge to yell at one's child). The clinician should also be creative and flexible. For example, an angry business executive became very cold and stern when angered, but had no idea of how he looked. He and his son agreed that every time the father needed to express negative feedback to the son for a two week period, they would sit on opposite sides of a table with the father facing a large mirror. His reflection provided direct feedback regarding the nonverbal features of his anger, which he recorded in a journal.

Although it may sound obvious, you shouldn't get so involved in other assessment and therapeutic activities that you fail to emphasize the importance of self-monitoring. If the client fails to see its importance and does little to record anger episodes you may miss valuable information and lose the chance to reinforce the value of self-monitoring specifically and homework generally. If at all possible, the clinician should make arrangements for the client to drop off his or her self-monitoring prior to the session for the clinician's review. This not only gives the clinician the opportunity to go over material and form impressions prior to the session, but it supports the collaborative alliance and underscores the importance of homework.

Self-Report Inventories

Questionnaires are open to the same forms of self-report bias as the interview. Since the source of data is the individual, responses are open to a variety of conscious and unconscious distortions. However, assuming that the client is reporting as truthfully as possible, they can provide normative and idiographic information with great efficiency.

During the session(s) devoted exclusively to assessment, using one or more of the self-reporting measures recommended in the overview can offer concrete data unavailable otherwise. These measures should be completed by the client in the first, fifth, and final sessions.

Other Assessment Information

A final source of assessment information is archival data. Records of anger expression and other pertinent data may already exist (e.g., school records and incident reports, write-ups at work, probation or other court records, etc.). The clinician should get the appropriate releases from the client and acquire as many relevant records as possible.

In summary, the therapist should supplement the clinical interview with a variety of other sources of information and develop with the client a beginning conceptualization and working picture of the client's anger.

Collateral Issues and the Larger Picture

Anger does not exist in isolation and shouldn't always be a primary target of intervention. The clinician should assess and integrate a conceptualization of anger issues with the following factors in mind.

Potential for Violence Toward Self and Others

Violence or aggression, directed toward self or others, should receive attention if you suspect it as a factor. You should engage in an assessment of potential for suicide, violence, or harm toward others, and/or child abuse or neglect. Although the prediction of violence is a difficult matter, clinicians should be aware that, in general, potential for violence increases with the following factors: 1) past threats of the behavior; 2) current threats of the behavior; 3) prior enactment of the threatened behavior (e.g., stalking another person, being found with a weapon, etc.); 4) clear and specific plans and means for implementing those plans; 5) mood and thought consistent with violence (e.g., depression, hopelessness, and suicidal rumination for self-directed harm, and anger, resentment, hostility, and thoughts or images of harm, assault, revenge, retaliation, etc. for violence or harm toward others); 6) current alcohol and/or drug involvement; 7) a history of illegal, violent, and/or antisocial behavior for violence toward others; and 8) a sudden change in behavior or atypical pattern of mood and interpersonal behavior. If violence or harm to self or others seems highly probable, then the clinician should shift focus to crisis intervention and initiate appropriate social system involvement (e.g., call police to initiate a seventy-two hour hold or protection for potential victims, make every effort to contact potential victims, or initiate contact with child protective services). Clinicians should be aware of and follow both ethical guidelines and state regulations involving these matters.

Anger as the Outcome of a Toxic Situation

Anger may be a reaction to negative, abusive, intimidating, coercive individuals or systems. For example, the individual may be a victim of spouse abuse or an economically unstable, turbulent, chaotic lifestyle at the hands of a spouse. The client may be exposed to sexual or other harassment in the workplace. These possibilities should be considered, assessed, and responded to appropriately. Treatment efforts may shift to crisis intervention and/or work to empower the individual in making and enacting decisions and setting limits.

Other Physical, Neurobiological, Medical, and Psychiatric Issues

Anger is not an independent response or issue. It arises within the context of basic physiological, neurological, medical, and psychiatric processes. Temperament, hormone, and basic neurological processes may set the tone and threshold for anger responsiveness and require special assessment. First, what has been the client's historical background regarding these processes? Has he or she, from very early in life, tended to be angry, irritable, thin-skinned, and impulsive, or has the client been much more calm, reflective, and able to exert self-control in the past? Second, what is the more recent history regarding basic physiological and neurological responding? Has there been evidence of head injury, tumor, major illness, disease, or disturbance of normal physiological processes that may have changed the threshold? Did problems with anger overreactivity start shortly after any such illnesses?

Another issue is the potential contribution of other medical conditions to anger. Coping with some chronic diseases, conditions such as chronic pain, and physical disabilities can place serious strain on the client's coping resources and lower the threshold to anger. Such conditions can be a direct source of frustration, which in turn elevates anger.

Medications and Drugs

Medications, too, can sometimes influence anger reactivity, either directly or indirectly. Direct effects may involve side effects of anger and irritability. Indirect effects can include side effects that influence anger reactivity, such as causing headaches that make the person more irritable and reduce coping resources. A quick review of prescription and nonprescription medications should be undertaken.

Additionally, typical patterns of ingesting common drugs (e.g., alcohol, tobacco, and caffeine) should be assessed generally and in relationship to anger. For example, conceptualization and perhaps treatment will change if anger problems appear primarily in the presence of alcohol consumption. Also check for the influence of cocaine or amphetamines. These are notorious for exacerbating or even creating anger.

Psychiatric History

A brief psychiatric and family history is also relevant. Taking a general psychiatric history that includes a family history of mental disorders (e.g., psychosis, depression, bipolar disorder, and substance abuse) can be very helpful in understanding potential biological and psycho-social vulnerabilities of the individual. The individual's psychiatric history also may help in conceptualizing anger. For example, anger in a person with a long history of dysthymia and major depressive episodes may have different treatment implications than the same anger in an individual without such a history (e.g., use of SSRI antidepressants may be of greater value to the first case). The clinician will also want to check psychiatric and psychological conditions that have a greater association with anger problems. For example, is there a family or individual history of conduct disorder, antisocial behavior, aggression or violence, impulse control problems, adolescent substance abuse, or other deviant behavior, etc.? Information about family and individual history may help the clinician rethink the nature of the person's problems over time to see if anger begins to fit the symptomatology of another disorder.

Anger as Part of Another Psychiatric Disorder

As noted earlier, anger can be part of or a secondary symptom of other Axis I DSM-IV disorders such as depression, bipolar disorder, posttraumatic stress disorder, schizophrenia, and some cognitive disorders. It can also be a salient element of Axis II disorders such as paranoid, narcissistic, borderline, and antisocial personality disorder. Anger may be involved in some Axis III conditions such as elevated blood pressure, coronary heart disease, and tension and migraine headaches. Moreover, anger is also an element of many interpersonal relationship problems (i.e., V codes, and some other Axis I disorders such as sexual dysfunctions). In such cases, anger shouldn't automatically be considered a primary target of intervention. Anger should be conceptualized within the larger context of other psychological concerns and symptoms, and appropriate treatment and referral plans should be developed and implemented.

Anger Is Comorbid with Other Conditions

Clients are complex and may bring a variety of issues that are comorbid or co-mixed with anger. Anger issues are often mixed with other psychological disorders, medical conditions, and/or substance use, whether reaching diagnosable levels or not. When anger is commingled with such issues, the clinician should attempt to disentangle them and understand their relationships. As noted previously, anger is sometimes an element of another disorder that should be the primary focus of treatment. In other cases, it appears primarily as a secondary reaction to some other disorder or issue. For example, a client may become very irritable with him- or herself after experiencing significant anxiety or depression secondary to chronic pain or stressful medical procedures. In such cases, the focus would again seem most appropriately on the primary issue. It if it were resolved, the reactive anger would decrease as a result.

You should bear in mind, however, that it's unwise to assume that anger is *always* secondary to other conditions. It is true that anger is sometimes secondary to depression (i.e., anger with one's self seems to follow periods of self-loathing and depression). However, it may turn out that depression is actually secondary to anger issues. That is, a person could become depressed at his or her inability to manage and modulate anger that has led to several key losses (e.g., loss of a job, important relationships, friends, or money, etc.). Sometimes, anger management can be adjunctive therapy so that the client can lower anger, feel better, and have more resources to address the primary issue. In still other cases, anger and other issues appear relatively independent of each other and deserve separate consideration and intervention.

A final consideration is that anger and other issues may be facilitative or contributing factors to each other. For example, an individual may be much more prone to anger and aggression when experiencing headaches or consuming alcohol. One may not lead directly to the other, but the interaction is more powerful than the effect of either alone. In such cases, anger management may be an appropriate intervention to lower anger's contribution to the overall combination of problems, but anger management should be integrated with interventions for the other issues. Additionally, the clinician should also assess whether comorbid conditions and/or their treatment will interfere with anger-focused treatment and how/whether concurrent treatment of anger and comorbid problems can be implemented and coordinated. From the perspective of psychological and medical triage, the clinician should carefully think about the prioritizations and staging of interventions to achieve the maximum coordinated benefit for the client.

Motivation for an Individually Focused Anger-Reduction Intervention

As previously noted, not all clients with anger issues are good candidates for an individually focused anger reduction intervention such as CRCS. Even those who own anger as a problem may not be highly motivated for change. Anger management is an undertaking that requires a significant commitment of psychological, emotional, time, and financial resources. The angry individual may be at a more pre-contemplative stage of readiness (Prochaska, Norcross, and DiClimente 1995) and not yet be motivated to commit to an action-oriented intervention such as CRCS. The clinician should assess the individual's degree of pain and consequences stemming from his or her anger and the degree of commitment and motivation for change. Anger-focused therapy requires a client who, at least to a significant degree, owns anger as a personal problem and who has suffered enough from the consequences of anger that he or she is ready for change. If the individual is not yet ready for an action-oriented intervention, then the focus of therapy might more appropriately be on enhancing readiness, rather than prematurely moving toward change.

The clinician should attempt to rule out individuals who are not ready for anger-focused therapy

- because of their immediate potential for violence;

- because of a near total lack of awareness of their anger, its impact on others, or the consequences it produces;

- because anger is so identity or role congruent as to prevent the client from desiring a change in anger;

- because anger and aggression are so highly reinforced as to preclude meaningful change;

- because anger is so thoroughly externalized that the individual does not own anger as any type of personal problem.

While clients falling into the categories above may have significant anger problems, they are currently not at a state of readiness for action-oriented change. If this is the case, the therapist may wish to develop an alternative therapeutic contract that focuses on these issues (e.g., Deffenbacher 1995; DiGiuseppe 1995; Miller and Rollinck 1991). The goals of such interventions would be to increase awareness of anger problems, provide a range of alternative anger scripts, and increase the motivation to address anger as a personal problem. At a later point, CRCS or other action-oriented interventions may become appropriate.

Assessment of Collateral Strengths, Resources, Social Supports, and Sources of Interference

Anger problems exist within the context of a person's strengths, values, relationships, and social systems. For example, an individual with anger problems who is generally intelligent, well employed, competent, possesses a sense of self-efficacy, has a history of making other changes, and enjoys a rich network of family and friends is generally in a better position to make change than an isolated individual who is less intelligent and competent and who is plagued with low self-esteem and doubts about self-efficacy. Such differential resources should be assayed so that, where possible, they may be integrated into anger-focused therapy.

On the other hand, the individual may possess other characteristics and/or relationships and systems that may work to undermine the therapy. For example, a drug-involved spouse may not want the partner to change. He or she may work to provoke anger and undermine therapy in order to keep the relationship in angry turmoil, thereby deflecting the focus from the substance-abuse problem. Cultural and social systems should be considered as well. If anger reduction leads the person to violate cultural or subcultural norms or role definitions, or to countermand important group norms, these forces may undermine treatment. For example, an adolescent who begins to significantly reduce his anger may lose sources of peer support and encouragement (e.g., support for giving lip to teachers). A parent who lowers her anger may find that the children escalate anger provocation because they have previously been able to manipulate the parent when she was feeling guilty about being angry. To the extent possible, you should assess such forces and evaluate their influence on therapy. Moreover, you should remain open to the possibility of outside sources of interference throughout therapy. When impasses have been reached or when interventions are not transferring well to the external world, the clinician can see these as cues to consider whether there are other forces and sources of reinforcement undermining the interventions. Your focus must then be to identify and alter these forces.

Involvement of Other Stakeholders

Angry clients may have other individuals who care about them and are invested in their treatment. However, anger may involve a number of different stakeholders in the individual's anger problems. The person may be in treatment because of the referral or mandate of these other stakeholders. For example, spouses or employers may have imposed conditions related to anger management if they are to continue the marriage or employment. The school system may have imposed conditions upon an angry adolescent's continuing or returning to school. The courts, too, may be involved. Judges, probation officers, and attorneys may all have stipulations on the individual's treatment.

The clinician should inquire about who and what systems are involved and then how these systems may have a formal or informal investment in the person's anger reduction. Has the client made any sort of contract with others regarding treatment? If so, there may be a very real question of "Who is (are) the client(s)?" You should think through how and whether you are willing to undertake the case within the constraints and expectations of the various individuals and systems involved. If you go forward with the case, it is strongly recommended that releases be signed and very clear contracts and understandings be negotiated with all involved. Furthermore, it is suggested that all releases, contracts, and understandings be written up and signed by the various parties prior to initiating further assessment and that the client clearly understands, in writing, the limits of confidentiality with any parties involved.

Your Conclusions

Because assessment is a collaborative process, you and the client have been exploring together each discovery about the client's anger. At this point in the session, you and the client *both* understand the triggers of anger, the pre-anger conditions, the appraisal processes, how anger is subjectively experienced, how anger is expressed, and its consequences. You've also explored together issues of frequency, intensity, and the client's best coping strategies. You've looked at the potential for violence, and the possibility of toxic influences, as well as physical, neurobiological, medical, and psychiatric issues. You've explored the level of motivation and shared your conclusions regarding the client's readiness for CRCS. Because assessment is an open process, your client should know much of what you know, and now be ready for clear treatment recommendations.

Treatment Recommendations

Providing treatment recommendations and rationale marks the transition from assessment to intervention. In making this transition, you will have made three decisions. First, you ruled out the range of issues (see earlier discussion) that would make the client a poor candidate for the type of intervention to be recommended. Second, you have decided that the client is motivated for and is at an action stage of intervention readiness. Third, you have decided that CRCS is an appropriate intervention or partial intervention at this time.

Treatment recommendations and rationales should attempt to achieve the following four things.

1. They should be a collaborative extension of the assessment activities. As much as possible, interventions should be linked to and seem to naturally flow out of the examples and issues discussed earlier in the session. In many cases, clients will have already described elements of treatment in general terms. For example, "I've got to calm down" can be related easily to relaxation skills or "I have to get my head clear" can be connected to cognitive change strategies. The clinician's job is to lift out these types of descriptions and link them to the intervention elements of CRCS.

2. The recommendations and rationale should be in clear, simple language that the client understands. The clinician should describe things in terms of what the client and therapist will be doing in the coming sessions. The treatment steps should also be described so that the client has an understanding of the progression of treatment and can cooperate more fully. You should resist the temptation to use professional jargon and to over-explain things. Generally, references to the treatment literature are inappropriate, unless the client asks for them or would appear to be reassured by them.

3. The rationale should impart positive, realistic expectations regarding the process, outcome, and time frame of therapy. The client should be told that anger reduction is achievable, but that it will take significant work on both the client's and therapist's part. This provides the opportunity to indicate that CRCS is an active process that involves work both within and outside the session. The importance of homework should be briefly described. Moreover, it should be emphasized that the interventions will not lead to an anger free world. The client will still experience significant frustrations and provocations (e.g., children, spouses, and coworkers will not always do what the client wishes; other people will sometimes be loud, rude, inconsid-

erate, and disrespectful; and other drivers will not behave the way the client wants them to). That is simply life, but the client can learn to manage anger and cope more effectively. The goal is anger reduction, not anger elimination. Moreover, anger reduction is likely to be a lifelong process. The frustrations and hassles will continue to be present, and the client will need to continue using anger-reducing skills. In the same way one needs to stay physically fit, the client will likely have to continue exercising his or her new anger-reduction skills. Sometimes, this can be presented in a kind of "good news" and "bad news" format. The good news is that anger reduction can be achieved, and the bad news is that it takes work. This explanation can help the client to set realistic expectations about the effort involved and creates a transition to discussing the amount of time needed. In this regard, the clinician should do two things. It should be clearly communicated that CRCS will take from seven to ten sessions and that the therapist is asking for a tentative commitment for that amount of time. It should also be indicated that the client will likely experience significant benefits in that time frame and that the client and therapist will undertake ongoing progress checks and a more complete review at the end of that time.

4. The presentation of the rationale should end with the opportunity for the client to ask questions and clarify things. Unless the client naturally summarizes his or her understanding or asks questions that indicate an understanding of the process, you should ask for a summary of the rationale and recommendations in the client's words.

A sample presentation of a treatment rationale is outlined below.

Therapist: Let me try to pull together what we've been discussing. When you get angry like you do when your wife or supervisor criticize you or when someone puts you down or questions your integrity, you get really upset. You're tense all over, but particularly in the stomach, and your heart pounds. You get into those angry thoughts like, "Who the hell does she think she is?", or "They shouldn't talk to me like that," or "I'm not going to take that kind of shit from him." When you're hot like that, you tend to become defensive, yell, and fight back verbally. You want to work on your anger at this time because it's hurting your relationship with your wife, and you've already been disciplined once at work. You're afraid that if you don't chill out, you might lose your job. Does that capture what we discussed?

Client: Yeah, and sometimes I become kind of physically intimidating too, because of my size.

Therapist: Good. We both see it about the same way. Sounds like you need some ways to calm down and strategies to help you think things through differently. Do you have any ideas about how you might do that?

Client: Well, I suppose I could just walk away when I get pissed.

Therapist: That's a good idea. It can be really helpful to take a time-out and get your head together before you respond to a provocation, and we'll work on that. But sometimes that's not so easy, like when you are right in the middle of work. Do you have any other ideas about how you might calm down or think about things differently?

Client: I don't really know. I just get so damned mad that I can't think straight. That's why I took the advice of the woman in human resources at work and came to see you.

Therapist: *(Not pushing him any further for his suggestions but instead linking treatment rationale to what he just said)* Well, I think you said a lot right there. You get so angry and upset that you aren't able to think clearly and calmly. It sounds to me like that's a good place to start—teaching you the skills to calm down and to think about things more clearly and less angrily. If you would like, I could take a minute or two to describe how we might do that.

Client: Okay.

Therapist: I think the first step would be to focus on calming down. Earlier, you said that you can calm down by reading or going for a walk. Well, we would try to help you get that kind of relaxed feeling, but in a different way. First, I'll show you a way to relax so that you can be really calm. Then, I'll show you some quick and easy ways of triggering that relaxation so you can relax away the angry feelings and chill out. That way you'll have some relaxation tools to fight anger with.

But knowing how to relax is not enough. It's important to be able to use relaxation tools when you're pissed. To do this, we will need to have you practice relaxing away the anger and chilling out here in the session and in real life. In the session, we will practice by having you imagine things that pissed you off, have you get pissed again, and then have you relax away the anger. Early on, I will help you with the relaxation, but as you get better and better at it, you'll do it on your on. Also, we will have you practice your relaxation when you get angry out in the world, like when you're angry with your wife or supervisor. We'll have you record your efforts at relaxing away anger and go over them to fine tune things. With practice, you'll get really good at chilling out. Now, that won't make all the hassles and anger go away, but it will give you one good way to calm down. Are you with me so far?

Client: Yeah, I think so.

Therapist: Good. The second approach will be changing those really angry thoughts. You described an example of doing that naturally the other day when you thought to yourself, "Oh, to hell with it. It's not that important anyway." When you did that, you said you were a lot less angry with your wife, even though you didn't agree with her. We will do much the same thing. We'll identify those thoughts that jack your anger up and then come up with calmer alternatives to them. These alternatives will be thoughts that make sense to you and that you can really believe in. Then, like relaxation, we'll have you practice them over and over until they become second nature. You'll do that by again imagining those situations and getting pissed, but thinking them through differently, with the calmer thoughts. Also, we'll have you practice thinking differently out there in real life when you're getting angry. Practicing both calmer thoughts and relaxation, you'll be able to chill out your head and your feelings.

My best estimate is that if you and I both do our parts, it will take us about seven to ten sessions to do this. In that amount of time, you should be experiencing significant anger reduction or something is wrong. We'll certainly talk about how it's going along the way, but I think it will take us about that amount of time to get the pieces in place and give it a fair chance to be successful. Does this make sense and sound like something that you would like to do?

Client: Sure. Sounds good to me.

Therapist: I laid out a number of different things and I would appreciate it if you would describe in your own words what you're agreeing to and what we will be doing over the next few weeks.

The clinician listens to the client's perceptions of the treatment contract, then moves on to briefly summarize the session. This review should include the reasons the client came to therapy at this time, the assessment of anger and other issues, the nature of treatment decisions made, and an overview of the treatment contract. For example, you might say something like:

In our session, we have clarified your reasons for seeking out therapy, and have worked together to understand your anger and how it affects your life and the lives of those around you. Although other people and things may contribute to anger, we have determined that you are ready for and committed to change how you deal with your anger. We have decided we will focus first on helping you learn skills to relax and calm down and to look at and think about things in less angering ways. We have outlined a plan for therapy that will take about seven to ten sessions. The first couple of sessions will focus heavily on developing relaxation skills. From then on, relaxation and cognitive change strategies will be focused on lowering anger both within and outside therapy sessions. You will be doing a lot of hard work in the session, but we will also use homework tasks outside the session to develop and consolidate your anger management skills in your everyday life.

Feedback from Client

Ask the client if they have any questions, comments, or concerns that he or she wishes to bring up at this time.

Homework

After the client has had an opportunity to voice concerns or questions you can contract homework, as appropriate (see below).

Therapist: Okay, we're near the end. We've done a lot of good work clarifying the nature of your anger, the situations that trigger it, and the things you do and experience when angry. Here toward the end, we agreed to some approaches for helping you lower anger. To help us continue to get a clearer picture of your anger and prepare us for next week, I would like to have you complete (give you) those questionnaires (State-Trait Anger Scale, Anger Situation, and Anger Symptom) we talked about earlier and have you start keeping the Anger Log. Okay? *(If the client does not have a client manual, give him or her a copy.)*

Client: Sure. Should I have them done by next week?

Therapist: Actually, if we can work it out, I would like to have you drop them by the day before our next session. That way, I will have a chance to look them over and be ready to talk about them with you in our next session. So, can you drop them off the day before?

Client: Fine.

Therapist: How about you put the log and the questionnaires in a large envelope and slide it under my door if I'm not here. That way your confidentiality will be protected if I should walk in with somebody. One final thing regarding the Anger Log; you should record every significant anger event—any time that your anger goes over 40 on our anger scale. Write experiences down as close to the time that they happen as you can. That will help us get as fresh and clear a picture as possible. Also, make an entry at least once a day, no matter how angry you become. So, even if you have a great day, at least put down the thing that annoyed you the most. So are you clear about what you're going to do?

Client: Yeah. I'm gonna put down everything that bugs me over 40 and add to the log at least once a day, even if everything is cool.

The dialogue above provides an example of how assessment-related homework might be given. The importance and general nature of homework was described in the overview.

Assignments at the end of session 1 include:

1. Completion of the State-Trait Anger Expression Inventory (STAXI) if it is being used, the Anger Situation worksheet and the Anger Symptom worksheet, with the appropriate number of worksheets completed.

2. Self-monitoring in the form of Anger Log I. The client records all anger experiences over 40 on the anger scale. Entries in the log should be made at least once per day, regardless of the level on the anger scale.

3. Read the introduction and sessions 1 and 2 from the client manual if this has not already been done. Encourage a review if the client has already done the reading.

Depending on the nature of the client's presenting issues, the clinician may also negotiate assignments that may involve the following types of things:

- Contracts regarding violence or other dysfunctional behavior

- Collecting information regarding insurance

- Talking with other stakeholders and providing the clinician with information needed to secure releases of information and make contact with them

- Making arrangements for providing the clinician with information needed to secure releases of information for the acquisition of archival data

- Making arrangements to talk with other individuals who may be able to provide information relevant to the client's anger

Generally, the session will end by signing any release forms, completing any treatment contracts the clinician may use, completing any other information required in the clinician's state (assuming these were not completed earlier in the session), and making any other arrangements necessary (e.g., making arrangements to talk with someone about the client's anger or to talk with the client's insurance or managed care system).

Clinician Summary and Case Conceptualization

You have collected a great deal of information in this session and made arrangements for the collection of additional assessment information (e.g., questionnaires, self-monitoring, etc.), but now comes the time for you to pull your thoughts and notes together. A form for recording your notes and case conceptualization is provided below. You can use this as is or modify to fit your needs.

Assessment of Change and Outcomes

Before leaving the topic of assessment, it is not too early to think about ongoing assessment and the evaluation of change. Assessing change and outcomes of therapy is critical to ongoing case management and clinical decision making and to making decisions about success and termination. However, it is never too early to start thinking about measuring change over the course of therapy.

Interview data from sessions will provide important information about how the client is doing and what kinds of changes are occurring. However, several of the other forms of assessment outlined earlier in this chapter not only provide initial assessment data, but also can be adapted to measure change. Examples are provided below.

- The Trait Anger Scale and the Anger Expression portions of the STAXI can be readministered at later points in time (e.g., mid-therapy, termination, and follow-up). Scores can be compared to the individual's earlier scores to assess change. Scores can be compared to norms to assess where the individual stands relative to others at each point in time and can be compared to the client's pretreatment score.

- The Anger Situation and Anger Symptom can be employed to measure change within the individual. The clinician can make a photocopy of the client's initial Anger Situations and Symptoms and white out the initial ratings on the copy. This can then be copied, and the client can be asked to rerate the situation and symptom according to how he or she experiences the situation or symptom at the present point in time. Pretreatment ratings can be compared to current ratings to assess intervention effects.

- The State Anger Scale can be completed for several days in a row at the same time (e.g., when the person first gets home from work) and compared to pretreatment levels completed at the same time of day. The State Anger Scale can also be completed immediately after the person encounters the same situation (e.g., performance feedback from a supervisor or difficult interactions with a spouse or child). This could also be done in response to role plays, simulations, or visualizations within therapy sessions. Comparisons to pretreatment levels in the same situations, role plays, simulations, or visualizations would provide markers of change of angry feelings and urges to aggress physically and verbally.

- Self-monitoring logs also can provide sensitive measures of change over time. The frequency and average intensity of ratings can be plotted on simple frequency and intensity graphs each week to get a sense of the frequency and intensity of anger. Change should be reflected in reductions in the frequency and/or intensity over time. The frequency and average intensity of ratings over 40 can also be calculated and plotted in a similar manner. This provides ongoing measures of the frequency and intensity of events that are more problematic. Again, positive change would be reflected in the number and average intensity going down over time.

Such assessment activities will provide information regarding intervention effectiveness and may strengthen client self-efficiency. Additionally, having clear outcome assessment plans may be helpful in writing reports and communication with systems such as insurance companies, the courts, and the like. So, start now and over the next week or two develop your outcome assessment plan.

Summary of Session 1

Client Name: _____ Date: _____

1. Anger Triggers (list as they apply)

External Situations:

Memories & Other Traumatic Events:

Thoughts/Ruminations:

Feelings/Emotions:

2. Pre-Anger State (other things that influence anger)

Physical & Emotional Condition:

General Attitudes & Beliefs:

Cultural Elements of Anger:

3. Appraisal Processes

Appraisals about Triggers:

Appraisal about Self & Coping:

4. Anger Experience

Emotional Arousal:

Physiological Arousal:

Cognitive Experience:

5. Anger Expression (note dysfunctional and functional forms of expression)

6. Anger Consequences (note what happens as function of client's anger)

7. Past Efforts to Cope and Positive Resources

8. Other Potentially Important Issues (note violence toward self or others, contributing biological, psychological, or social issues, psychiatric history and comorbidity, medication, etc.)

9. Client Goals for Therapy

10. **Case Conceptualization and Treatment Plan**

11. **Homework (list specific assignments)**

12. **Other People or Systems Involved (list name and other relevant information)**

Anger Log I

Date/Time	Situation	Reactions Rate 0–100

Anger Situation

Instructions: Please describe, in detail, the one *ongoing* situation that creates the greatest feelings of anger for you. By ongoing, it is meant that the situation occurs fairly often, say at least once a month or more. Pick out the most angering, ongoing situation. Be very specific. For example, do not say "work" or "parents," but instead describe what particular part of work or parents produces anger for you.

Description of Situation:

1. How much anger do you experience in this situation? Rate the amount of anger **on the average** that you feel in that situation. Use a 0-100 scale where 0 = little or no anger and 100 = maximum level of anger you could ever experience.

   Rating (0–100): _____

2. How often do you experience this situation? In the blank below put a number to indicate how often you experience this situation in a **month's** time, i.e., how often per month do you experience it.

   Frequency: _____

3. When you become angry in this situation, how long does the anger typically last? In the blank below, put a number to indicate about how many minutes the anger **generally** lasts in this situation.

Length: _____

4. How much does anger in this situation interfere with your life? Rate interference on a 0–100 scale where 0 = no interference and 100 = extreme interference.

Interference (0–100): _____

Anger Symptom

Instructions: Identify the physiological symptom of anger that you experience most frequently and list it in the space below. Examples of symptoms include things such as sweating, fast pulse, shaky feelings, trembling, headaches, shoulder tension, upset stomach, clenched jaws, flushed face, back tension, etc. **List the symptom that is *most* frequent for you.**

Symptom: _____

1. How severe is the anger symptom? Rate severity on a 0–100 scale where 0 = no problem at all and 100 = extremely severe.

   Severity (0–100): _____

2. How often do you experience this anger symptom? In the blank below put a number to indicate how often you experience this symptom in a **month's** period of time, i.e., how often per month do you experience this symptom.

   Frequency: _____

3. When you experience this anger symptom, how long does it typically last? In the blank below put a number to indicate about how many minutes this symptom **generally** lasts when you experience it.

Length: _____

4. How much does this symptom interfere with your life? Rate interference on a 0–100 scale where 0 = no interference at all and 100 = extreme interference.

Interference: _____

Relaxation Skills

Monitoring of Current Status

The clinician should ask about the client's reaction to the assessment and evaluation procedures experienced during their first session. Inquire about thoughts and reactions to beginning an anger-management program, and encourage the client to share any doubts and concerns about learning anger-management skills. Listen for and clarify any misunderstandings about anger or the processes of therapy the client may have. The client may want to share specific responses to daily monitoring using the Anger Log, but these can be dealt with when you review the homework.

Agenda

The agenda for this session includes homework review, orientation to relaxation, progressive relaxation training, and relaxation image construction. The session will end with a relaxation handout to facilitate home practice and a homework assignment to use the new relaxation skills and keep a Relaxation Log.

Review of Homework

The clinician should review homework assigned from the previous session, either producing the Anger Log because the client dropped it off before the session or asking to look at it if log was not dropped off. If you did receive the log beforehand, indicate that you have examined it, supporting the notion that you do your homework just as the client does theirs. Verify with the client that all anger reactions greater than 40 on the 100-point scale of anger arousal were recorded. Also make sure that at least one entry was made per day (even if there were no anger experiences over 40 on that date). If the homework has not been done, or only partially completed, emphasize that the acquisition of anger-management skills will depend on home cooperation. Abundant research suggests that clients achieve more positive outcomes in a much shorter period of time if they comply with homework assignments.

Let the client know that the problems they're struggling with and the positive changes they wish to achieve will be directly related to their personal investment in daily practice of their new skills. Identify any blocks to completing homework assignments: inability to remember, lack of time, tiredness, fear of being observed, and so on. For each reported problem, develop a collaborative solution with your client. For example, a client who forgets to practice might write practice times into his or her appointment book. If tiredness is the issue, they might practice earlier rather than later in the day. Someone who has difficulty with motivation might contract with a friend to do a daily check-in about homework practice. Some clients might even need to leave messages on your voice mail reporting about homework practice before coming in for their next session. Knowing they'll have to describe homework efforts in a message helps maintain practice throughout the week.

Look for Themes and Triggers

If the log has been completed, go over each situation to identify themes and typical anger triggers. Ask clients about what they noticed in observing anger during the past week. Help them to identify patterns in the situations experienced. For example, some clients may only get angry at work, with intimates, or where they feel controlled. Also, help them identify patterns in their anger reactions. For example, clarify that they tend to engage in intense emotional and physiological arousal and loud, insulting, verbal aggression following a challenge to their authority. Or that they sit on intense angry feelings at the time of provocation, ruminating for long periods of time afterwards, and experiencing stomach upset and tension in the shoulders.

The clinician should also look for contrasts in the client's experience. For example, the client may have become very angry on one occasion, but much less angry in another very similar situation. What accounts for the difference in experience? Sometimes there are situational differences that are important for both the client and clinician to understand. However, on other occasions the difference is primarily in perception, attitude, or the way the client thought about the situation. If so, a clarification may serve as a helpful prelude to cognitive change strategies introduced in future sessions. Below is a client-therapist exchange that exemplifies this.

Therapist: Bill, I when I looked over your Anger Log, I noticed here (*pointing to the log*) on Thursday you got really mad at James (*his son with whom he had frequent outbursts*) for not having cleaned up the family room after school, which was his after school chore for that day.

Client: Yeah, he really pisses me off when he ducks his responsibility and then tries to blame it on not having enough time.

Therapist:	Really pushed your buttons on Thursday, huh? But, I noticed here on Sunday evening that you were only somewhat mad (35-40 on log) when he went off with his friends without cleaning up his room.
Client:	Uh-huh.
Therapist:	So help me understand the difference. On Thursday, you're really pissed when he doesn't do a chore, but on Sunday, it's not a big deal. So how is Sunday different from Thursday?
Client:	Well, I was tired on Thursday. He always gets to me more then.
Therapist:	So, he gets to you more when you're tired. Anything else that's different about the two situations?
Client:	Well, I don't know. Sunday was just such a good day. The weather was nice, but I was also in a good mood. Jane and I went out Saturday night and had a good time without the kids. I just woke up in a good mood and decided not to let things get to me.
Therapist:	So, on Sunday when you were in a good mood and when you *decided* not to let things get to you, you were only frustrated with James. I guess I don't quite know what you mean by "decided." How did you "decide" not to let things get to you.
Client:	You know, like I thought about things more rationally.
Therapist:	Could you explain that a bit more. What do you mean rationally?
Client:	You know, like it's a nice day, no need getting all upset. He's just a kid anyway. Kids don't always do things. I know I didn't always do my chores when I was a kid. Hell, I don't even do all of them now. Also, I remember thinking that I'm always on his ass and should give him a break. I also remember something you and I had talked about last time about maybe learning not to take things so seriously. You know, making a mountain out of every molehill. It just didn't seem so bad.
Therapist:	So when you were thinking calmly and rationally, kinda putting things into realistic perspective on Sunday, things didn't seem so bad. Thinking that way helped you be only frustrated with James rather than angry, is that it?
Client:	Yeah.
Therapist:	Bill, that's a really important point that we'll be becoming back to. We'll be exploring how we can help you be more rational and realistic so that you can have more days like Sunday, rather than the storm of Thursday. We'll zero in on this in a session or two.

This brief exchange opened two things. First, exploring a naturally existing contrast in client experience provided a prelude to cognitive interventions. The clinician can use the example or look for similar ones to help introduce and illustrate cognitive interventions. Second, the exchange identified the potentially important connection between being tired and getting angry. This may be important for the therapist to track. If anger consistently happens when the client is tired or at the end of the day, then the clinician can assist the client to recognize this vulnerability. The client can then employ cognitive and relaxation strategies to deal with anger directly or with stressors and frustrations that lead to increased fatigue and irritability.

The clinician should use homework to develop collaboratively an understanding of the client's anger over time. In this way, assessment is not fully completed in the first session or two. Through the use of homework it becomes an ongoing, developmental, shared understanding of what the client is experiencing, thinking, and doing and the consequences of the client's behavior. The client and therapist continually revise and reformulate their understanding of the client's issues, leading to changes and shifts of emphasis in the intervention.

Bridge to Relaxation Training

Toward the end of the Anger Log review, the clinician may want to focus specifically on emotional and physiological reactions. This serves as a natural bridge to relaxation training (i.e., developing relaxation in order to lower arousal). For example, the therapist might summarize the most frequent emotional and physical anger reactions and indicate that the client cannot experience these and be calm and relaxed at the same time. That's why the relaxation skills learned today are so important—they give the client skills to remain calm in the face of provocation.

Concepts and Skills

Psychoeducation

Rationale for Relaxation Training

Motivating your client to learn relaxation procedures is critical for a positive outcome. You can encourage full compliance with relaxation training by saying something like the following:

Learning to relax is essential to anger management. That's because getting angry requires two things—physical tension or stress plus anger-triggering thoughts. Half the anger battle can be won by simply learning to relax the physical tension that develops in provocative situations. If you can relax your body, and keep it relaxed, it's almost impossible to get angry. Combating stress using the skills you're about to learn can help you calm down, think straight, and handle situations that could make you mad in an effective, positive way. The goal is to be so good at relaxing that you can let go of tension anytime, anywhere, in thirty seconds or less.

The first step is to learn how to create effective relaxation imagery. After that you'll learn a technique called progressive relaxation training that involves tensing and releasing your muscles.

Skill Building

Relaxation Image Construction

One way clients can defuse anger is by visualizing a personal relaxation scene or image, one that triggers significant relaxation for them. The scene should capture a real life, concrete moment from the client's past. The scene should be real rather than fantasy because fantasy images are more easily modified by clients and may take on angry or other negative qualities. Also, if the client has experienced the relaxing situation many times (e.g., frequented the same beach or lake), the clinician should ask the client to pick a specific time that stands out most clearly or produced the greatest amount of relaxation. Sometimes, if the scene is not a specific memory or event, clients report switching around between several images, in which case they don't get one clear and relaxing scene. Images should be a specific, concrete moment in time, like a snapshot from the person's memory. They should be rich in sensory detail, using visual, auditory, kinesthetic, and temperature information closely tied to the affective experience.

To begin developing the scene with the client, the clinician might say something like:

> In a few moments we'll go through the tensing and releasing of the muscles that we talked about a moment ago. But before we do that, I would like to take a few moments to develop a personal relaxation image with you. Later, after you've tensed and released each muscle group, I will have you bring this relaxing image to mind, increasing your relaxation. So, could you take a moment and think back to a time when you were really relaxed, a time when you were calm and peaceful? It could be at the beach, the mountains, in meadows, or in your childhood bedroom. Anchor your memory of this place to an exact instant in time. Try to see it as it was at that moment—the shapes and colors, the quality of light. Notice the sounds in this place—birds or waves or babbling water. Feel the temperature of this place—is it cool or warm? Feel the textures of whatever you touch.
>
> Now feel the emotions of this place. Notice the feelings of safety or calmness or gentle longing that it evokes in you. Let yourself be aware of the special qualities of this place—what you see or hear or feel—that gives you the greatest sense of peace or tranquillity.

Two client scenes are provided below as examples. The first scene is from the relatively recent past, whereas the other is from the distant past. Both types of scenes are fine. The requirements for relaxation images are that they be clear, concrete, easily visualized, and *relaxing*.

Relaxation Scene 1: It is that day about three weeks ago when you and your brother were out on the lake fishing (*general setting detail*). It was one of those perfect days. Your brother always makes you laugh and feel good (*general emotional detail*). You've been fishing most of the morning and now have moved over into Jayne's Cove. The two of you have anchored the boat about seventy-five yards off shore. You're laying crossways on the seat of the boat. You aren't talking but can sort of feel your brother's presence as you lay on your back with your hat covering your face. You have your eyes closed *(more specific setting details)*, but there is warm orange light coming through your hat and onto your face *(visual and temperature detail)*. You can just feel that early fall warmth on your body, not too hot but warm. The boat is rocking gently with the slight breeze. It's like you are gently swaying in a hammock *(kinesthetic detail)*. You can hear the water lapping quietly against the side of the boat and the occasional sound of a gull somewhere overhead *(auditory detail)*. You're warm, but not hot, and totally relaxed *(temperature and emotional detail)*. You have that sense of being totally at peace with the world. You're thinking that if you died right then everything would be right with the world *(more emotional detail)*.

Relaxation Scene 2: It's that time many years ago, the summer that you were eleven, and you and your cousin, Mary, were visiting your grandparents' farm in rural Georgia *(general setting detail)*. You loved it there, always feeling free and truly loved by your grandparents *(general emotional detail)*. You and your cousin were up in the loft of the barn. She was on your right about an arm's length away, and the two of you were talking. You were laying there in the loose hay, looking out through the open doors onto the area your grandfather had recently plowed up. You looked across a plowed field to the pasture and then to the pine trees beyond *(more specific setting detail)*. You can smell the air, dry and mildly dusty smelling *(olfactory detail)*. The air is warm and very still *(temperature detail)*. It is starting to rain. Both of you are dry, but can hear the rain gently coming down on the metal roof *(auditory detail)*. Best of all, the rain is making that wonderful "wet earth" smell come up from the ground just out back *(more olfactory detail)*. You just love that smell. Everything is still, peaceful, and relaxed as you rest there in the barn with your cousin at your grandparents'.

Deep Breathing and Progressive Relaxation Training

In giving the treatment rationale in the preceding session, emotional and physiological arousal were noted as a significant part of the individual's anger response. Treatment was linked to helping the client lower anger arousal by becoming more calm and relaxed. Progressive relaxation training is now introduced as a means to help the client lower overall arousal. Explain that learning to relax is a learned skill, like learning to ride a bike or play tennis. It's something that may feel foreign at first, but with practice it becomes easier and more automatic.

Progressive relaxation training is a straightforward process that involves systematically tensing and releasing the muscles of the body. Muscles become more relaxed after they have been tensed and released completely. The clinician may want to use the analogy of how relaxed people feel after exercising (i.e., muscles have been tensed and released and feel more relaxed than before).

The therapist then shows the client how to tense and release each muscle group. The client just watches at this point. Modeling reduces confusion and decreases the chances that clients will open their eyes during the relaxation procedure. The clinician might introduce this by saying something like the following:

In a moment, I'm going to have you tense and release the muscles of your body, but first I'd like to show you what it looks like so that you will know what I'm asking you to do. First, we'll start with both hands. I'll have you clench both hands into tight fists. You'll hold that for about ten seconds, and then I'll ask you to release those muscles. When I do, I want you to let the muscles quickly go limp, like this (demonstrating). Just let the tension flow out quickly and focus on the difference between tension and relaxation. I'll have you focus there for about thirty seconds, and then we'll go to the next muscle group, the muscles of the forearms. Push your hands out in front of you (demonstrating), bending your hands back at the wrists like you were pushing a heavy object away. (Continue in this manner, introducing and demonstrating the following muscle groups in order):

- *Upper arms by bending the arms at the elbows and tightening the upper arms like the Charles Atlas pose*

- *Shoulders by shrugging, like trying to bury the shoulders in the ears*

- *Forehead by frowning or lifting the eye brows upwards* (give client a choice)

- *Eyes and bridge of the nose by squinting very tightly, like the client walked out of a dark room into the bright sun*

- *Cheeks and jaws by drawing the mouth back into a wide, wide grin* (preferred over clenching the jaws because of dental problems)

- *Lips and mouth by pressing the lips together firmly*

- *Back of neck by bending the head downwards and backward firmly*

- *Front of the neck by bending the head forward, trying to touch the chin to the chest*

- *Chest and upper back by taking a very deep breath and holding it, then exhaling*

- *Middle and lower back by leaving the hips and shoulders in the same plane and arching the back*

- *Stomach by pushing the stomach out into a hard wall*

- *Hips and buttocks by clenching the buttocks together firmly*

- *Thighs by lifting the feet a couple of inches off the floor and clenching the thighs*

- *Shins by lifting the feet a couple of inches off the floor and trying to touch the toes to the knee caps*

- *Calves by pointing the toes down and away*

The foot and leg exercises provide a nice transition for a summary and the asking of questions. For example the clinician might conclude as follows:

Now, be careful with this exercise. It's easy to have the big toe or arch of the foot cramp up. With all of these exercises, I want you to tense firmly, but not to the point of pain or cramping. Hold the position for about ten seconds, focusing on the feelings of tension, and then release it quickly and focus on the feelings of relaxation that replace the tension. Any questions?

The clinician answers questions and clarifies issues as needed and then continues with the progressive relaxation procedures. The transition may start with deep-breathing induced relaxation as a way of both making the transition to progressive relaxation and introducing breathing as a natural way of relaxing. The clinician might say something like:

Okay, now let's begin tensing and relaxing the muscles. First, settle yourself comfortably in the chair with your arms and legs uncrossed (the latter is done so that the muscles are less likely to fall asleep). *Just close your eyes and settle down* (5 to 10 seconds to do this). . . . *Okay, now let's have you start to relax by taking three or four deep breaths. Take a big deep breath* (clinician takes a big deep audible breath to cue the client). . . . *That's it, now just exhale and relax . . . just letting yourself relax more . . . Now another big deep breath, holding it for a moment . . . and now exhale and relax . . .* (Clinician repeats three to five times total.) *And now let's start tensing and releasing the muscle groups. . . . First, we'll start with the hands. So, tense up both hands into tight fists . . . That's it . . . Feel the tension in and around the fingers and knuckles . . . Okay, now relax and let that go quickly, tuning into the feelings around the fingers, knuckles, and hands . . . Notice how they feel as the tension flows out . . . They may feel tingling, even jump and twitch a little as they relax more and more . . . Just notice the feelings, perhaps warm feelings in the hands and fingers . . . Okay, now let's move to the muscles of the forearms . . . Tense these by* (continuing to tense and release the muscles as outlined above) . . .

After the muscles up through the shoulders have been tensed and released, the clinician may conduct a brief review of the muscles without tensing them (see below for sample instructions). This foreshadows relaxation without tension in the next session. Such a mini-muscle review is also conducted for the muscles in the head-neck region (i.e., forehead through front of neck), chest, stomach and back, and buttocks and lower legs.

(After the shoulders are complete but prior to tensing the forehead) *Okay, let's take a moment and review the muscles we've just been through and let them relax a little more, but without tensing each one. When I mention a muscle group, I want you to focus your attention there and let it relax a little more without tensing it at all. So focus on the muscles around the neck and shoulders. . . . Just letting those muscles relax a little more without tensing them. . . . It may feel like a wave or flow of relaxation soaking in around the shoulders. . . . Now let that wave of relaxation flow down through the biceps . . . loosening and relaxing the biceps and upper arms. . . . Let that flow of relaxation move on down through the forearms . . . loosening and relaxing the forearms. . . . Now let that relaxation flow into your hands and fingers . . . and let the remaining tension drain right out the end of your fingers. . . . Take a moment to enjoy the feelings of relaxation you've been creating and which you can use to reduce anger* (the clinician is giving a self-control suggestion here). . . . *Now shifting our attention to the forehead, tense this area by . . .*

When the tension-release sequence is completed, the relaxation scene is introduced for the first of two repetitions. It is suggested that the relaxation scene be initiated twice because visualization is sometimes difficult on the first presentation, and the second presentation greatly increases the chance that the client will be successful in visualizing the scene. A sequence of relaxing with three to five deep breaths may be interspersed between the first and second visualization. The relaxation scene might be introduced as follows:

> *Now let me help your relax in a different way, this time by having you visualize your personal relaxation scene. In a moment, I am going to ask you to switch on your relaxation scene involving* (brief reference to the scene content). *When I do, I want you to put yourself right back into the scene, like it's happening to you right now. When you're visualizing it and are relaxed, signal me by raising your right index finger* (or whatever signal the therapist and client work out). *So right now, you are* (clinician provides scene detail and prompts for a signal) *... Okay, I see your signal. Now just continue visualizing the scene and relaxing more....* (Approximately ten seconds after the signal) *Okay, now switch that scene off. Just erase it from your mind and refocus your attention on your breathing. To relax even more, let's have you take three big, deep breaths and relax as you exhale. So, a big deep breath in—exhale and relax ...* (repeat two times).

The relaxation scene is then repeated in a similar manner as before and then the session may be terminated by counting backwards from five to one, as follows:

> *You're probably feeling more relaxed now than before we started. I would like to bring you gently back from that state of relaxation by counting backwards from five to one. On the count of four, stretch your arms and legs gently to help them become more alert. On the count of two, open your eyes and look around. On the count of one, you will feel much more alert, but still retain that sense of being relaxed and refreshed. So, I will now begin counting ... five ... four ... just wiggle your arms and legs, letting them become more alert ... three ... feeling now any aches or pains ... two ... opening your eyes and looking around ... and one ... alert and refreshed* (giving the client ten to twenty seconds to sit up and reorient and then moving to debriefing the relaxation experience).

During the debriefing of the relaxation experience, the therapist should inquire first in an open-ended way how the client experienced progressive relaxation. Common positive experiences include a sense of relaxation, calm, peacefulness, sleepiness, and the like. Reinforce these feelings and attribute them to the client's effort. Some minor negative experiences that are common include physical sensations such as twitching, itching, jumpiness, and the like. Others that are more attentional or psychological include distractibility, mind wandering, and losing track of the tension-release sequence. Clients should be told that these are common experiences and that they tend to go away with practice. The therapist should note them mentally, but not pay too much attention to them as they typically drop out with practice. Rarely, clients will experience relaxation induced anxiety (i.e., relaxation exercises bringing a strong sense of anxiety). This can often be circumvented by the following: 1) shifting to another form of relaxation such as autogenic relaxation or temperature biofeedback training; 2) breaking progressive relaxation procedures down into smaller steps and gradually exposing the client to each; 3) counterdemand instructions in which clients are told that anxiety is a common experience and that increased tension often occurs before relaxation is experienced [see Deffenbacher and Suinn (1988) for further detail and procedures].

Inquire about areas that were easy to relax and any that may have been more difficult. Difficult areas may also be those in which the client feels anger physiologically (e.g. the abdomen or shoulders). Inquire about relaxation imagery experiences, paying particular attention to the second visualization as it is typically most representative of what clients will experience. If minor problems are encountered, tell clients that these commonly occur and tend to dissipate with practice. Then move to the summary, feedback, and homework activities.

Session Summary

The three relaxation skills you have learned this week can have a major impact on anger. Progressive relaxation training, if you do it every day, can reduce overall tension. And relaxation imagery and deep breathing can help you face specific situations that threaten your calm.

Feedback from Client

Ask the client for feedback about the session and each of the three relaxation procedures with a question like: "Any special problems or reactions you want to report?" Ask the client what he or she enjoyed about the relaxation procedure. Explore ways that it might have been fun or rewarding. If the exercise was reinforcing, this bodes well for homework compliance. Clarify and answer any questions before assigning homework.

Homework

1. Using Anger Log II (which includes a column for thoughts), have the client continue daily monitoring, paying attention to situations that elicit anger. Encourage the client to note trigger thoughts and the reactions to these thoughts, particularly emotional and physiological. As before, all angry reactions greater than 40 on a 100-point scale of anger arousal are to be reported, and at least one entry per day is to be made.

2. Give your client the relaxation-training handout to facilitate home practice. Ask the client to practice progressive relaxation training, deep breathing, and the relaxation image at least five of the next seven days. Practice is to be recorded in the Relaxation Log (see handout).

HANDOUT 1
Relaxation Practice

Relaxation is very important to your anger reduction efforts. Since you cannot be very angry and relaxed at the same time, you will be learning ways of relaxing quickly and easily so you can relax and reduce tension and anger. Relaxation is a skill, and like any skill, it becomes better and easier with practice.

The first step is practicing at home the skills you learned in the session. For each practice session, set aside about thirty minutes in which you will not be interrupted. You may not need the full thirty minutes, but you don't want to feel rushed with one eye on the clock. Pick a time that is convenient for you. However, do not practice relaxation within the last hour before you go to bed. Many people get a kind of second wind after relaxing, and you don't want that just when you're trying to go to sleep. Pick a place that is quiet and comfortable, but not so comfortable that you go to sleep. Generally, sitting in a comfortable chair works well. Follow the general sequence below. With one hand on your abdomen (just above the belt line) and the other on your chest, breathe in such a way that the hand on your chest moves little or not at all, while the one on your abdomen goes up and down with the breath. If you have difficulty doing deep, abdominal breathing, push on your abdomen with your hand. Breathe so the air seems directed to where you are pushing with your hand, forcing it to rise.

1. *Start with four to five slow deep breaths.* With one hand on your abdomen (just above the belt line) and the other on your chest, breathe in such a way that the hand on your chest moves little or not at all, while the one on your abdomen goes up and down with the breath. If you have difficulty doing deep, abdominal breathing, push on your abdomen with your hand. Breathe so the air seems directed to where you are pushing with your hand, forcing it to rise.

2. *Tense and release muscles* (tense for about ten seconds focusing on the tension and then relax for about 20-30 seconds, focusing on the feelings of relaxation, and then go to the next muscle group). Below is the order and means of tensing the muscles.

   - Hands, by clenching them into a fist
   - Forearms, by bending them at the wrist and pushing away hard
   - Upper arms, by bending them at the elbows and flexing them
   - Shoulders, by shrugging them
     (Review shoulders, upper arms, forearms, and hands without tensing)

   - Forehead, by frowning or raising eyebrows (whichever works best for you)
   - Eyes and bridge of nose, by squinting eyes tightly
   - Cheeks and jaws, by grinning ear to ear
   - Mouth and lips, by pressing lips together firmly

- Back of neck, by pressing backwards and downward firmly
- Front of neck, by pressing chin forwards and downward
  (Review head and neck muscles without tensing them)

- Chest and upper back, by taking a deep breath and holding it, then exhaling
- Middle and lower back, by arching back
- Stomach by pushing it out into a hard wall
  (Review chest, back, and stomach without tensing)

- Hips and buttocks, by clenching the buttocks together firmly
- Thighs, by lifting feet from floor and clenching thighs firmly
- Shins, by trying to touch toes to knees
- Calves, by pointing feet down and away
  (Review legs and lower body without tensing)

3. *Turn on personal relaxation image one or more times.* Vividly imagine your personal relaxation scene. Construct it as quickly as possible, focusing on shapes and colors, sounds, and physical sensations. Pay particular attention to what makes you feel really peaceful and safe in this scene. Hold the image for about a minute, then erase and repeat.

4. *Count backwards from five to one and come to alertness.*

Relaxation Log

Instructions: Put a check mark under all relaxation exercises completed on each date.

Date	Progressive Relaxation Training	Relaxation Imagery	Breathing-Cued Relaxation	Cue-Controlled Relaxation	Relaxation Without Tension

Anger Log II

Date/Time	Situation	Thoughts	Reactions Rate 0–100

Session 3

Relaxation Coping Skills

Monitoring of Current Status

The therapist should ask about reactions to the relaxation training provided in the preceding session. Also note the average anger levels for this week, seeing if there has been any change from last week. Because the very act of measuring anger can tend to reduce both its frequency and intensity, the client may describe (and the Anger Log may support) reductions in overall levels of anger. Try to clarify with the client what he or she is doing or thinking differently (e.g., trying not to take potential triggers as seriously). Such gains are something to celebrate with the client, who may feel a beginning sense of efficacy and control over angry affect. But it's also a chance to offer a warning that these gains may be temporary unless there is consistent effort in the weeks ahead.

If anger levels have remained constant or increased, this is an opportunity to explore exacerbating factors and learn more about the client's anger triggers and nature of the anger response.

Agenda

The agenda for this session includes a review of homework, as well as the new skills of breathing-cued relaxation, cue-controlled relaxation, and relaxation without tension. The client will also have the opportunity to practice all components of the relaxation training in sequence.

Review of Homework

Verify that the Anger Log has been completed with an entry for each date since the last session. As you did in session 2, focus on themes and similarities that occur across various anger situations. Again, note which thoughts, physical responses, and behavior occur most typically in this client's anger reactions. If the client is having difficulty identifying trigger thoughts, ask key questions to help them do so. "What did you think he or she had done to you?" "How had he or she been wrong, or caused you pain?" Any high amplitude anger responses should receive particular attention. Where did they occur, with whom, at what time, and after what event? Also, what were the outcomes or consequences?

Review the Relaxation Log and check to see if the client has practiced relaxation at least five days of the week. If there is noncompliance, or minimal compliance, it's recommended that you assess with the client all blocks to completing the homework. When the blocks have been identified, make a specific plan for overcoming each obstacle. Have the client make a written contract for completing the homework if he or she is still having difficulty at this point.

There are many reasons for noncompliance. A common source of noncompliance is falling asleep. If this happens, encourage the client to find another time and/or less comfortable environment in which to practice relaxation (e.g., switch from relaxing on the bed at 7:00 P.M. to sitting in a straight back chair at 5:30-6:00 P.M.). Another common problem is a misunderstanding of when to practice relaxation. Some clients think that they should relax only when they are stressed and tense. This misunderstanding should be clarified. Indicate that they can practice relaxation methods when stressed and may experience some benefit, but relaxation is a skill, and must therefore be practiced nearly every day (at least five of seven days), whether the client is stressed or not. Another common issue is having other commitments and not spending the necessary time on relaxation practice. This should be addressed directly by assisting the client to clarify the importance of and their commitment to anger reduction. Another source of noncompliance is current life stress and problems that interfere with relaxation practice. These should be explored briefly. If stress is actually very high (e.g., the breakup of a relationship), then explore and address these issues directly. If, however, the current level of stress is characteristic of the client's life, then address it as a time-commitment issue.

Some clients may question the value of relaxation for anger management. Here's an example of how you might respond to this concern.

Client: I'm not sure I see the point of this. I'm never going to be able to do that progressive relaxation stuff, tensing and relaxing my muscles, when I'm in the middle of some big hassle. And what's it gonna do anyway? A few critical remarks from my wife is all it takes to wipe out a whole hour of these exercises. I'm instantly tight as a rubber band.

Therapist: If you do the progressive relaxation exercise every day, that'll help reduce your overall tension and make you less irritable. But you're right. It isn't enough. You need a way to relax your body during an actual upset.

Client:	Yeah, that's my point. How do I do that?
Therapist:	In two weeks we're going to do an exercise to help you practice relaxing quickly in the face of provocation. We will have you become angry in the session and relax away the anger. We're going to keep practicing until it's "overlearned," which means it's so natural you don't even have to think about it. Like riding a bike or driving a car.
Client:	So I shouldn't worry that I can't relax my body when my wife is on my case?
Therapist:	No. It's all about practice. When you've practiced relaxing again and again and again while imagining provocative situations, you get really good at it. The key is to keep rehearsing so when your wife really ticks you off, relaxing and deep breathing becomes a reflexive, natural response.

Concepts and Skills

Skill Building

Provide a brief overview of the four basic relaxation coping skills—relaxation without tension, breathing-cued relaxation, relaxation imagery, and cue-controlled relaxation (each described in this section). Indicate that the client will become able to use one or a combination of these to lower anger and other stress reactions such as anxiety, guilt, and depression.

Review Progressive Relaxation Training

Ask your client to go through the entire progressive relaxation sequence without prompting on your part. Verify that he or she has either memorized the sequence or is able to use the relaxation handout. Assuming tension-release practice has gone well, tell the client you will be doing relaxation practice today without tension.

Review Relaxation Imagery

Have your client close his or her eyes and describe out loud the key relaxation image. Notice if the image has sufficient visual, auditory, and kinesthetic detail to be evocative. Ask the client which part of the image is particularly helpful for relaxation. You may wish to collaborate with the client to add more details in order to make this part of the image even more powerful. Develop a new scene as needed.

Breathing-Cued Relaxation

Breathing-cued relaxation is an extension of the deep breathing procedures from the last session. Have your client take deep, diaphragmatic breaths. This can be accomplished by having the client place one hand on the abdomen (just above the belt line) and the other on the chest. During a deep, diaphragmatic breath, the hand on the abdomen should move while the one on the chest should move slightly or not at all. Continue practicing the slow, deep breaths until the client can reliably "push" the breath into the abdominal area. If, after reasonable practice, your client continues to struggle, have him or her press on the abdominal area and try to direct the air down to where the hand is pushing. Other strategies include having the client lie down with a phone book placed over the abdominal area. The goal is to make the phone book rise and fall with each breath.

Here's how you can introduce this exercise to your client:

Start by putting one hand over your chest and the other over your abdomen, just above your belt line. Try taking a deep breath, way down into your belly. Really try to push your belly out with the breath. As you breathe in, the hand on your abdomen should rise, while the hand on your chest remains relatively still. Focus all your attention on your belly—send your breath down, down, down to fill your belly. Let your breath slightly stretch and relax your abdomen. Each breath stretches your diaphragm and sends a message to your brain that all is well, there's nothing to worry about.

Cue-Controlled Relaxation

At this point you can introduce the concept of the cue word or phrase paired with a deep, diaphragmatic breath. Cue-controlled relaxation gives the client tools to relax the entire body in a minute or less. Typical cue words or phrases include: Relax; relax and let go; peace; calm control; calm and relaxed; one; love; or Om.

Instruct the client to verbally repeat the cue word or phrase while exhaling a diaphragmatic breath. The cue can also be said subvocally or be merely a thought. Here's how to introduce this skill to your client:

Now it's time to select a word or phrase that will cue deep relaxation each time you repeat it. The word could be "relax" or "letting go" or "peace." It might be a color, such as "green," or a feeling, such as "love." One or two syllable words seem to work best. (Client selects cue word)

I am going to say the word "relax" (or other cue word) slowly, and each time you hear it, just let yourself relax more. . . . So, just let yourself "relax." . . . (Wait approximately ten seconds between repetitions. The clinician can use the client's slow rhythmic breathing as a rough cue for the repetitions.). . . . "Relax" . . . "Relax" . . . "Relax" . . . more and more "Relax". . . . (Repeat a total of ten times). . . . Now take a few moments and continue to relax your body as you slowly repeat the word "relax" to yourself. Say "relax" as you breathe out slowly and regularly . . . (pause approximately 20 seconds). . . . That's it, just relaxing more each time you say the word "relax" to yourself . . . (pause approximately twenty seconds).

Okay, discontinue saying the word "relax" and just take a moment to enjoy the feelings of relaxation that you're creating for yourself.

Relaxation Without Tension

Take clients through the major muscle groups in exactly the same sequence as the progressive relaxation training. But on this occasion don't have them tighten anything. Instead, have them scan each major muscle group for tension and relax away any tightness noticed in the target area. The key phrase *notice and relax* can be used frequently throughout this exercise. Sample instructions might sound like this:

Focus on your arms and notice any tension you may feel there. Now relax away the tension. Just let it go. Notice and relax the tension. Feel the difference as you relax your arms.

Now turn your attention to your upper face. Notice any tension and relax it away. Let it go. Notice and relax the tension. As you relax, really feel the difference in your upper face. Notice any tension in your jaw, and relax. Relax it away. Notice what it feels like for your jaw to let go, to be really loose.

Combined Relaxation Skills

At this point the client can learn to use relaxation skills in combination. Have the client sit back and get comfortable, closing their eyes. The sequence of training is up to the clinician, but the following order works well. Start with breathing-cued relaxation. Follow this by relaxation without tension. Then, follow with a trial of relaxation imagery and cue-controlled relaxation. Then another trial of relaxation imagery, followed by breathing-cued relaxation and cue-controlled relaxation. Repeat other skills as time allows, and then terminate by counting backwards as done in the last session.

The combined relaxation exercise should take about fifteen minutes.

Session Summary

Briefly review with the client the four relaxation coping skills—relaxation without tension, relaxation imagery, breathing-cued relaxation, and cue-controlled relaxation. Indicate that different people will find specific strategies or a certain combination of strategies more effective than others for reducing anger. But this can only be learned with practice. Emphasize the importance of over-learning—mastering skills to the point where they seem natural, even automatic.

The combined relaxation exercise is another key to anger mastery. Essentially, you are combining breathing-cued relaxation, cue-controlled relaxation and relaxation without tension in a single exercise while alternating it with relaxation imagery. Put together, these components are a powerful and effective relaxation armamentarium.

Feedback from the Client

Ask the client about his or her experience during each component of the relaxation training. Explore which components felt easiest and most natural. Praise the client's willingness to try new things and learn new skills.

Homework

1. Ask the client to continue self-monitoring anger using the Anger Log II handout. Give the client additional handouts if needed.

2. Clients should practice the full relaxation sequence once per day (i.e., relaxation without tension, relaxation imagery, cue-controlled relaxation, and breathing-cued relaxation). This is to be done in the quiet of the client's home as progressive relaxation was done the week before. It typically will take about ten to fifteen minutes, but clients should allow plenty of time so that they're not hurried. Practice should be recorded in the Relaxation Log.

3. At least once per day (more often if possible), clients are to practice one of the relaxation coping skills in nonstressful, everyday circumstances (e.g., watching TV, waiting for a friend at lunch, riding the bus, etc.). These efforts should be recorded in the Relaxation Log. The goal here is to help the client be able to initiate relaxation coping skills in vivo. Some clients will ask if they can or should apply relaxation coping skills when they're angry or stressed. Answer a cautious "Yes" to this question. The caution is that their skills are not fully developed yet and therefore may not successfully lower anger. The client will be gaining a great deal more practice in coming sessions, but if he or she wants to try now, that's fine. However, tell your client not to become discouraged if the skills don't work perfectly yet. The goal is to try and see what happens, not necessarily to bring anger under control at this point.

4. Ask the client to identify and make notes of two occasions where he or she was anticipating or ruminating about an anger situation that was likely, but had not yet happened. For example, anticipating dealing with parents, boss, or coworker about a tense issue; waiting for a roommate or partner to come home so that an issue could be dealt with; or knowing that something upsetting was about to happen at work. Clients should be instructed to focus on all of the external (situational and behavioral details) and internal (cognitive, emotional, and physiological) components of the provocative circumstance. The emotional intensity level of these two scenes should be approximately 50-60 on the 100-point scale. These scenes will get further attention in homework following session 4.

Session 4

Cognitive Restructuring

Monitoring of Current Status

Celebrate any gains the client reports in terms of frequency or magnitude of anger reactions. Check to see if the client has encountered any stresses during the week that may have exacerbated anger. Clarify and troubleshoot these as possible. Explore with your client any reactions to the relaxation component of the treatment.

Agenda

The agenda for this session will begin with a review of the homework. New material will include an introduction to cognitive concepts, a listing and description of anger distortions, and practice recognizing and labeling distortions in the Anger Log.

Review of Homework

Review the Relaxation Log. Each component of the relaxation program should have been practiced at least five out of seven days. If there have been barriers to maintaining a regular practice schedule, identify them and devise a collaborative coping plan. Should it become apparent that the client is not invested in doing homework, you will need to confront his or her readiness for the treatment program. Here's how you might approach this issue:

Therapist: I'm concerned that you're not getting enough practice at home.

Client: Yeah, well, you know how it is. There are lots of things I gotta do. I'm sure this relaxation is good to do and all, but it takes a lot of time.

Therapist: About twenty minutes, or so. You may need to make an appointment with yourself to do it at a specific time each day.

Client: I try, but things come up.

Therapist: Here's what worries me. I know you've had some fights where you and your girlfriend nearly split up. And there have been a couple of recent jobs you've lost after blowing up. (*Remind your client of any recent anger episodes that had serious negative consequences.*) You came in to see me because you wanted to change that pattern; you didn't want to risk losing what's important to you.

Client: Right, we already talked about all that.

Therapist: We did, and I realized as I listened how much you wanted to change the way you react to upsetting situations. But here's the problem. Unless there's a way to find time for practicing at home, you won't be able to learn these new anger-management skills. Nothing will change. Your anger will stay on a hair trigger.

Client: Look, I'm trying, but I don't have a lot of time.

Therapist: I know you really want things to be different. If you put in the practice, there's a very good chance they *will* change. But without daily practice the new skills simply won't get learned. Can you commit yourself to doing the home practice a minimum of five out of seven days?

Client: If this won't work without it, I guess so.

Therapist: I'm afraid it won't, so I'm glad to hear your willingness. Let's see if you can write in your appointment book the practice times for this week.

It's important to be clear and unambiguous in stressing that the success of therapy depends on the homework practice. But avoid framing this punitively. You are "worried" and "concerned" about the risks and potential losses if anger management fails. The issue is not a lack of effort on the client's part, the issue is the *danger* that habitual anger responses pose to the client's well-being.

The therapist may confront these issues in other ways as well. For example, you may ask the client if he or she has really wanted to change their anger responses in the past, and inquire if anything actually changed. Typically, clients report promising themselves or others to change and even making a few efforts in that direction, only to be disappointed when nothing really happened. The clinician should follow up with an inquiry about why lasting change didn't occur. The usual report is one or both of two things: Either the person was counting on others to change and these people did not, or the client didn't continue sustained efforts at change. At this point you can clarify to the client the probable reasons these strategies didn't work. First, it is unlikely that others will change exactly the way the client wants them to, clearing up any potential anger triggers. Even if they do, you can point out that it's unlikely that things will stay changed. Second, changing anger is like changing any behavior—it's hard work. If it were easy, the client would have already changed and wouldn't be in therapy. Suggest that therapy is not like New Year's resolutions; it isn't effective to simply say you're going to do it but not follow through with significant effort. Therapy must be undertaken with resolve if change is to occur.

Alternatively, anger reduction may be likened to weight loss. The individual must, like the dieter, engage in behaviors that lose and keep off the weight of anger. It can be done, but it's hard work. The therapist should ask the client what he or she is going to do to make sure that the resolution to reduce anger or "lose the weight" of anger will be achieved. How will the client find the necessary time, energy, and commitment for these tasks?

A second strategy is to ask the client if he or she ever undertook learning something new like a foreign language, tennis, sewing, and so on. Analogies should be attuned to the culture, gender, and individual background of the individual. The goal is to seek out a complex, new task that the individual undertook successfully. The clinician should ask the client how this was done. The usual report is that the person received some lessons or assistance and then practiced the elements to get more proficient. The therapist can use this information by drawing a parallel to anger management. First, the client is getting some lessons or assistance in the form of therapy (i.e., getting training in the skills necessary for anger reduction). However, like any new task, it takes practice to really improve. You can then ask the client what he or she is willing to give up in order to have time for practice and improvements.

Look over the week's Anger Log to verify that there is a notation for each date. Notice if the average anger level is changing relative to previous weeks and pay attention to any situation that continues to evoke high levels of anger. As you have in previous sessions, let the log be a springboard to identify physical responses, thoughts, and behaviors that are frequent components of the anger response. Because this week you will be introducing cognitive concepts, it may be helpful to emphasize important triggering thoughts the client describes in the log. Look for contrasts or examples that provide a lead or transition into cognitive elements.

Concepts and Skills

Psychoeducation

Introduction to the Cognitive Model

Remind your client that anger has two components: arousal (both emotional and physiological) and automatic thoughts. While arousal management through relaxation is important, it isn't enough. It's also crucial to understand the role of automatic thoughts—how cognitions trigger and shape angry feelings.

Explain the ABC model of emotion, where A (event) leads to B (thought, interpretation, assumption, appraisal), which in turn leads to C (emotion).

> *When you get swept up in anger, it seems as though someone or something is making you feel that way—they are causing your anger. But really what happens is that an event starts you thinking about how bad or unjust a situation is, how someone has harmed or taken advantage of you. And it's the thought that sets off your anger. In your mind, you label someone's behavior*

as "wrong," "bad," or "unjust." They've deliberately caused you pain. It's these assumptions and interpretations of the event that trigger your feelings. (If possible, link this back to a specific example from current or past homework. This personalizes the general issues.)

As an experiment, ask your client to rate his or her current anger level on the 0 to 100 point scale (0 = calm, no anger; 100 = furious, as angry as you've ever been). Now review some key experiences recorded in the Anger Log. Pay special attention to the anger-triggering automatic thoughts. Have the client elaborate on these thoughts, focusing on any appraisals of wrong or unjust behavior. Have the client think out loud about the situation. Now ask the client to rate his or her level of anger. It will almost certainly have gone up.

This exercise can provide more evidence that thoughts affect feelings. Point out to the client that nothing happened in the room to create anger. The triggers were 100 percent cognitive—the rehearsal of old, negative interpretations. Suggest that anger would likely be even higher if the client were in the actual situation having the "hot" thoughts and recycling them rapidly along with other "hot" thoughts, images, and feelings.

Cognitive Visualization

You can expand this theme with a visualization experience. Ask your client to close his or her eyes and imagine having recently lost an important relationship:

Imagine a situation where you have suffered a romantic rejection. After dating for a number of months, your partner tells you that the chemistry feels wrong and describes feeling that something is missing in the relationship. Your partner conveys appreciation for you and talks fondly of things enjoyed during your months together. As you listen, you're thinking about the lovely times that are over and about the many things you'll miss. You tell yourself that it'll be a cold day in hell before someone like this comes into your life again. You start to ponder some of your failures and limitations as a person that may have affected the relationship. This was a special person, a good relationship, and now it's lost because of your mistakes. Life is empty, meaningless without him or her. And it's all your fault. If you hadn't screwed things up, maybe you'd still be together. Maybe he or she is better off without you.

Ask the client to describe any feelings while imagining this scenario, and then ask them to rate these feelings on the scale from 0 to 100. Write the feelings and ratings down. Then have the client imagine the situation again but thinking about it differently.

Now imagine the same situation: Your partner tells you the chemistry is wrong, that there is something missing in the relationship. He or she appreciates you and remembers many good times, but doesn't feel able to get closer. As you listen, you tell yourself that this is bullshit. Your partner never really tried to get close or work any of the problems out. You're getting thrown away because he or she is too uncaring and too damned lazy to put effort into the relationship. Out of selfishness and complete lack of regard, your partner has taken away the one good thing you had, something that felt special. You have been screwed over and cheated, and you don't have to be nice about it. You've been jerked around, and nobody should be treated that way.

Once again ask the client to describe any feelings that came up during the visualization. Rate their intensity from 0 to 100, and write both the feelings and ratings down. Then tell the client that there's one last piece to the exercise. With eyes closed, have the client visualize the situation again, getting in touch with the feelings he or she is having.

It's the same situation with your partner where you're told the chemistry is wrong, there's something missing, the relationship doesn't feel close enough. Your partner appreciates and values you but would like to end it. As you listen, you tell yourself that this is sad and something you're going to have to deal with. For a while, you may feel hurt and sad and lonely, and you probably will for some time to come. But it's not the end of the world. You'll need to rally your friends and get some support. You're going to find other things to do, such as take a cooking class, join a singles' bike club, and stop turning down party invitations. In your next relationship, you decide you're going to get feedback at regular intervals and make sure you stay more aware of how your partner is feeling. If you learn about a problem early enough, chances are you can do something about it. This is sad and hard, but you can cope.

Have the client describe and rate any feelings that came up during this scenario. Write them down. Now show the client the paper on which you've written their emotional responses to each visualization. While every scenario described the same basic situation, the emotional response to each was probably quite different. The reaction to the first is generally depression, and to the second, anger. The third scenario, with its focus on rational thinking and problem solving, usually elicits realistic sadness with a determination to cope with the outcome. Point out that the affect changed while the situation remained the same. What made the difference was automatic thoughts—how the situation was interpreted.

Now turn your attention to the intensity of affect ratings. Ratings on the 0 to 100 scale of intensity are generally 70 to 100 for the first two scenarios, and 25 to 50 for the third. Rational thinking and problem solving clearly modulate emotional intensity.

This exercise underscores the importance of cognitions and serves to introduce the notion that life provides many frustrating, disappointing, irritating events, but that high levels of anger are constructed by cognitions that make bad situations worse. Point out to the client that life serves up many "crummy" things, and people can actually make them worse by the way that they think or the attitudes they hold. But, on the other hand, people can also learn to cope differently. The key to coping is to recognize the power of automatic thoughts and learn to change them. Changing thoughts, just as in the scenarios, can reduce anger. The good news is that change is real and possible. The bad news is that it takes vigilance and practice—lots of practice. The first step is learning to recognize anger-triggering automatic thoughts.

Anger Distortions

Introduce the six types of anger distortions and go back to the Anger Log to find examples, if you can, of each.

Magnifying/Catastrophizing. Magnifying and catastrophizing are ways of thinking that make every problem bigger and worse. When a person is magnifying or catastrophizing they often phrase their thoughts using words like "awful," "disgusting," "terrible," "can't stand it," "horrendous," "devastating," "sickening," and so on. The person then reacts with extra anger to the exaggerated reality they've created, rather than to the "real" reality (which may be frustrating enough). Descriptions that magnify tend to exaggerate the painful aspects of a situation while leaving out everything that's tolerable or even good. The rational alternative to magnifying is to describe each situation accurately and specifically. The dinner that was "horrible and totally overpriced" can be talked about more accurately: "The entree was $16 and the fish tasted bland." You might describe magnifying and catastrophizing to your client in the following way:

> *Magnifying and catastrophizing is the tendency to perceive things as worse than they really are. Events are thought of or described as "awful," "terrible," "disgusting," or "horrendous." "She's awful with the whole support staff." "This is going to be a horrible mess next week." These magnifications will crank up your sense of outrage and the feeling that you've been victimized. When you exaggerate a problem, you feel overwhelmed by the unfairness. You feel wronged.*
>
> *There are three things you can do to control the tendency to magnify. First, be realistically negative. Life often serves you up crummy, frustrating, difficult, hassling things. You are likely to get your share, just like everyone else. So call it what it is, a pain, a hassle, a loss, or whatever. Feel those negative feelings. But don't blow it out of proportion. Use words like "annoying," "frustrating," "disappointing," "sad," and the like and keep things where they really are. Second, try to use very accurate language. Rather than words such as "disgusting" or "horrible," describe exactly and specifically what the problem is. The bill isn't "outrageous," it's "$40 more than I expected." Your "obsessive" boss could be more accurately described as "detail and mistake oriented." The third way you can control magnifying is to look at the whole picture. Step back and consider everything. There is a downside and an upside to every situation or relationship. Your friend is late for most dates, but on the other hand, is a good listener when you need support. Focusing on the positive aspects of a person or a situation puts a natural break on magnifying.*

Overgeneralization. Angry individuals tend to draw broad, general conclusions that go well beyond the details of specific events. This anger distortion is built on words such as "always," "all," "every," "never," "everybody," and so on. The terms make an event that happened once or twice feel like something that's constant and eternal. As with magnifying, overgeneralization makes the problem feel bigger than it is and helps the client ignore all moderating and contradictory experiences. "He's *always* handing me things at the last minute" distorts reality because it obscures the many occasions when tasks were assigned with ample warning. The key to overcoming this anger distortion is to avoid terms that generalize. Once again, clients should be encouraged to stay with and use accurate, specific descriptions of fact. It's also important to look for *exceptions* to the generality. Was there ever a time when the opposite happened? Has the offending person ever behaved differently from the stereotype?

> *Overgeneralization is a big trigger for anger. You can always tell you're overgeneralizing when you use words like "all," "always," "every," "never," "everybody," "nobody," and so on. They're the tipoff that you're exaggerating or going beyond the facts of a situation or problem. Using these words will make you angrier because it makes the problem seem constant and overwhelming.*
>
> *The keys to stop overgeneralizing are: 1) try to avoid generalizing terms, 2) use specific and accurate descriptions of a situation ("You were late twice this week" instead of "You're always late," and 3) look for exceptions to the rule (what were specific times the person acted differently or the situation was reversed?). Looking for exceptions is perhaps the most important antidote for overgeneralization. When you take the trouble to recall how people sometimes act contrary to their tendencies, it makes things less enraging. It puts things in an overall context, maybe a frustrating one, but you can cope with that.*

Polarized or dichotomous thinking is a special subset of overgeneralization. In the case of this cognitive error, the client codes events in broad, overinclusive, dichotomous ways. Things are judged to be at one or the other end of a continuum. These continua have significant positive or negative emotional polarities. For example, things are good or bad, right or wrong, people are winners or losers, strong or wimpy, people love me or hate me, and the like. When the person encounters evidence that the positive end of the continuum is not true (e.g., something is not good or right, the person is not a winner, or not powerful), the negative polarity is triggered, and he or she reacts with intense anger in response to this perceived highly negative state of affairs. The antidote for such dichotomous thinking is for your client to employ more qualifying adjectives and adverbs (e.g., a little, somewhat, a lot, etc.) and phrases that introduce the shades of gray into the black-or-white world. A second strategy, parallel to addressing other elements of overgeneralization, is for the individual to look at multiple dimensions of the situation. For example, in addressing a situation in which the client is tempted to think of a coworker in terms of a love-hate dichotomy (the coworker is either all good or all bad), exploration of the relationship may reveal that the client actually likes one thing about the person, strongly dislikes another, and couldn't care less about a third. The client can be shown that a love-hate dichotomy does not apply as there are multiple dimensions involved in each relationship, each with its own valence.

Demanding/Commanding. With this distortion, the person elevates him- or herself to be a god or goddess. The person elevates personal preferences and desires up to the level of dictates and commandments of themselves, others, and the world. These are the "ought to," "have to," "need," "gotta," and "expect" kind of thoughts. In terms of anger, the client is imposing his or her will on some element of the world and *insisting* that things be a certain way, the way they "should" be. Unnecessary anger eventuates when these commandments are broken or unfulfilled.

These demands, commandments, or "shoulds" are often accompanied by a sense of entitlement, the feeling that one's needs *ought* to be gratified. Many people believe they're entitled to feel emotionally and physically safe, to always rest when they're tired, to never be alone, or to have their work always appreciated. One of the biggest entitlements is the expectation that people will know one's needs without asking.

You can introduce the notion of replacing demanding/commanding thoughts with personal preferences or wants. Suggest that it's very important to hold personal preferences and values, to care about them and work hard for them, and to experience the natural frustrations, irritations, and disappointments that come from not getting them met. But make it clear that raising these preferences to the level of a demand leads to heightened anger, because the other person is always seen as wrong and bad. Change "you should" thoughts to "I'd prefer that you ..." requests. Some confrontations with shoulds may come from a series of questions such as, "I understand that you're frustrated, but why 'shouldn't' you have to experience that?" Others may need to be more pointed, such as "Who appointed you God?" These can be followed by an explanation of the rigid, "godlike" role of the person's commandments.

Another key to dealing with shoulds is to recognize that people inevitably do what *they* want to do, not what *we* think they should do. The clinician may wish to introduce the "paradox of freedom" here. The therapist asks the client if he or she always does what others ask or tell them to. The usual response is an incredulous look and an emphatic "No." The client is then asked, "Why not?" Typical explanations include something to the effect that the person has the right to make his or her own mind up and act accordingly. Then, the clinician points out the paradox. That is, they are free to decide, but when they make demands, they assume that others are not. In a free world, the client is free, and so are others—free to pursue their goals and desires and not live according to the client's dictates. Others have the right to be wrong. The client is free to choose how he or she will deal with that, but has no right to impose demands/commands on others.

> *Anger is often triggered by a judgment based on a set of rules about how people should and should not act. People who behave according to the rules are right, and those who break the rules are wrong and bad. Angry people think that others know and accept their rules but deliberately choose to violate them.*
>
> *The first problem with shoulds, however, is that people with whom you feel angry rarely agree with your rules. Their perception of the situation leaves them blameless and justified. Other people's rules always seem to exempt them from the judgments you think they deserve. The second problem with shoulds is that people rarely do what they should do. They do what they need or want to do. They take care of themselves. Shoulds can be thought of as one person's needs and values imposed on someone else who has very different needs and values.*

The key thing to remember about shoulds is that people do what they want to do, not what you think they should do. Your needs are not their needs. Because you want something or believe in something, it doesn't mean that they have to agree with you. And while shoulds make you feel righteous in the moment, they'll often push your anger out of control. The best way to cope with shoulds is to think of them as personal preferences or wants. It's better to think "I'd prefer he left the party with me," rather than "He should always leave with me."

Common commandments often involve the following themes:

1. *Perfectionism:* I or others should do it right, perfectly, correctly, etc.

2. *Others (key people) should love me:* A certain person or persons should love, like, approve or support me.

3. *Others (key people) should not dislike me:* (not the same as #2) Other people should not express dislike, disapproval, criticism, or negative feelings toward me.

4. *Things should be just and fair:* It's not right when things are not just, fair, kind, courteous, respectful (whatever a person's standards or rules for behavior are).

5. *Bad things shouldn't happen to me:* I shouldn't have to experience, deal with, cope with, or put up with pain, frustration, delay, etc. (a kind of narcissistic rule that the person be exempt from the difficulty of normal living).

In addressing demanding and commanding, the therapist should be ready to focus on two issues. They may not necessarily come up in this session, but in case they do, they are introduced here.

The client may say or imply that since the therapist is not endorsing his or her shoulds and rules for living, the therapy is "worthless," and hence can be ignored or dismissed. The clinician should address this directly. It should be pointed out that the client has every right to endorse whatever values he or she wishes to hold. It's healthy to have values, to hold them dear, to work hard for their implementation, to feel good when they are achieved, and to feel natural frustration when they are not implemented or achieved. However, it's when the individual elevates his or her values to the level of moral dictates on others that problems and anger ensue. So the therapist is not endorsing a valueless position. Quite the contrary, you support the client's right to values and encourage their pursuit. What you are questioning is the rigid demand that others live by the client's rules.

The second issue is the client's attempt to trap the therapist into disproving his or her values, rather than having the client prove why the world should meet these commandments. Angry clients are often adept at assuming the position that what they say is true, challenging the therapist to try and prove them wrong. Therapeutic time is likely to be wasted, and true therapeutic impasses may ensue if the therapist accepts this challenge. It is suggested that the therapist assume the opposite posture, namely that it is the client's job to prove his or her position convincingly. More specifically, you can use reflections and summaries to highlight the client's position, then use open-ended questions that push the client to explore and justify this belief.

In so doing, the client is forced to explore underlying assumptions, rather than asserting them as a fact. Examples might include:

I understand that you find it really upsetting and frustrating when others don't agree with you, but why should they automatically agree with you?

You really want to do it that particular way. It would be much better and more convenient for you. But, why shouldn't he be able to do it his way?

You want her love and approval, but why does she have to give it to you?

Have you ever decided not to love someone or not to go out with them?... So you had the right to choose that for yourself, but why doesn't he have the same right?

Sounds like you expect yourself to do everything perfectly. But why? Why do you have to be perfect? Why can't you make a mistake every now and then?

Inflammatory/Global Labeling. This is a major trigger for the anger prone individual. Typical of global labeling are the highly negative, often obscene attacks such as: "freak," "bastard," "sonofabitch," "jerk," "slob," "ass," "asshole," "idiot," and so on. Other global judgments include: "stupid," "selfish," "screwup," "loser," "worthless," "ugly," "evil," and "lazy." Such labels condemn a *person*, rather than specific behavior. The key is to replace the global attack with accurate and specific descriptions of the individual or problem behavior. The landlady isn't a ripoff artist; she has asked for a hundred dollar increase in the rent. A broker isn't stupid; rather, he has made several bad investment decisions.

A global label makes sweeping negative judgments. Typical global labels include terms like "stupid," "selfish," "asshole," "jerk," "loser," "liar," and so on. Global labels fuel your anger by turning the target into someone who is totally bad and worthless. They are like a cup of mental gasoline on an angry fire. Instead of focusing on a particular behavior, you indict the entire person. Global labels are always false because they exaggerate a single characteristic and imply that it's the whole picture.

Some labels are just plain funny when you think about it. Take, for example, calling another driver an "ass." If you look it up, "ass" has two meanings—burro and buttocks. Now, how do burros or buttocks drive? Visualize it for a moment. See how absurd that is. Stay with the facts—a scary, discourteous, unsafe, etc., driver. That's bad enough, but not infuriating.

The way to overcome global labels is to be specific. Replace the label with an accurate description of the offensive behavior. Leave the person out of it, describe what he does, not who he is.

Misattributions/Single Explanations. Angry individuals often jump to egocentric conclusions or interpretations about the motives, beliefs, and feelings of others. They then respond angrily as if these conclusions are true, whether they are or not. The underlying belief is that others are often motivated by a desire to harm. They are out to get the client, things have been done intentionally or on purpose. One way to explore misattribution is to discuss the problem of mind reading. How often has the client been convinced that he or she knew exactly what someone else was thinking and feeling, only to discover later how wrong that assumption was? Encourage your client to remember and list some of these mind-reading errors. Suggest that there may have been many other times when a mind-reading error was made but never discovered. Explore, in terms of the client's actual history, some of the negative consequences of misattribution.

There are helpful antidotes for misattribution. First, encourage clients to do reality checks. When you hear your client make assumptions about the motives and feelings of others, work collaboratively to develop tactful verifying questions. "I've a feeling you're a little withdrawn because I got home late, is there anything to that?" "It occurred to me that maybe you think I was kind of stupid to have sold the car. Am I imagining things, or is there some truth in that?" "Was there a reason for going to the game without me?"

Secondly, whenever your client is doing any kind of mind-reading, you should work to develop alternative explanations. Look for different interpretations of the problematic behavior; make a list of other possible motives. You can even encourage your client to generate far-fetched explanations (e.g., the other person is an alien) in order to help break the assumptions.

> *Misattribution is basically mind-reading. A friend excessively brags about a promotion, and you feel like he's trying to annoy you. Or you assume that your mother's putting you down if she asks where you got a certain piece of furniture. When people hurt or annoy you, it's easy to imagine that it was deliberate and meant to upset you. But how can you know a person's true motives? Unless you ask and get a direct answer there's a real chance you could have gotten it all wrong. Can you remember any times when you made an assumption about someone else's motives or feelings toward you, and you learned later it was way off? Have you ever made an assumption about someone's intentions, found out you were wrong, but had already acted in a way that caused a big problem?*
>
> *The best way to avoid misattributions is to pay attention when you're making assumptions about people's motives. When you catch yourself, try to find a way to test the truth of your beliefs. You and I together could plan some of the questions you might ask that wouldn't be too embarrassing, to check out those assumptions. Another way to overcome misattribution is to develop as many possible alternative explanations for people's behavior as you can possibly think of. Don't believe everything you assume. Think of your assumptions as one of many possible hypotheses to explain someone's behavior.*

In dealing with misattributions and one-track thinking, the clinician should be prepared, now or later, to deal with the possibility that the client's attribution may be accurate. For example, the client may be right that a partner does not really care for him or her, that a coworker does have it in for the client, or that a parent really is cruel and abusive. Occasionally, malevolent, negative attributions are accurate and must be considered. If it's discovered that the negative attribution is true, then the clinician's focus shifts from cognitive restructuring to support and problem solving.

If the situation is dangerous or highly aversive, the clinician may need to shift to a crisis intervention modality in order to prevent harm to the client or others. For less dramatic, but more probable conditions, the usual first step is to outline the nature of the choices open to the individual. The client may not be able to do much to change the negative situation, but he or she does have some choices about how to react. Sometimes these choices are difficult and painful (e.g., to stay with or leave an intransigent spouse/partner, or to continue or terminate a stressful job). Anger management may free resources to help the client calmly think about and decide a plan of action, but no amount of anger management will remove the need to make painful and difficult choices. This is one of the developmental and existential aspects of living. Some clients have a "should" that they be spared making difficult choices. This can be addressed as a demanding/commanding form of cognitive distortion. Then start problem solving.

Blaming. Blaming is a major anger distortion. The key belief underlying blaming is that the client's pain is someone else's responsibility. The client is blameless and has no responsibility. The problem is externalized; the client righteously and angrily blames and attacks the perceived source. Realistically, however, the pain a client may be in won't change unless he or she finds alternative coping strategies. Putting the blame on others obscures the need to find new, more effective responses to a problem situation. The client stays helpless and waits for the other person to "fix things."

Blaming constructs a world in which people are deliberately doing bad things. A more realistic view is that people always choose the action that seems most likely to meet their needs. They always choose the *apparent* good. Can we blame anyone for choosing what seems to be the best available option?

The key to overcoming blaming is to address the client's helplessness. Make a collaborative coping plan to change a painful situation. It may be helpful to introduce the difference between the "elegant" and practical solutions. In the elegant solution, everyone else changes (e.g., no one ever drives in your lane, children and spouses are always supportive and cooperative, coworkers are always understanding, timely, and do their part perfectly, etc.). The practical solution is developing a plan for coping when this fantasy is not fulfilled, which it rarely is.

> *Blaming comes from a belief that the other person* did it to you. *Whatever pain you feel, whatever hurt or fear or loss, they did it to you. One problem with blaming is that it leaves you feeling helpless. Whatever is wrong, whatever is hurting you, it feels as though the power to solve the problem lies with others. When you get stuck in blaming, it's easy to forget that you often have the ability to make the situation different. Because you're focused on trying to change the other person's behavior, you forget that there are choices you* can *make.*
>
> *The other problem with blaming is that people are mostly doing the best they can. Everyone tends to choose the action that seems most likely to meet their own needs. And very often that can hurt or disappoint others. When we blame others for what they're doing, we're blaming them for taking care of themselves in the best way they know how at the moment.*

In the course of describing the six anger distortions, it's helpful to weave in examples from the client's Anger Log. The easiest way to do this is to ask clients to think of any examples from their own recent experience of each type of distortion.

Therapist: Nearly everyone does some inflammatory labeling now and then. Thinking back to some of the anger situations you wrote down in your log and the thoughts you had in those situations, can you recall any examples of inflammatory labeling?

Client: Well, when I was mad at my son's teacher, I was thinking how *lazy* and *stupid* she is. She's such a bitch.

Therapist: When you thought those things, did it seem to feed your anger?

Client: Probably. She was on his case for the quality of his writing but wasn't showing him how to improve. It pissed me off.

Therapist: And thinking she was a stupid, lazy bitch, did that make you more pissed?

Client: Yeah. It puts it all on her, I guess.

Therapist: Makes her to blame? If you were going to replace the labeling with a specific description of the problem, how would you do that?

Client: Just what I said, I guess. She gave my son low grades on his essays, but I want her to teach him specific techniques. He needs to learn how to improve.

Therapist: When you put it that way, what happens to your anger?

Client: I guess I feel a little more rational. I start thinking about what to do. You know, have a meeting with her or something.

Here's another example with misattributions:

Therapist: Do you remember any time in the last few weeks when you made some assumptions about another person's motives, feelings, or attitudes toward you?

Client: I don't remember.

Therapist: Let's look over your Anger Log and see what we find. *(The client and therapist together start looking through the pages.)* Do you see anything?

Client: Maybe I was assuming something about my brother when I got mad about him not coming for Thanksgiving. I was thinking he probably doesn't like our house and the neighborhood and everything. Like it's too low class for him.

Therapist: Yeah, that thought could hurt *and* make you angry. Is there any alternative explanation for why he didn't come?

Client: Yeah, well, he went to my uncle's house, and he says he got that invitation first. Another explanation might be my uncle's been cheerleading him to get a CPA degree. They're pretty close.

Therapist: So, maybe there are other simple explanations, like getting another invitation first. When you think of those alternative explanations, what happens to your anger?

Client: It's a little better. Hell, last year we went to my wife's sister's place, even though we were invited to my folks' place first.

Skill Building

Recognizing Triggers

Go through one of the weekly Anger Logs with your client and ask him or her to circle the main anger-triggering thoughts listed in the log. Next to each circled thought, have your client write in which anger distortion it represents. Let them know that more than one distortion may be involved. If a client has difficulty labeling a trigger thought, use Socratic questioning:

Therapist: You've circled the thought, "She's screwing me up; I'm too upset to get my work done now." Which anger distortion does that sound like?

Client: I don't know. Global labeling?

Therapist: When you think, "She's screwing me up," are you labeling her in some way?

Client: She's got me all messed up, but I'm not really labeling her.

Therapist: What's the other part of the thought doing—"I'm too upset to work"?

Client: Blaming my problem on her. Oh, I see. The whole thing is blaming.

Therapist: What makes it blaming?

Client: I got a problem and I'm saying she did it.

Therapist: Like you're helpless and she's got to fix it?

Client: Yeah, I want her to chill out and let me get some work done.

Therapist: If you stop blaming her and feeling so angry, is there a chance you could solve the problem yourself?

Client: I could say, "We're both upset. I've got to go in this room here and close the door and calm down. If I don't do that, I won't be able to get the work done, and I'm going to be crazy all night."

Therapist: Now it sounds like you're not so helpless. You could take a time-out, go to the other room and calm down. Then, when you feel less angry, you can get caught up in your work. You've got a plan to deal with the problem.

Session Summary

Remind your client that the main focus of this session has been exploring the role of thoughts in creating or intensifying angry feelings. The exercise where the client rehearsed angry thoughts from the past is an example of how cognitions can definitely influence and increase anger ratings. The exercise where the client imagined three different interpretations to the same situation is more evidence that stereotyped thoughts produce specific emotions and determine level of emotional intensity.

Knowing the six types of anger distortions is a key step toward being able to modulate anger. Labeling a trigger thought is a way of distancing from it and can open the door to alternative interpretations and more accurate perceptions.

Feedback from the Client

Ask the client what they think about the concept that thoughts can create or intensify feelings. Explore his or her response to the six anger distortions. Notice particularly if the client is feeling defensive and under attack. If so, emphasize that everyone uses these triggers at one time or another. They are as common as grass. Depending on your style, you might share an example or two of your common distortions. Rather than feeling blamed or wrong, encourage the client to see him or herself as way ahead of most people. Most folks use the distortions unconsciously and don't realize their impact. By recognizing the triggers, the client has taken a major step toward being able to control them.

Homework

1. Ask clients to continue monitoring their anger by using the Anger Log II. Instruct them to circle key automatic thoughts on the log and outline them in detail (using a separate sheet of paper, if necessary). Then write next to them the name of the anger distortion. They can use the Anger Distortions handout as a reference.

2. Have clients review the two anger scenes they developed in last week's homework. If they have not completed this homework, have them do so this week. Ask clients to identify key automatic thoughts in each scene and label the type of distortion it represents. These two scenes will form the cornerstone of next week's session, so it's very important that the client completes the assignment.

3. Ask clients to practice relaxation without tension, relaxation imagery, breathing-cued relaxation, and cue-controlled relaxation at least five of the next seven days and keep a record in the Relaxation Log.

4. Ask clients to apply relaxation coping skills at least once per day in nonstressful situations. The goal is to get clients competent and comfortable in initiating relaxation coping skills in vivo. Clients can apply relaxation in the face of anger but should be cautioned that full effects may not be felt yet, and that they should not be discouraged.

Anger Distortions Handout

Our thoughts play a key part in both generating anger and increasing it. Below are listed several types of thoughts that commonly increase anger. Following each are some alternative ways of thinking that help manage anger and deal appropriately with frustrating, irritating, and disappointing situations.

Magnifying/Catastrophizing

This is the tendency to make things worse than they really are. Events are often described as "awful," "terrible," "disgusting," or "horrendous." When you magnify, you are more likely to respond angrily and even go on the attack, as if things really were as bad as your magnification makes them seem.

Examples

- This is the worst thing that's ever happened.

- My job is totally screwed up.

- I can't stand the way that he or she is talking to me.

- He behaves so horribly it made the whole party a nightmare.

- This is total shit.

There are three things you can do to control the tendency to magnify. One is to be realistically negative. Call it what it really is—"crummy," "disappointing," "frustrating," "a hassle," etc. If it still seems awful, ask yourself, "How bad is it really?" Then answer that question honestly and realistically. The second strategy is to use very accurate language. The bill isn't "outrageous," it's "forty dollars more than I expected." Your "disgusting" boss could be more accurately described as "detail and mistake oriented." The third way you can control magnifying is to look at the whole picture. There's a downside and an upside to every situation or relationship. Your friend is late for most dates, but on the other hand, he or she is a good listener when you need support. Focus on the positive aspects of a person or a situation to balance or neutralize your anger.

Helpful Coping Thoughts for Magnifying

- It's not the end of the world. It's just frustrating.

- It's just not worth getting all pissed about it.

- I'll just take the best out of the situation that I can.

- Hang in there. It'll be over soon.

- Getting all bent out of shape doesn't help, and it actually adds to my problems. When I lose my cool I've got to deal with the situation at hand *and* being all angry.

- Hang loose and cope. Don't let it get you down. It's not worth it.

- Why should I get all upset? Who will know or care in a week anyway?

- Look, I'll do what I can. If it works, great. If not, well, I did my best. No need to go crazy about it.

- Shit happens, but I can develop a plan about how to deal with it.

Overgeneralization

You can make a problem seem bigger than it is by using words such as "always," "all," "every," "never," "total," "everybody," "nobody," and so on. These go way beyond what is really true. These terms make an event that happened a few times feel like something that's continuous and bigger than life.

Examples

- You never get home on time.

- Everybody was very unhappy.

- You pick a fight with me every day.

- He's always handing me things at the last minute.

- Things like this always happen when I'm in a hurry.

- Nobody ever gets things done on time.

- Nobody ever does it right.

The three keys to stop overgeneralization are, first, to try to avoid generalizing terms; second, to use specific and accurate descriptions of a situation ("You were late twice this week," instead of "You're always late"); and finally, to look for exceptions to the rule (what were specific times the person acted differently or the situation was reversed?). Looking for exceptions is perhaps the most important antidote for overgeneralization. When you take the trouble to recall how people sometimes act contrary to their tendencies, it makes things less upsetting.

Helpful Coping Thoughts for Overgeneralization

- Be accurate. How many times has this *really* happened?

- Sometimes things go a lot better than this. I'm going to think about that, too. Put the whole thing in perspective.

- No need to get upset. I'll think about exceptions when _____ acted a lot better than this.

- I'll keep my mind on the facts—exactly what happened and how often.

- Generalizing makes things worse. Relax and you'll get through it soon.

- If I don't make this bigger than it is, I can relax and let it blow over.

- Stay with realistic negatives. No need to make things bigger than they are. They're bad enough as it is, but I can figure out a way to cope with that.

Demanding/Commanding

This is the tendency to make your wants into demands for yourself or the rest of the world. Shoulds are typically couched as "ought to," "have to," "need to," "gotta," "expect," and "must" kinds of thoughts.

Anger is often triggered by a judgment based on a set of rules about how people should and should not act. People who behave according to the rules are right, and those who break the rules are wrong and bad. You might think that others know and accept your rules, but the people with whom you feel angry rarely agree with you. Their perception of the situation leaves them blameless and justified. Common commandments often involve the following themes:

1. *Perfectionism:* I or others should do it right, perfectly, correctly, etc.

2. *Others (key people) should love me:* A certain person or persons should love, like, support, or approve of me.

3. *Others (key people) should not dislike me:* (not the same as #2) Other people should not express dislike, disapproval, criticism, or negative feelings toward me.

4. *Things should be just and fair:* It's not right when things are not just, fair, kind, courteous, respectful (whatever a person's standards or rules for behavior are).

5. *Bad things shouldn't happen to me:* I shouldn't have to experience, deal with, cope with, or put up with pain, frustration, delay, etc. (a kind of narcissistic rule that the person be exempt from the difficulty of normal living).

Examples of Commanding/Demanding

- He or she should have known that would hurt my feelings.

- They should not have done that.

- This has gotta be done by 5:00 P.M.

- She should have known I'm overwhelmed with work.

- He isn't being fair; he needs to listen to me once in a while.

- He knows better than that; I expected more of him.

The biggest problem with shoulds is that people rarely do what they *should* do. They do what they need or want to do. They take care of themselves. There is no absolute reason why things "should" be the way that you want. Because you want something or believe in something doesn't mean that others have to agree with you. The best way to cope with shoulds is to think of them as personal preferences or wants ("I prefer . . . ," "It would be nice if . . . ," "I'd like it if . . ."). It's better to think

"I'd like him to leave the party with me," rather than "he should always leave with me."

Stay with your wants, desires, and preferences—not shoulds. It may be frustrating, disappointing, and inconvenient when you don't get what you want, but it isn't because of someone's moral failure. Stay with the disappointment; you can cope with that better than the righteous anger.

Helpful Coping Thoughts for Demanding/Commanding

- So what if I don't get what I want? Sometimes I do and sometimes I don't. There's no guarantee. No reason to blow up about it. Stay cool.

- People do what they want to do, not what I need them to do.

- This is disappointing, and I would prefer things to be different. But I can cope and make the best of it.

- Forget the shoulds, they only get me upset. I don't like how they act, but I can accept and live with it.

- There are problems, fears, needs that influence his or her behavior.

- No reason why he or she should do it my way, other than that I want it that way.

Inflammatory/Global Labeling

A global label makes sweeping, negative judgments. Typical global labels include terms like "stupid," "selfish," "jerk," "loser," "liar," and so on. Many labels are obscene: "bastard," "sonofabitch," "asshole," "f---up," and so on. Global labels fuel your anger by turning the target into someone who is totally bad and worthless. Instead of focusing on a particular behavior, you indict the entire person. Global labels are always false because they exaggerate a single characteristic and imply that it's the whole picture. Some are just plain funny when you think about it.

Examples of Inflammatory/Global Labeling

- That salesperson is an idiot.

- The bastard can go to hell.

- He's a little Hitler at work, a complete asshole.

- Why are you so selfish?

- My stepson has been a lazy loser since the first grade.

- She's a total bitch.

The way to overcome global labels is to be specific. Focus on behavior, not the person as a whole. Describe the offensive behavior specifically. What exactly occurred? How many times? What was its effect on you and on others? But leave judgments about the person's worth out of it. Also, concretely define your terms (e.g., bitch = female dog; son of a bitch = male dog; and asshole = anus or space between cheeks of buttocks).

Helpful Coping Thoughts for Global Labeling

- He or she is not an ass, just a person with whom I have a disagreement.

- An ass? Now that's funny. He or she is not a burro or buttocks.

- No one's bad—people do the best they can.

- What exactly is bothering me? Stick to the facts.

- Why am I swearing? It's just frustrating and not the way I want it, but I can cope with that.

- It's just a problem, that's all.

- I'm upset and it's a hassle, a hassle I can deal with.

- Children make mistakes. That's their job. Boy, is he (or she) doing the job well!

Misattributions/Single Explanations

This is about mind-reading. When people hurt or annoy you, it's easy to imagine that it was deliberate and meant to upset you. You jump to conclusions and assume to know the person's true motives. Rather than thinking about the multiple reasons for why things could have happened the way they did, you focus on a single negative explanation.

It's easy to guess at people's motives, but unless you ask and get a direct answer there's a real chance you've jumped to the wrong conclusion. Think of times when you made an assumption about someone else's motives or feelings toward you and you learned later you were completely wrong. Sometimes misattribution may have caused real harm. Have you ever made an assumption about someone's intentions, found out you were wrong, but had already responded in a way that caused a big upset?

Examples of Misattributions

- He or she is doing that to get to me.

- They wouldn't have done that if they were my friends (which means that they don't care about me).

- The whole purpose of what she did was to embarrass me.

- He corrected what I said to make me look stupid.

- He did that to piss me off.

The best way to avoid misattributions is to pay attention when you're making assumptions about people's motives. When you catch yourself, try to find a method to test the truth of your beliefs. Check out the facts. Find a diplomatic way to ask about the other person's intentions. If you're reluctant to check out your assumptions directly, try to keep an open mind. Tell yourself that you don't really know what's in the mind of another. Another tactic is to ask other people how they think about situations like the one you are dealing with. You'll often hear very different assumptions about what's going on.

While sometimes your interpretations may be true, there are often other reasons or explanations for people's actions that you haven't thought of. Your anger may be inappropriate or exaggerated because you don't see the whole picture. A very good way to overcome misattribution is to develop as many alternative explanations for people's behavior as you can possibly think of. Think of your assumption as one of many hypotheses that could explain how another person acts.

Helpful Coping Thoughts for Misattributions

- Don't jump to conclusions. Check out the facts.

- I'd better check it out first, before going off half-cocked.

- I may not have all the facts.

- Getting angry doesn't help me figure out what's going on.

- Where's my evidence that this is the only reason?

- Stop the mind-reading.

- Don't second guess the motives of others.

Blaming

This anger distortion gets people really hot. Blaming comes from a belief that the other person *did it to you*, often on purpose, and that he or she shouldn't be allowed to get away with it. Whatever pain you feel, whatever hurt or fear or loss, they did it to you. While blaming feels very good at times, it also leaves you feeling helpless. The power to solve the problem always seems to lie with others. They have to fix it. You keep waiting for them to change their bad behavior, but they never do. While so focused on changing the other person, you may forget that there are choices *you* can make. Also, when you blame, you often become judge, jury, and executioner. You attack and punish angrily. The other person will then pull back or counterattack. You now have two problems—the initial one and messed up relations from your anger.

Examples of Blaming

- You want breakfast in the morning, and that always makes me late.

- I could enjoy this vacation if it weren't for your constant negativity.

- This house looks like a pigsty because you never lift one finger to clean or fix it.

- I could have gotten the job if you had bothered to proofread my résumé.

When bad things happen, when you're in pain, it feels better in the short run to point fingers. But your pain will continue unless you find a way to solve the problem yourself. The key is to make a coping plan, something that either changes the situation or how you respond to it. Do something that doesn't require any cooperation from the person you blame. Leave them out of it.

A second way to overcome blame is to realize that people are mostly doing the best they can. Everyone tends to choose the action that seems most likely to meet their own needs. The people you blame may be doing nothing more than taking care of themselves in the best way they know how.

Helpful Coping Thoughts for Blaming

- I'm not helpless—I can take care of myself in this situation.

- I'll make a plan to deal with this myself.

- Blaming makes me feel helpless. What can *I* do about the problem?

- I may not like it, but they're doing the best they can.

- It's disappointing to me, but they're just taking care of themselves.

- They do what they need to do, I'll do what I need to do.

- Nobody appointed me the punisher. I just need to take care of myself and leave the blame and punishment to others.

General Coping Thoughts Handout

- Take a deep breath and relax.

- Getting upset won't help.

- Just as long as I keep my cool, I'm in control.

- Easy does it—there's nothing to be gained in getting mad.

- I'm not going to let him/her get to me.

- I can't change him/her with anger; I'll just upset myself.

- I can find a way to say what I want to without anger.

- Stay calm—no sarcasm, no attacks.

- I can stay calm and relaxed.

- Relax and let go, no need to get my knickers in a twist.

- No one is right, no one is wrong. We just have different needs.

- Stay cool, make no judgments.

- No matter what is said, I know I'm a good person.

- I'll stay rational—anger won't solve anything.

- Let them look all foolish and upset, I can stay cool and calm.

- His or her opinion isn't important—I won't be pushed into losing my cool.

- Bottom line, I'm in control. I can always leave rather than say or do something dumb.

- Take a time-out. Cool off, then come back and deal with it.

- Some situations don't have good solutions. Looks like this is one of them. No use getting all bent out of shape.

- If they're trying to make me mad, boy, are they going to be disappointed.

- It's just a hassle. Nothing more, nothing less. I can cope with hassles.

- Break it down. Anger often comes from lumping things together.

- I got angry, but kept the lid on saying dumb things. That's progress.

- It's just not worth it to get so angry.

- Anger means it's time to relax and cope.

- I can manage this; I'm in control.

- I can't expect people to act the way I want them to.

- I don't have to take this so seriously.

- I have a plan to relax and cope.

- This is funny if you look at it that way.

Session 5

Coping Skills Training

Monitoring of Current Status

Evaluate with your client his or her reaction to tracking anger distortions. Note which distortions the client has been aware of during the week. Has there been an attempt to restructure anger triggers using coping thoughts from the handout? Explore with the client any reactions to using the coping thoughts. Are they foreign or alienating? Do they feel sensible and helpful to the client?

Agenda

This is the prototype session for the remainder of treatment. Coping skills training is introduced. Anger will be aroused by visualizing anger scenes, and the client will reduce this anger through the application of relaxation and cognitive coping skills. In the future sessions, the amount of therapist assistance in initiating coping skills will be reduced while in-session anger arousal will be increased. The client has already prepared two anger scenes for this session that involve anticipating a likely anger experience that rates 50 to 60 on the anger scale. Later sessions will involve scenes where anger intensity is 75 to 100 on the scale. A variant is not to specify the type of anger-provoking scene (e.g., preparing for or ruminating about a provocative situation) for each session and to just increase the intensity about 10 or 15 units per session. Otherwise, procedures are the same.

Review of Homework

Look over the week's Anger Log. If there are changes in the frequency, intensity, or duration of the anger experienced, underscore these shifts in the overall anger profile. At this point, clients will very often report having greater control in certain anger-provoking situations. Ask for details about coping thoughts or impulse control strategies the client may have used. The key intervention here is to keep exploring what the person is doing differently now than in the past. Keep these in mind and adapt them to future situations. Get excited; praise and support these changes.

Check the Relaxation Log and verify that the client has practiced relaxation without tension and cue-controlled relaxation during the week. Ask if the client has used any of the relaxation strategies in real life settings, such as waiting in the doctor's office, riding in the car, watching TV, and so on. Ask if the client has used them to cope with anger. If so, support, encourage, and clarify success. Reiterate caution that relaxation strategies, particularly early on, don't always work to defuse anger.

Is the client beginning to combine relaxation and cognitive coping elements? If not, encourage them to use both relaxation methods and coping thoughts as soon as a provocative situation occurs. Caution them that these skills may not always be successful at this point, but that trying is very important. Let them know that from now on the focus of therapy will be practicing relaxation and cognitive coping skills together.

Concepts and Skills

Skill Building

Making Anger Scenes Real

Review the client's two anticipatory anger scenes. Ask for specifics. Make sure you have visual, auditory, and kinesthetic details to flesh out the scene. Also draw from the client cognitive, emotional, and physiological reactions that are occurring during each scene. Write down the key elements of what you've heard so you can remind the client during visualization exercises. Here's how you might frame some of these questions:

> *During our work today we need to recreate your two anger anticipation scenes so that they feel vivid and real. To do that, we have to collect some details, specific things you saw, heard, and felt physically during the scene. We also need to key in on any anger triggering thoughts you may have had and any emotions that may have welled up. Close your eyes for a moment. Try to imagine a vivid picture of your first anger anticipation scene and tell me what you see. . . . Notice the environment and describe for me the highlights. . . . Now notice what you hear—what sounds go with the scene? What are people saying? Now be aware of any physical sensations you have—the temperature or texture of the environment. . . . Notice any feelings you may have inside*

your body as anger starts to mount, sensations such as tension in your shoulders or a tightening of your stomach. Tell me the main things that you're aware of. . . .

In this scene you're anticipating that you'll get angry, but haven't blown up yet. Notice the thoughts you have as you look forward to the potential upset. Try to stay in the scene and tell me your trigger thoughts.

The therapist should use summaries of cognitive processes and open-ended inquiries (e.g., "Are there any other thoughts going through your head while you're there?") to flesh out additional cognitive content.

Which of these thoughts is the most provocative for you? Now notice if there are any emotions other than anger. Are you anxious? Sad? Guilty? Ashamed?

After you've written down the details for each of the two scenes, explain to the client that coping skills training works best when the images are clear and strong. That's why you need so much detail, and that's why it helps if the client really concentrates on the image to make it as evocative as possible. Add that the details will help generate more anger for your client to practice relaxation and rethinking skills with.

Development Of Cognitive Counterresponses

For each of the two scenes you're working on, return to the key automatic thoughts the client identified in their homework assignment. Ask the client about any anger distortions they may represent. Now work collaboratively with the client to develop coping thoughts that could diminish anger intensity. If the client has any ideas, write them down. Otherwise, look together at the Anger Distortions Handout to find example coping thoughts for particular distortions. Also check the General Coping Thoughts Handout to see if any of these more generic responses might be helpful. Here's how you might say this to the client:

I've written down some of the trigger thoughts you have in that scene. (Therapist reads one of the trigger thoughts) What do you make of that one? Does that fit into any of the anger distortions we've talked about? If we can identify a distortion, that might make it easier to find a coping thought. Which distortion would you say it is? (The client suggests a particular distortion) That sounds right. It's natural when you're anticipating an anger situation to have thoughts like that, but the problem is it makes your anger worse, and then things escalate.

Recalling what you read in the Anger Distortions Handout, is there any coping thought that might be helpful in dealing with this particular distortion? Is there some way we can talk back to the automatic thought to make it less upsetting? (Any coping responses the client suggests should be written down) Okay, let's look up this distortion in the handout and see if we find any other helpful counterresponses there. Also let's look at the General Coping Thoughts Handout for ideas on how you might talk yourself through the beginning feelings of upset.

Here's an example of how to work on a particular trigger thought:

Therapist:	Let's take a look at your first scene where your husband's late getting the kids at preschool and you get a call saying no one's picked them up. I wrote down a couple of your trigger thoughts, but I wonder which one really sends you through the roof?
Client:	It's when I think that he doesn't give a damn about anything. All he cares about is himself. He just wants a family to be fun; he never takes any responsibility for the work involved.
Therapist:	Do any of those trigger thoughts ring a bell in terms of the anger distortions we talked about last week?
Client:	I guess when I say he never takes any responsibility, it's overgeneralization.
Therapist:	Anything else?
Client:	I don't think so.
Therapist:	What about, "He doesn't give a damn about anything. All he cares about is himself."
Client:	That's the way it seems to me.
Therapist:	Right. Some of his behavior does make it seem that way. But what are you assuming with that trigger thought?
Client:	I'm assuming that's how he really is inside. That's my husband!
Therapist:	And when you assume you know a person's true feelings and motives, what's that?
Client:	(Pausing for a minute to look through the handout) I guess it's misattribution. But I don't think I'm misattributing anything. I think that's a fact.

Now the therapist has three tasks: 1) developing coping thoughts to respond to the anger distortions, 2) opening the client to the possibility that her thoughts may not be totally accurate, and 3) helping the client find some general coping thoughts to manage arousal in the scene.

Therapist:	Okay, let's start with overgeneralizing. Remember in the handout there were a couple of ways to deal with that. One was to replace the generalization with a more accurate description of the problem.
Client:	(Thinking) All right, he's late picking up the kids at least once a week. It embarrasses me, and sometimes I have to get them myself. He lets me do most of the limit setting. And when there are struggles with the kids, I'd say at least half the time he disappears.
Therapist:	Good, you're turning the generalization into a statement that's more specific and accurate. Now, let's do the second part. Are there exceptions to this behavior? Times he seems to be trying, or times he hangs in with a tough situation?

Client:	Well, obviously, four out of five days he does get the kids on time. I tend not to think of that when he's late. And maybe a third of the time he sticks around when the kids are acting up, and he'll tell them to listen to me, or he'll carry one of them into Time Out.
Therapist:	How about other ways he might be supportive to you and the kids?
Client:	Well, he gets them breakfast in the morning, he reads them bedtime stories, he does some playing with them. I'd like it to be more. There are times when he listens to me when I'm crazy and overwhelmed and need to let off steam.
Therapist:	Okay, how could you remind yourself of these exceptions to the generalization? Just a sentence or two.
Client:	I'd like him to do more, but he does make some effort with the kids.
Therapist:	And sometimes he supports you.
Client:	He does make an effort and sometimes he supports me. Okay, I can say that.
Therapist:	What happens to your anger when you think that?
Client:	It softens, I guess.

Now the therapist tackles misattribution.

Therapist:	Let's look at the thought, "He doesn't give a damn about anything." One of the ways to cope with misattribution is doing what we've already done with overgeneralizing—looking for exceptions. When you think back on the exceptions you uncovered, how does it affect the "He doesn't give a damn" thoughts?
Client:	I guess he does care *some* or he wouldn't do those other things, the exceptions.
Therapist:	So you may be assuming something with that thought which isn't entirely true?
Client:	Yeah.
Therapist:	Another thing we do with misattributions is look for alternative explanations for people's actions. Can you think of anything else, other than not caring, that might contribute to your husband's lateness, or escaping during high stress times with the kids?
Client:	Well, he's late for everything—parties, even work. I've noticed that he has a hard time with transitions, leaving one situation for another. He's also a big conflict avoider. He'll do anything not to have a fight. So maybe that's what's going on when I'm disciplining the kids and he disappears.
Therapist:	I see. So those are very different explanations for his behavior. How could you remind yourself of them during the upsetting scene?

Client: I don't know. *(Pauses)* I guess I'd just say that he does make an effort sometimes and there are other reasons for his behavior than not caring.

Therapist: What happens to your anger when you think that?

Client: I'm not very angry right now, but I think it would help when I was.

Finally, the therapist looks for additional resources in the General Coping Thoughts Handout.

Therapist: Would you take a look at the General Coping Thoughts Handout? Do you see anything there that might be helpful to remember during this scene?

Client: I'd say the most important one is, "Stay cool, make no judgments."

Therapist: Okay, so we have three important coping thoughts to use during the scene. *(Writing them down)* We'll need to try to remember these:
1. He does make an effort and sometimes supports me.
2. There are other reasons for what he does besides not caring.
3. Stay cool, make no judgments.

How Clients Can Develop Cognitive Counter-responses at Home

Clients can develop coping thoughts at home appropriate for both anger scenes and real life provocations. Since no therapist will be on hand to ask key Socratic questions, the Creating Coping Thoughts Handout has been developed to provide a structure to help generate counterresponses (see example at the end of this session). This handout starts out by having clients list up to three trigger thoughts that are associated with an anger scene or situation. Next, clients identify the anger distortion that lies behind each trigger thought. To recognize distortions, they are encouraged to refer to material in the Anger Distortions Handout.

The third and most crucial step involves indentifying a "counterresponse plan" for each trigger thought. Once again the client uses information from the Anger Distortions Handout to name a specific strategy for challenging and rewriting trigger thoughts. Counterresponse plans include strategies such as "looking for exceptions," "alternative explanations," "preferences not shoulds," "being specific and accurate," "looking at the whole picture," "being realistically negative," etc. After the counterresponse plan has been named, the client attempts to revise the trigger thought using the plan as a general guide.

The final step in this process is for the client to find appropriate coping thoughts in either the Anger Distortions Handout or the General Coping Thoughts Handout, writing one down for each trigger thought. A completed sample of the Creating Coping Thoughts Handout is provided at the end of this chapter so you can see how a client might utilize it.

Coping Skills Rehearsal

Coping skills rehearsal (also called stress inoculation) is a guided rehearsal of cognitive and relaxation coping skills. Anger arousal is induced by visualizing each of the anticipatory anger scenes the client developed as part of the homework. Then the client learns to relax and use coping thoughts in response to the scene.

The general format is as follows:

1. Assuming relaxation is going well, have the client relax by whatever method or methods work best for him or her and signal you when relaxed. This generally takes one to three minutes. If a signal is not seen in approximately ninety seconds, prompt the client by some comment such as, "And signal when you're relaxed." If relaxation is lagging, then the therapist will instruct the client in relaxation without tension.

2. Now ask your client to vividly visualize one anticipatory anger scene and to become involved again as if it were happening at that very moment. Remind your client of the visual, auditory, and kinesthetic imagery in the scene. Instruct him or her to pay particular attention to the physiological reactions that are associated with rising anger. Repeat one or two key anger- triggering automatic thoughts. Ask the client to signal by raising a hand when they have become angry.

3. When the client signals, instruct him or her to stay in the scene and try to focus on the experience so anger intensifies. Have the client pay attention to the internal cues of anger arousal and keep recalling automatic thoughts. When he or she has experienced anger for approximately thirty seconds, ask the client to erase the scene. Now have clients begin relaxation coping. Have them engage relaxation imagery and one of the other relaxation techniques (i.e., cue-controlled relaxation, breathing-cued relaxation, or perhaps relaxation without tension) to reduce the anger arousal. Have clients signal when once again relaxed. After relaxation, and prior to the next anger scene, ask clients to think about the anger situation more calmly by rehearsing two or three of the anger-lowering cognitions identified, which you can provide verbatim.

4. Repeat the entire sequence using the second anticipatory anger scene.

   Now continue to alternate the two scenes until you get as many as four to six repetitions of each. During the first few repetitions specifically remind clients of each cognitive counterresponse so they don't have to struggle to remember their coping thoughts. In later repetitions, fade your concrete modeling and present more general categorical instructions, such as: "Remember your coping thoughts; talk back to the distortions."

   In each rehearsal, use two of the briefer relaxation procedures as described above. It's important that clients learn to rely on brief techniques such as cue-controlled relaxation in response to genuine anger.

   Check to see which of the coping thoughts worked best. Eliminate or modify thoughts that aren't working.

When clients report that certain coping thoughts don't work, this is important information. Take the time to uncover what about the coping thought may not be believable. Collaborate with the client on ways to change the thought so that it feels more valid and powerful. Don't hesitate to eliminate a thought that has minimal impact and find something more meaningful in the General Coping Thoughts Handout.

Here are sample instructions for presenting the coping skills rehearsal sequence to clients:

> (Client has signaled that they're relaxed.) *In a moment, I'm going to have you turn on that first anticipatory anger scene, the one involving (brief reference). When I do, let yourself really be there. Put yourself right into it, like it was happening at this very moment. Then signal me by raising your hand when you're starting to feel angry. So, right now, turn on that first anger scene . . . (describe visual, auditory, and kinesthetic details). Notice the feelings that the scene creates in your body . . . stay with it and let it build. Now listen to your anger triggering automatic thoughts . . . (therapist repeats one or two key automatic thoughts) . . . keep pushing, keep pushing up the anger. Really be there, feel the annoyance mounting, the upset growing in your body . . . keep reminding yourself of your automatic thoughts* (Repeat them.)

Continue in this vein until the client signals an anger reaction. Keep the anger level up for approximately thirty seconds, continuing to instruct the client to focus on arousal. Then, switch the scene off and focus on coping.

> *Okay, now switch off that scene. Erase it from your mind. Switch to your relaxation imagery (describe briefly the relaxation scene). Now begin some cue-controlled relaxation or another relaxation coping skill. Go ahead and take deep breaths, noticing any tension in your body and relaxing it away. . . . That's it. Let yourself really let go of the anger arousal. Retrieve the feeling of relaxation. Enjoy your relaxation image while breathing deeply and saying your cue word. You're becoming more and more relaxed, your whole body letting go of tension and arousal. (As a variant between anger scenes you can also use breathing-cued relaxation or relaxation without tension) Now leave your relaxation image and try taking a different perspective on that situation. Remind yourself of your coping thoughts. (Therapist specifically mentions two or three counterresponses) Notice which thoughts work best . . . . When you feel calm again, go ahead and raise your hand. In the meantime, just continue to remind yourself of your coping thoughts. . . . You can also take a deep breath and use your cue word whenever you want to give an added boost to relaxation. . . . Keep relaxing and remembering your coping thoughts. (Repeat one of two or the coping thoughts.)*

When clients signal that they are completely relaxed, check in about the effectiveness of each coping thought and collaboratively make appropriate modifications. Repeat the whole sequence with a second anticipatory anger scene.

Clients who have difficulty getting relaxed again after the anger scenes need special attention.

Therapist:	I noticed it took a while to get calm again.
Client:	Yeah, I'm not sure I'm totally calm yet. Once I get upset, it seems to have a life of its own.
Therapist:	How's the cue-controlled relaxation working?
Client:	I can do that pretty well. It relaxes my stomach where I usually feel the anger.
Therapist:	Good. How about the coping thoughts? Are they helping?
Client:	A little.
Therapist:	You don't sound sure. Do they seem believable to you?
Client:	I keep telling myself, "Getting upset won't help," and "Don't jump to conclusions." And that works okay for the moment.
Therapist:	But somehow there's a problem.
Client:	There is, because you know what? The old automatic thoughts keep cropping up. I start calming down, and then all of a sudden they're coming at me again.
Therapist:	So that's making it hard to get rid of the anger arousal. What's the main automatic thought that keeps coming back?
Client:	Bill (a coworker) is just plain lazy. That's why he keeps shoveling more work on me.
Therapist:	Sounds like we need to find something to say back to that. A new coping thought. Your automatic thought sounds like our old friend, global labeling, with a little bit of blaming thrown in. Do you remember that with blaming it helps if you can see that the person is doing the best they can?
Client:	Well, Bill's wife just had a baby, and he's still taking night classes. On top of that, I always thought he was a pretty anxious personality. Maybe he's trying to get out of stuff because he's sinking, overwhelmed.
Therapist:	Sounds very possible. Could you try using that coping thought on the next repetition: "He's trying to get out of stuff because he's sinking and overwhelmed."
Client:	Yeah, I think that would help.
Therapist:	Maybe you could check that out and see if he really is overwhelmed. Would you be willing to do that?

Session Summary

Remind your client that the main focus of this session has been rehearsing coping skills. While thoughts can trigger anger, they can also help calm it. Putting relaxation skills and cognitive coping together makes a powerful anger-management tool. This process of identifying automatic thoughts, recognizing anger distortions, and developing coping thoughts will be a prototype for the coping skills training done throughout the remaining sessions.

Feedback from Client

Explore with clients any reactions to visualizing anger-evoking scenes. Invite responses to the process of developing and modifying coping thoughts. Learn how it feels for the client to put the relaxation and cognitive coping skills together at the same time.

Is there any concern or discomfort with multiple repetitions of the anticipatory anger scenes? Has the client felt blamed or insulted when automatic thoughts are labeled as distortions? Clarify and answer any questions before assigning homework.

Homework

1. Ask clients to practice relaxation without tension, cue-controlled relaxation, breathing-cued relaxation, and relaxation imagery at least five of the next seven days and to keep a record in the Relaxation Log.

2. Clients should now apply cognitive and relaxation coping skills once or more daily to all types of stressful situations, especially anger. They should note these efforts in Anger Log III, which has an additional column for recording coping strategies. (See Anger Log III handout.) Caution clients against expecting success in every application of these skills, but stress the importance of simply trying. Since many stressful situations occur spontaneously and can't be planned for, encourage clients to memorize three or four of the general coping thoughts that could be effective in any upsetting situation.

3. Clients should develop two moderate (50 to 70 on the 100-point anger scale) anger scenes. Rather than the anticipatory scenes you've been working with up until now, these should be scenes where the client is right in the middle of a problem interaction. They should be events that happen often enough that the client can easily bring them to mind and get a clear image of the situation. When developing the scenes, clients should be instructed to focus on all the external (situational and behavioral) and internal (cognitive, emo-

tional, and physiological) components of the provocative circumstance. The more detail they can generate, the better.

Encourage clients to develop counterresponses to trigger thoughts (automatic thoughts) in each scene using the Creating Coping Thoughts Handout.

4. Remind clients that all significant anger experiences, whether coping efforts were made or not, should be recorded in Anger Log III. It's still important to keep track of every anger situation that is greater than 40 on the 100-point scale.

5. Ask clients to fill out the Anger Situation and Anger Symptom measures in the waiting room, and return them to you before leaving.

Anger Log III

Day/Time	Situation	Thoughts	Reactions	Coping Efforts (what did you do, how did it turn out?) Rate 0–100 before and after

Creating Coping Thoughts Handout

Complete the following for each significant trigger thought (automatic thought) in an anger scene or situation:

1. Trigger thoughts that inflame my anger:

   a.

   b.

   c.

2. Anger distortions that underlie my trigger thoughts:

   a.

   b.

   c.

3. Counterresponse plan for each of my trigger thoughts (e.g., looking for exceptions, alternative explanations, preferences not shoulds, and so on). Rewritten trigger thought based on each counterresponse plan.

   a. Counterresponse plan:

      Rewritten trigger thought:

   b. Counter-response plan:

      Rewritten trigger thought:

   c. Counterresponse plan:

      Rewritten trigger thought:

4. Helpful coping thoughts (see Anger Distortions handout or General Coping Thoughts Handout in session 4):

   a.

   b.

   c.

Creating Coping Thoughts Handout

Complete the following for each significant trigger thought (automatic thought) in an anger scene or situation:

1. Trigger thoughts that inflame my anger:

    a. *He's a selfish jerk.*

    b. *He never pays attention to my needs.*

    c. *He always shows up late because seeing me is a low priority.*

2. Anger distortions that underlie my trigger thoughts:

    a. *Inflammatory/Global Labeling*

    b. *Overgeneralization*

    c. *Misattributions/Single Explanations and Overgeneralizations*

3. Counterresponse plan for each of my trigger thoughts (e.g., looking for exceptions, alternative explanations, preferences not shoulds, and so on). Rewritten trigger thought based on each counter-response plan.

    a. Counterresponse plan: *Focus on specific behavior; be realistically negative.*

       Rewritten trigger thought: *His lateness and not wanting to do some of the things I like really bothers me. He's just terribly different from me.*

    b. Counterresponse plan: *Be specific and accurate; look for exceptions.*

       Rewritten trigger thought: *He won't shop with me or do outdoor things, but has taken me to Vegas, helped me with my taxes, and given me some generous gifts.*

    c. Counterresponse plan: *Alternative explanations*

       Rewritten trigger thought: *A major reason he might be late is he works sixty hours per week; another is he seems very disorganized about time in general.*

4. Helpful coping thoughts (see Anger Distortions handout or General Coping Thoughts Handout in session 4):

    a. *He's not a jerk, just someone I have a disagreement with.*

    b. *I can't change him with anger; I'll just upset myself.*

    c. *Don't jump to conclusions; there are other explanations.*

Coping Skills Training — Moderate Anger Scenes

Monitoring of Current Status

Review the results of the Anger Situation and Anger Symptom measures, which your client filled out before leaving the last session. Note if there are any changes compared to the initial assessment. If levels of anger are declining, celebrate this fact. Ask the client to speculate on what he or she is doing to reduce levels of anger. If anger levels are unchanged or climbing, make this a launching place for discussion of what may be blocking the client's utilization of the anger-management skills they've learned. For further explanation of how to manage this issue, see the sample therapist-client dialogue in the "Review of Homework" segment of this session.

Scores on the Anger Situation and Anger Symptom measures may be low for another reason. The client simply may not have been very angry because he or she was in the therapist's office and not highly aroused at the time. Therefore, low anger is an accurate report that isn't necessarily indicative of a problem. As an alternative or addition, the therapist should follow up by reviewing the frequency and intensity of anger from the various Anger Logs. Daily frequency can be plotted over the weeks from the beginning of therapy to the present or, alternatively, average daily frequency can be plotted for each week. This may provide a graphic picture of beginning anger reduction for clients who experience frequent anger episodes. If the client's anger issues are fewer in frequency, and more in the intensity or form of anger expression, then this type of graph may have little relevance, as the client was already at low frequency.

The clinician should also ask the client to estimate the level on the 0 to 100 scale of anger intensity where anger begins to cause problems (e.g., for many clients this is a rating of approximately 40). Then plot the frequency and average intensity of entries on the Anger Log that are above this point. If anger management is beginning to take place, then the frequency and intensity of such events should decrease across sessions. For example, the frequency of events greater than 40 may go from 3.7 per day with an average intensity of 68 to 1.3 and an average intensity of 50 over the course of therapy, which would represent good external application and anger reduction.

Explore with the client any reaction to the coping skills training introduced in session 5. Did the practice of anger-management skills following provocative imagery help the client feel more confident using relaxation and cognitive coping strategies? If so, clarify and reinforce. If not, clarify and inquire as to what would have made a difference. Try to build those elements into the session. Be encouraging that anger management will increase over time.

Agenda

This session is essentially identical to session 5. Anger will be aroused by visualizing anger scenes, and the client will reduce anger through relaxation and cognitive coping procedures.

Coping skills training this week will center on the two moderate (50 to 70 intensity level) anger scenes that the client identified as part of the homework assignment. Unlike the *anticipatory* anger scenes in last session, these will involve a problematic interaction where two or more people are getting upset. If the client has not developed two moderate anger scenes, you'll have to do that together now.

Review of Homework

Once again review the Anger Log. The main focus at this point should be the client's use of coping strategies during real life provocations. Clients should be using, or trying to use, their new skills in the majority of anger situations. If they aren't, it's time to explore and confront this:

Therapist: I notice quite a few anger events where you aren't finding a way to use some of your new coping skills. Could we explore this for a minute to see what might be getting in the way?

Client: Okay.

Therapist: You've worked hard to learn cue-controlled relaxation, for instance, and you practiced it during coping skills training last week. But you don't often use it when there's an upset. What do you think keeps you from taking those cue-controlled breaths?

Client: I don't seem to think of it, I guess.

Therapist: Okay, it's hard to remember in the heat of the moment. Anything else?

Client: Yeah. It's a little weird trying to take those deep breaths when you're right in front of somebody. I don't know. They might notice and think it's odd.

Therapist: So you're concerned the cue-controlled breathing might be a little obvious. Okay, let's tackle one problem at a time. Do you have any ideas how to remind yourself to do the cue-controlled breathing?

Client: Tie a string on my finger? *(Laughs.)*

Therapist: Something like that could actually work.

Client: I'd look stupid.

Therapist: Any reminders that might be more subtle?

Client: *(Shrugs)* It's hard to think of anything.

Therapist: How about a new ring or a piece of jewelry that would remind you to breathe and relax? Something you'd notice on your hand or wrist that would cue you?

Client: My daughter gave me a friendship bracelet that I've never worn. Maybe I could use that. It's kind of pretty.

Therapist: When you saw that bracelet during a provocation, could you tell yourself to chill out and do cue control?

Client: I could try. I'll put it on.

Therapist: Every time you look at it, remind yourself of the cue-controlled breathing and your plan to use it the next time you get angry. Will you commit to doing that?

Client: I guess so. I'll wear it and remind myself.

Now the therapist turns to the second problem that the client identified:

Therapist: Good. Now on to the problem of maybe looking odd during cue-controlled breathing. Let me do one in front of you, and you tell me if it looks odd. *(Therapist takes a deep breath and lets it out with a slight sigh.)*

Client: It's not that bad, I guess.

Therapist: A lot of people do that naturally when they're upset. Take a deep breath and sigh. You just take it in slowly. *(Demonstrates)* Do you think anyone would notice that as weird?

Client: Not really.

Therapist: And you can let it out slowly *(demonstrating)*, while thinking your cue word and trying to let the tension release. Is that really noticeable?

Client: It's actually okay. But what if you're talking?

Therapist: You can pause like you're thinking and do it *(demonstrates)*, or take a deep breath while the other person's talking. Why don't you try it right now while we're conversing?

The therapist and client role play cue-controlled breathing as they talk further. At this point the conversation might move to the question of using cognitive coping strategies.

Therapist: Let me check in with you about using coping thoughts. You're not mentioning that in the log.

Client: I just don't think of it. I don't think you realize how hard all this is to do in the moment, you know? It's easy for you to *tell* me to do this stuff. *Doing* it is another thing. *(Getting angry.)*

Now the therapist needs to join the client in appreciating the depth of frustration. It's also important to acknowledge the reasons why this client came to therapy to begin with.

Therapist: You're right. It's easy for me to make suggestions—but I'm not in the middle of these upsetting situations. I'd find it a whole lot harder if I was caught in the middle of one. So I totally agree with you. *(Pause)* You told me in the first session some of the things that have happened when you lost control of your anger. So you have important reasons why you're here and working on this. Can we look at the coping thoughts and see if there's anything we can do to strengthen them?

Client: Okay.

Therapist: Take this situation *(pointing to something in the Anger Log)*, can you think of a coping thought that would help here?

Client: I don't know. Maybe just, "Calm down, don't blow a gasket."

Therapist: Would that help?

Client: Not really.

Therapist: Can you tell what the anger distortion might be here? Let's look at the handout.

Client: I'm thinking she's a total flake, so I guess it's magnifying.

Therapist: I was wondering, is there a way to pull back and look at the whole picture here?

Client: Like times when she doesn't screw up?

Therapist: Yeah.

Client: I'm never going to think of that when I'm upset.

Therapist: How about something more general, a better way to think about mistakes? Like getting a kind of a philosophy about them.

Client:	(After a silence) You mean like, "Sometimes things go okay, and sometimes they don't. And I don't have to get upset about it"?
Therapist:	Yeah. Does that seem true to you?
Client:	I guess so.
Therapist:	How would it feel to say that to yourself in this situation?
Client:	If I remembered, it would be okay.
Therapist:	Then, how could we make this thought something you'd remember?
Client:	I'd have to think of it often.
Therapist:	Like if you saw it in a sign around your house?
Client:	Maybe.
Therapist:	Where? Shaving (vanity) mirror? Closet door? Wallet (purse)?
Client:	You think I should put that coping thought up on a sign?
Therapist:	It's a very good thought that I think would help if you could remember to. Where could it go?
Client:	On the mirror would be Okay.
Therapist:	Sounds like a good plan. Think about it and see if you can figure out other ways this coming week to remind yourself of your anger lowering thoughts. You may figure out some ways we've not even thought about. (Therapist makes a note to check back on this next session.)

Remind clients that they can develop coping thoughts at home using the Creating Coping Thoughts Handout (introduced in session 5). An additional copy of that handout appears at the end of this session.

Don't forget to check the Relaxation Log as part of the homework review. Sometimes, at this point in the protocol, the relaxation component gets lost and clients stop practicing. It's unwise to let this happen because relaxation is such a critical anger-management skill.

Concepts and Skills

Skill Building

Coping with Moderate Anger Scenes

As you did in session 5, flesh out the visual, auditory, and kinesthetic details of each of the two anger scenes the client identified as homework.

Anger scenes should be concrete and detailed in order to maximize the scene's clarity and elicit as much anger as possible. Examples of several different types and levels of anger arousal are provided below to show the kind of detail that may be included.

Scene 1: Waiting for a Provocative Event. (Scene level 60) It was last Friday evening, about 6:00 P.M. I'm home alone in the kitchen of my apartment, pacing around waiting for my roommate, Sarah, to get home so that I can talk to her about her share of the phone and utility bills and the rent. I have tried to talk to her about this several times over the last week, but she's always busy or has some excuse for why she can't talk about it when I bring it up. I think she's ducking me and that pisses me off. I'm pacing around the kitchen, fiddling with the mail on the counter. I have that knot in my stomach and can feel a burning sensation across my face and chest. I'm angry that she won't come clean and just talk with me. I am also a bit worried about what I'll do if she isn't able to come up with her portion of the bills. I can cover it, but I really don't want to. Damn it, roommates aren't suppose to treat each other this way! I'm there waiting for what seems like forever, even though I have only been home about twenty minutes myself.

Scene 2: Clear External Event—Moderate Anger. (Scene level 65) I was on my way to work last week, on Thursday. I'm first in line in the lane that turns onto the on-ramp of the freeway. The light has just turned, and I'm starting to accelerate when a woman in a blue Ford appears out of nowhere and races in front of me, right into my lane. She doesn't even seem to notice what she did. I hit my brakes to keep from hitting her. My anger surges. I can feel everything tense up, especially my hands tightening around the wheel. My arms and shoulders tense, and I clench my teeth as I yell at her, "What in the hell are you doing? Watch where the hell you are going. You're going to get all of us killed. Stupid bitch! They should take her damned license away if she's going to drive like that." There I am, tense and shaking, as I'm pulling onto the on-ramp.

Scene 3: Clear External Event—Higher Anger. (Scene Level 85) It was a week ago, Wednesday. I had just come into the house from work. It had been a hard day at work, and I had come home tired but in a good mood. I was just coming around the corner into the family room where I could hear the television was on. As I come into the room, I encounter Dan, my son, and his mess. He's laying on the couch, and there is stuff all over the place. His coat, backpack, and trumpet case are in a pile in the middle of the room. There are two pop cans on the floor, and a couple of videotape boxes; the phone is out of the cradle and on the floor, and there is a bunch of other stuff on the floor, too. It's like a surge of electricity goes through me—I'm instantly mad. That hot flash sweeps across me, and I'm tense all over. I'm thinking, "Jesus Christ, here we go again. How many times do we have to talk about the general rules about putting stuff away before watching TV. Lazy little shit! He always does this kind of stuff. He gets what he wants and then leaves it to his sister and me to clean up after him. I am not going to put up with any more of this shit! I've had it with being nice." I just want to come across the room and jerk him up off the couch. I start to yell at him.

Scene 4: External Event and Anger at Self. (Scene Level 80) I was in my office four or five weeks ago. It's right after the project-managers meeting where we had been going over the production schedules and the financial statements for the last quarter. Both sales and production were down in my area. I'm sitting there with my feet on an open lower drawer of my desk and looking out the window. I just can't stop thinking about the meeting and how unfair it was. I'm thinking things like, "What the hell do they expect from us. They take all of the computer support away and then wonder why things aren't getting done. Idiots! If they don't give us the resources, we can't do our jobs. Same old same old. They make these types of decisions to save a few dollars and then blame us, the people who have to try to make their dumb decisions work. It makes me so mad. And once again, I just sat there and took it. I didn't even *once* try to tell them what I thought about their plans and what I thought the consequences would be. I didn't stick up for my people or myself. I get so pissed at myself for being such a wimp. I always wimp out at key points like this."

I'm just sitting there at my desk in an angry stew. My stomach's burning and churning, and I feel like I can't breathe, like there's a big weight on my chest. I feel one of my headaches coming on and that kind of tight "mask" feeling across my face. God, I hate that feeling, feeling angry and out of control, but just sitting there doing nothing. I want to hit something or yell or something, but all I do is sit there and take it.

Scene 5: Angry Rumination. (Scene Level 85) I'm doing it again. It's one evening at about 11:00 P.M. I've been sitting at my desk trying to get my school work done, but haven't gotten a thing accomplished for a couple of hours. All I can think about is Jane, how she dumped me, how angry I am, how hurt I am, and how she's probably out screwing some other guy. I'm thinking about how much I miss her, how lonely I am, but the point when I get the angriest is when I flash back on seeing her over at our favorite pizza place last weekend. There she was with a bunch of our old friends, having the time of her life, laughing, drinking beer and having a good old time. There I was miserable and barely even able to get Fred to go for a beer. Man, when I think of that I get really angry. It's like reliving it all over again. I get that hot knife in the gut feeling, like it's slowly twisting and turning. My body feels like somebody is twisting it, like wringing me out. I just wish I could make her feel as bad as I do. I just want to shake her and make her feel what she did to me.

Recording the Scenes. You should be sure to write down key emotional, cognitive, and physiological reactions that occur during each scene. You may also include urges or impulses to do something (e.g., "I wanted to yell at him") but not actual dysfunctional behavior. When you have each scene on paper, and the descriptions seem vivid and real, it's time to develop cognitive counterresponses.

Identify key automatic thoughts for each of the two scenes and work with your client to name any anger distortions that show up. As described in session 5, work collaboratively to develop coping thoughts drawn from both the Anger Distortions Handout and the General Coping Thoughts Handout. Invite the client, through questions, to generate alternative new coping thoughts. (See therapist-client dialogue under "Development of Cognitive Counterresponses" in session 5.) Make sure alternative responses are in the client's language and are believable to him or her.

Some of the work develop coping thoughts for the anger scenes may already have been done at home. The client manual includes copies of the Creating Coping Thoughts Handout and encourages clients to fill one out for each anger scene prepatory to session 6.

With cognitive counterresponses in place, begin coping skills rehearsal using the five-step format described in the last session. Continue coping skills rehearsal until approximately five minutes before the end of the session. Alternate the two scenes with the goal of getting four to six repetitions of each. During the first few repetitions, remind the client to use specific coping skills: cue-controlled relaxation, breathing-cued relaxation, relaxation imagery, relaxation without tension, and particular coping thoughts. On the third repetition, you should be using only general reminders like, "Catching these shoulds and replacing them with your preferences"; "Telling yourself to focus on the situation as a problem and starting to develop a plan for dealing with it"; "That's it, not giving in to anger and blowing things out of proportion, just staying real"; "Remember your coping thoughts"; "Deeply relax"; "Using whatever relaxation method works best for you"; and so on. By the final repetition, it would be quite appropriate to say, "Go ahead and cope using whatever relaxation and rethinking methods work best for you." No other instructions should be necessary at this point.

As you have in the past, evaluate the usefulness of coping thoughts after several repetitions. Do any counterresponses need to be modified or replaced? Work with the client collaboratively to generate new coping thoughts whenever old ones seem inadequate. Also, have your client generate and write down more situation-relevant coping thoughts as part of the homework.

Session Summary

As in the previous session, the main focus has been rehearsing coping skills. The client is learning to put relaxation skills and cognitive coping together in an anger fighting armamentarium.

Feedback from Client

Explore reactions to visualizing the anger-evoking scenes. Ask for feedback about how the client feels putting the relaxation and cognitive coping elements together during provocative scenes. Any discomfort with multiple repetition of the anger scenes? Does the client have any concerns about his or her progress?

Homework

1. Clients should continue practicing relaxation without tension, cue-controlled relaxation, and relaxation imagery five out of seven days in the week. Results should be recorded in the Relaxation Log.

2. Clients should apply cognitive and relaxation coping skills once or more daily to a variety of stressful situations, including anger. These efforts should be noted in Anger Log III. Stress that clients will not always remem-

ber to use their new skills, but if they keep trying, the new coping strategies will start to become automatic. Encourage clients to keep using three or four of the more effective general coping thoughts in response to unanticipated upsets. To the extent that clients can anticipate provocative situations in advance, they should be planning specific coping thoughts and strategies to remember cue-controlled breathing. Encourage clients to do after-the-fact analyses for situations that went poorly or not as well as they would like. Have them identify anger-engendering thoughts and write out new alternatives or counterresponses. They can utilize the Creating Coping Thoughts Handout for this. Also, have clients write down ways they could have triggered relaxation during and after the event (or before, if relevant).

3. Clients should develop two moderate to high (60 to 80 intensity level) anger scenes. These scenes may involve anger after a situation is over or where a problem is unresolvable. Examples of such scenes include: 1) a high anger situation where the client is brooding angrily sometime later (e.g., brooding about a relationship breakup); 2) a memory of a past event where anger is still high and intrusive (e.g., memory of an abusive parent); 3) a time just after a highly disturbing anger event (e.g., right after a big argument with spouse or boss); 4) situations where the event is over quickly but anger remains (e.g., someone cuts in front of the individual in traffic); and 5) an event in which the person has chosen not to speak up (e.g., an injustice at work or a problem at home where anger might have serious negative consequences).

   When developing scenes, clients should always write down the external (situational and behavioral) and internal (cognitive, emotional, and physiological) components of the situation. Encourage lots of detail. Also, remind clients to develop counterresponses to trigger thoughts in each scene using the Creating Coping Thoughts Handout.

4. Remind clients that all significant anger experiences, whether coping efforts were made or not, should be recorded in Anger Log III. As in the past, the criterion for noting an anger situation is that it rates greater than 40 on the 100-point scale.

Session 7

Coping Skills Training — Moderate to High Anger Scenes

Monitoring of Current Status

Evaluate with your client his or her overall sense of how the program is working. Is anger a less frequent problem? Continue to plot anger frequency and intensity from the log if you began doing so in the preceding session, noting any success made on the log. Is the client getting feedback from peers about any changes in his or her anger response? Is the client able to stop angry interactions before they escalate to a destructive level? How often is the client able to modulate anger? Are there certain strategies that are working effectively and consistently? If the client has found specific techniques to be effective, take time to understand exactly what the client does that helps. Ask the client how he or she could use them even more effectively, more of the time, and as early in the buildup of anger as possible.

Agenda

This session will continue with coping skills training. Anger will be aroused by visualizing moderate to high intensity scenes. The client will then diminish anger levels using relaxation and cognitive coping skills. This session will introduce a new structural element to coping skills training. Now, instead of erasing the scene after thirty seconds of anger, clients will continue to visualize the provocative scene while utilizing cognitive and relaxation coping skills. In other words, clients will simultaneously generate images that evoke anger and use multiple coping strategies to diminish angry affect. Therapist input gradually fades as you move the client to greater self-control.

Review of Homework

Look at the Relaxation Log. If practice has slacked off, collaborate with your client on a plan to maintain more consistent practice levels. As described earlier, look for a reminder system, a desirable reward, or some kind of peer support to keep practice frequencies up.

A key element of last session's homework was to apply cognitive and relaxation coping skills to everyday stressors. These could be anger situations or virtually anything that is physically or emotionally stressful. Focus on the good news. Encourage and support use of any of the anger-management skills to smooth out stressful encounters. Make sure that clients recognize specifically what they have done to make these changes possible. Link positive changes in their anger response to increased personal awareness and to the specific cognitive, emotional, and behavioral shifts they are making. In the following sample dialogue, a therapist helps a client name critical changes in thinking and behavior that are altering chronic anger patterns:

Therapist: From what you've noted in the log, I can see that you've been using some of your new skills to deal with several different stressful situations. That very critical coworker, for example, who started to get on you about cleaning your coffee cups. There was a time when that might have ended in a blowup. What did you do differently last week?

Client: I just tried not to get upset, kind of talked myself into not going overboard.

Therapist: Was there a specific coping thought you used?

Client: I just thought, "Don't let her get to you. Getting pissed at her is just not worth it."

Therapist: So you kind of stepped back mentally and told yourself to stay cool. Did you do anything to try to relax?

Client: Let me remember. Well, yes. It's actually pretty automatic now, as soon as something bothers me I take a deep breath and say to myself, "Let go."

Therapist: Your cue phrase.

Client: Right.

Therapist: Did you do anything else in terms of what you said, or some action?

Client: Yeah. I just mumbled, "Right," instead of making some smartass remark. Then I got up from my desk to get away from her for a minute.

Now the therapist draws contrasts between new and old patterns of response:

Therapist: That's good, taking a time-out. What did you used to do instead of getting away?

Client: I'd get sucked in. I'd feel irritated and sit there thinking of things I could say to dig back at her.

Therapist: So you used to hang right there trying to get the fight started. Now you're distancing yourself so it won't start—that's a big difference.

Client: Yeah, I guess it is.

The therapist looks for specific coping responses to any automatic thoughts.

Therapist: When she got on your case about the dirty coffee cups, you had to have a few automatic thoughts, even if just a flash of something.

Client: I guess so. I don't exactly remember, but what I'd typically say to myself is, "I've taken enough crap from her. I'm always getting attacked."

Therapist: How did you keep thoughts like that from igniting you in this situation?

Client: (Pause) I keep thinking—since the therapy—"It's no big deal," which means stop exaggerating, stop making this bigger than it is.

Therapist: How does that affect automatic thoughts like, "I've taken enough crap," and "I'm always getting attacked"?

Client: I just tend to see them as an exaggeration and try not to run with it.

Now the therapist summarizes key changes.

Therapist: I'm glad we talked about this because I can see how many different ways you're coping. You're saying to yourself, "Don't let her get to me." You're dealing with automatic thoughts that magnify things by saying to yourself, "It's no big deal." On top of that, you're stopping yourself from coming back at her with a provocative remark, and physically getting away from the situation.

In exploring examples of real life coping, you may want to put some labels on themes so clients can more readily identify them. Effective coping strategies can be named. For example, the "no big deal" response from the previous dialogue can be referred to again and again over the course of therapy. Anger distortions that show up frequently can be given a funny name. Here are several examples of labels clients have created:

1. My "everybody's an idiot" reaction. *Global labeling.*

2. "Demanding perfection." *Shoulds.*

3. I've got my "crystal ball" again. *Misattribution.*

4. There's my "God-awful button" again. *Magnifying.*

Verify that the client is continuing to use Anger Log III. Pay particular attention to any high anger situations that have come up in the past week. Here is an example dialogue:

Therapist:	There was a big blowup with Diane (the client's sister) this week. You wrote down, "the usual," under automatic thoughts.
Client:	Yeah. The old, "Nobody cares that my life is shit" thoughts. Diane's just putting all this pressure on me.
Therapist:	And you're assuming she doesn't care.
Client:	Right. That's where I always go—nobody cares.
Therapist:	Not only Diane, but nobody anywhere cares. How could we head that thought off so it doesn't end in a hurtful blowup?
Client:	That's the thing, I know she cares. But in the moment, I just see her as the enemy.
Therapist:	Okay. How do you know she cares?
Client:	'Cause she's done a million things for me. She came down to Memphis and took me home with her when I was getting abused by some jerk.
Therapist:	She's done lots of things for you and gotten you out of a bad situation. How are you going to remember that next time?
Client:	Just say inside myself, "This is my sister. She loves me."
Therapist:	Will that work?
Client:	It has to. I just can't do that with Diane again.
Therapist:	Yes, but you've told yourself not to blow up before, and it hasn't worked. Let's see if we can't figure out how to make it work this time. Remember how, with misattribution, we try to find alternative explanations for upsetting events? Why else might Diane be pressuring you besides not caring?
Client:	'Cause she's worried. She knows sometimes I let my life go in the dumper. She's scared she's gonna see that happen again.
Therapist:	What will you say to yourself if an issue comes up with her again?
Client:	She's just scared for me, because she really does love me.
Therapist:	So you can practice thinking things like: "She really loves me. She really cares. That's probably why it feels like she's pressuring me. Pressure from someone loving and caring is pretty cool." How about if you made a list of these kind of thoughts before next session? Say it in as many different ways as you can think of. Okay? *(The therapist makes a note to check this list next session.)*

Before beginning coping skills rehearsal, make sure the client has two moderate to high anger scenes (60 to 80 intensity) that involve incomplete, unresolved, unfinished, or aftermath anger situations. If the client hasn't yet developed the scenes, do it now.

Concepts and Skills

Skill Building

Coping with Moderate to High Anger Scenes

As in past sessions, identify visual, auditory, and kinesthetic details to flesh out the two anger scenes (see session 6 for examples). Write these down along with cognitive, emotional, and physiological reactions that the clients can imagine having during each scene.

Develop cognitive counterresponses for each of the two scenes, as described in session 5. Work collaboratively with your client to develop coping thoughts using the Anger Distortions Handout and General Coping Thoughts Handout as resources. Because the capacity to create counterresponses is such an important skill, take your time to create believable, forceful coping statements. By this time you should be pushing clients to take more initiative in this process. You can ask questions to point them in the right direction ("Can you think of a way to question this assumption?" or "What's another way you can think about that?"). Are there coping thoughts the client has used in the past to effectively deal with similar situations? At this point in the program, the client has to take more responsibility for brainstorming counterresponses that are unique and appropriate for them. See session 5 for a therapist-client dialogue that illustrates this process.

As noted previously some clients may be using the Creating Coping Thoughts Handout to prepare calm responses for the anger scenes at home. This should be encouraged. An additional Creating Coping Thoughts Handout appears at the end of this session.

New Coping Skills Rehearsal Structure

The focus now is on the practice of cognitive and relaxation coping skills in somewhat more angering situations, and on greater client control. The intensity level for the current scenes is in the 60 to 80 range, so clients are being asked to manage higher levels of affect. Improved self-control will now be taught through a change in the scene presentation format. In sessions 5 and 6, the scenes were erased after thirty seconds and *then* coping skills were applied. In this session, and for the remainder of treatment, clients will be instructed to stay in the anger scene *while* they actively employ the cognitive and relaxation coping skills to reduce anger. This better parallels real life; the client has to stay in the situation and cope. When anger is felt, clients are required to use whatever relaxation and cognitive coping skills work best for them—and keep using them—until they have successfully controlled their anger.

The signal system will be altered to reflect these changes. Clients have signaled by raising their finger or hand when they experienced anger, but now they will continue to keep their finger or hand raised as long as anger is felt. They will remain in the scene, coping and relaxing until anger has abated. Only then will they lower their hands and erase the scene. The therapist clears the scene and provides general support for coping. For example, as the client signals anger reduction by lowering his or her hand, the therapist might say:

Good. I see by your signal that you have lowered your anger. Stay with that a moment. Feeling good about relaxing away the anger and rethinking the situation in calmer, more clearheaded ways . . . (ten-to-fifteen-second pause) . . . okay, now erase that scene from you mind, but keep that sense that you can manage your anger with you.

Once the scene is erased the format returns to its traditional structure. Clients continue to apply the cognitive and relaxation coping skills between scenes until instructed to get ready for the next anger scene presentation. As in prior sessions, you should alternate back and forth between the two scenes with the goal of four to six repetitions.

Here's how the therapist's instructions for the new rehearsal structure might sound:

As we have in the past, I'm going to describe the anger scene to you with as much detail as I can. I'm going to remind you of the situation and some of your automatic thoughts, and your job is to focus on the visualization and try to get fully immersed in it. Let the anger rise and notice it. When you start to get angry, just raise your hand and signal me. This is the point where things will change. Now, instead of being angry for thirty seconds and switching off the scene to cope, you'll continue to visualize the scene while coping. In other words, you'll do cue-controlled relaxation and remind yourself of key coping thoughts while continuing to visualize the upsetting scene.

And here's another thing. You'll keep your hand up the entire time you're feeling angry. As long as you're angry, your hand will stay in the air. Only when you've successfully controlled your anger using relaxation and cognitive skills will you lower your hand. At that point I'll ask you to erase the scene and we'll continue to relax for a while (using cue-controlled breathing and relaxation imagery) before starting the next scene.

This is a bit complicated, I know, because you're going to have to do two things at once. You've got to generate anger imagery and cope with your feelings simultaneously. But it can be done, and after several scenes you'll get used to it.

It may take a while to cope with some of these scenes. Don't worry about that. However long it takes is fine. Just keep coping—breathing and using your counterthoughts—until you feel calm again. Then you can lower your hand, and we'll hit the erase button on the scene.

During the first presentation of each scene, it's fine to continue giving detailed suggestions about coping—reminding the client to use cue-controlled breathing and other relaxation skills and suggesting specific coping thoughts. During the first presentations in the new format, you may also have to remind client of the new signal system—hand up, scene and anger on; hand down, anger managed, scene still on. But very soon you should fade detailed cognitive counters and relaxation instructions and encourage clients to take responsibility for their own coping process. Let them apply the thoughts they think will be most helpful to each scene and relax in ways that work best for them. When clients are encouraged to take this initiative, they're more likely to remember coping skills during in vivo provocations.

As I've done before, I'll remind you to use some of your specific coping skills during the first scene or two. But after that, I'm going to encourage you to cope in a general way and let you decide how best to do that. You can see what works best for you to manage your anger. I'm confident that you'll get better and better at coping as we practice in these scenes.

Session Summary

The main focus of the session has been rehearsing coping skills while the client has been encouraged to take greater and greater initiative in the process. An additional effort has been made to identify effective coping strategies the client has used during real life stressors. If the client is still experiencing major anger events, time has also been taken to focus on key anger distortions and counterresponses for these situations.

Feedback from Client

Explore with clients any reactions to the new coping skills rehearsal format. Invite feedback about the emphasis on client-initiated coping. Since you're making fewer specific suggestions for coping during the scenes, is the client taking more responsibility for his or her own coping process? Does the client feel able to come up with coping skills alone? Is coping harder without specific suggestions from the therapist?

Homework

1. Have clients continue to practice relaxation without tension, cue-controlled relaxation, and relaxation imagery at least five out of seven days and keep a record in the Relaxation Log.

2. Clients should look for opportunities to practice cognitive and relaxation coping skills during anger as well as other kinds of stress situations. If angering or stressful upcoming events can be identified (e.g., dealing with an angry teenage son about skipping school, or going to the dentist), then contract to use specific coping skills before, during, and after these events. Any coping effort should be recorded in Anger Log III. Clients should continue to use the Creating Coping Thoughts Handout to develop cognitive counter-responses for specific provocative situations.

3. Clients should develop two high anger scenes (75 to 100 intensity). They are free at this point to use virtually any anger scene or situation that rates at least 75 in intensity.

   Encourage clients to develop counterresponses to trigger thoughts in each anger scene using the Creating Coping Thoughts Handout.

4. As always, remind clients that all significant anger experiences (40 or over) should be recorded in the Anger Log whether they were with coping skills or not.

Session 8

Coping Skills Training — High Anger Scenes

Monitoring of Current Status

Continue to evaluate your client's reaction to coping skills rehearsal. After three sessions of visualizing and coping with anger scenes, is there any noticeable change in how clients react to real life provocations? Are they using the relaxation skills and coping thoughts when stressors occur? What works best? Have they found a particular set of coping responses that are generally effective? Overall, are clients subjectively less angry? Are they experiencing fewer occasions of lashing out with verbal attacks? Continue to graph frequency and intensity of anger, if this is being done.

Agenda

This session will attempt to synthesize some of what has been learned in the past by introducing "best coping thoughts" categories. Reviewing the coping thoughts that seemed most effective during the visualized anger scenes and situations at home, therapist and client work collaboratively to fit these thoughts into categories. They can then expand the options available by identifying additional thoughts from each category that might also be effective. In addition to this new conceptual work around cognitive counterresponses, the session will continue coping skills rehearsal using the two high anger scenes developed as part of the previous weeks' homework.

Review of Homework

Review the Anger Log, focusing mostly on coping responses that worked and celebrating success. Each time a client has applied relaxation or cognitive coping skills during a distressing situation, acknowledge this as evidence of significant behavior change. To help reinforce these gains, explore with the client how he or she *remembered* to use the skills and what, specifically, was said or done to cope. How did the client overcome previously described roadblocks that may have gotten in the way of coping in the past? Be encouraging and supportive of success and positive changes. However, since a shift toward greater self-control has taken place, the therapist may wish to shift the emphasis of support to reflecting the client's sense of accomplishment. For example, "So you're feeling good about letting it go, not being sucked into the anger, but relaxing and going on."

Review the Relaxation Log and once again emphasize the importance of maintaining these skills.

Verify that the client has prepared two high anger scenes (75 to 100 intensity). If this homework was not completed, develop these scenes now.

Concepts and Skills

Psychoeducation

Best Coping Thoughts Categories

This is a good point to review the coping thoughts that have worked best for your client. Working together, look back over the past three sessions of coping skills rehearsal and write down each of the effective coping thoughts in the appropriate category of the Best Coping Thoughts Handout. The handout has nine categories of coping thoughts. Each category has several example coping thoughts, and a blank space for you to fill in coping thoughts of that type that your client has developed. The client will continue adding thoughts to this handout outside of therapy.

The categories are:

1. *Cool thoughts.* These include emotional palliatives and self-instructions to initiate relaxation coping skills. Example: "Just stay cool, getting all pissed off won't help."

2. *Problem-solving thoughts.* Provocations can be thought of as problems to be solved or challenges to be overcome. The idea is that anger is just a signal that it's time to look for alternative solutions. Example: "It's not the end of the world, just a problem to be solved. Focus on that. What's my problem here?"

3. *Escape routes.* Taking time out and removing oneself from provocative situations is often very appropriate. Self-instruction to walk away from something upsetting, perhaps coming back later when things are calm, is a good

way to stop things from escalating. Example: "I can always walk away rather than totally lose it."

4. *Self-efficacy thoughts.* This type of coping thought is a reminder that the client is competent to handle the situation, that he or she has the skill to manage upsetting feelings. Self-efficacy thoughts should support coping and trying, attribute change to self, and set realistic plans for future coping. Example: "I can handle this—I've done it before."

5. *Reattributions.* Here the effort is to find alternative explanations for people's behavior rather than assuming they are being intentionally provocative. Why else might they be acting as they do? Humorous reattributions are particularly effective. For example, an individual's grouchy, irritable behavior might be attributed to "chanelling Attila the Hun again" rather than to a personal attack on the client. Another's forgetfulness and oversights might be attributed to the person "slipping into brain fog" rather than intentional neglect. Whether reattributions are serious alternative explanations or rely on silly humor, they help the client break the hold of anger distortions. Example: "They're probably just (scared, overwhelmed, confused, out of the loop, hurting, brain dead, etc.)."

6. *Seeing the whole picture.* This category is about the quest for exceptions. Coping thoughts redirect the client's attention to information and events that counterbalance negative automatic thoughts. Example: "Look at the other side."

7. *Getting accurate.* These are self-instructions that remind the client to stay with the facts, to avoid catastrophic thinking and exaggeration. This often involves the client being realistically and mildly to moderately negative (e.g., frustrated, hurt, disappointed, etc.). Example: "Cut the angry crap, tell it like it is."

8. *Preferences, not shoulds.* This category of coping replaces absolute should statements with the language of desire and preference. The intent is to soften the angry expectation that other people must live by the client's rules. Rules become personal wants, desires, and preferences, rather than dictates. Example: "What I want and what has to be are two different things. So, let me stay with my wants. That's hard enough."

9. *People are doing their best.* This coping category acknowledges that people are trying to survive and manage the circumstances of their lives as best they can. They make mistakes, they behave in self-serving ways, but they are ultimately doing their best to manage their pain and get what they need. Example: "He or she is only doing what they know how to do."

When you've finished writing the client's coping thoughts into the various categories, explore other coping thoughts in each category that might be helpful. Are there categories of coping thoughts the client hasn't used? Develop collaboratively two or three coping thoughts in these heretofore unutilized categories. Here is an example of how you might present the handout to your client:

This is something new for us to work with (hands the client the Best Coping Thoughts Handout.) *This organizes coping thoughts into nine categories and shows examples of coping thoughts in each. What I'd like to do now is go back to my notes where I've written down the coping thoughts you used during the last three sessions of coping skills rehearsal. I'll read off the coping thought, and you can tell me whether you experienced it as helpful. If it was, we'll write it down under the appropriate category of the handout. I want to get all of the most effective coping thoughts you've developed together in one place. Also, I'd like to develop some new ideas for coping thoughts that you can use in the future.*

Okay, here is the first coping thought (reads it aloud). *Was this something that worked for you?* (The client thinks it did) *So let's write it down in the category where it would belong on this handout. Where do you think it should go?* (The client selects a category and the therapist writes in the coping thought) *Good. Now would you look at the example coping thoughts in that category? Do you think any of those would be helpful?* (The client selects one and the therapist puts a star by it) *Any other ideas for helpful coping thoughts in this category?*

Now the next coping thought from my notes is (therapist reads it). *Where would you put that one on the handout?*

The therapist and client continue working together, placing each coping thought in the appropriate category and putting a star by any example coping thought that might also be useful. When this task is completed, it's time to examine the categories where nothing was written. Would any of these be useful in provocative situations? Look over the example coping thoughts in these categories. Are any appealing to the client?

You notice that there are some categories of coping thoughts that we haven't used. Do you think any of the example coping thoughts listed in those categories might be helpful? (The therapist stars any thoughts the client identifies as helpful) *I'd like to give a little thought to one or two of these categories and see if we could develop some coping thoughts of our own in them. Which category feels like the best place to start?* (Client points to one of the categories) *Okay, how could this category of coping thought help you in some of the anger situations you've been facing? Can we put our heads together and come up with a new coping statement or two?*

Later the therapist says:

This handout is going to be especially important to you after this therapy program is over. I'd suggest keeping it by your bed and reading it over each night. And add any new coping thoughts that you develop over time into the appropriate category. It'll help you stay very conscious of how you've learned to talk back to your anger and will remind you of specific coping statements that have worked best.

Skill Building

Coping with High Anger Scenes

Follow the new structure for coping skills rehearsal outlined in session 7. Flesh out the two anger scenes with visual, auditory, and kinesthetic details. Write these down along with any significant cognitive, emotional, or physiological reactions that the client might anticipate experiencing in the scenes.

If the client hasn't already done so, develop several cognitive counterresponses for each scene. Use the Best Coping Thoughts Handout as a resource. If you wish to encourage the client to use new categories of coping thoughts, this may be a good place to do it. For example, if a client has never developed any thoughts that fit into the problem-solving category, and one of the anger scenes cries out for problem-solving, you might have the following conversation:

Therapist: Let's think about the scene where your girlfriend leaves mail and junk all over the surfaces in the kitchen so you can't cook. This might be a good situation for some problem-solving thoughts. We haven't developed any in that category so far. Can we try?

Client: Okay.

Therapist: You see the examples of problem-solving thoughts on the handout. Could we come up with something similar for this scene in the kitchen?

Client: How about, "Don't go crazy; let's make a plan"? *(Laughs.)*

Therapist: Would that work for you to calm down?

Client: I don't know. Not really.

Therapist: Do you need a specific plan to back it up? Something you figured out that might solve the problem?

Client: Yeah, but . . .

Therapist: What could you do with all that junk? Could you put it somewhere?

Client: I could suggest that we get a basket, and if junk and mail got on the cutting boards, I'd throw everything in the basket.

Therapist: So what would the coping thought be?

Client: "Don't go crazy; I've got a plan." Then in the back of my head I'd know what it was.

Once the cognitive counterresponses are in place, start the coping skills rehearsal procedure. The client relaxes using relaxation without tension, cue-controlled or breathing-cued relaxation, and relaxation imagery. The first high anger scene is described in detail until the client raises his or her hand signaling an anger response. The client is instructed to remain in the scene, visualizing the provocative situation, and to *cope*. You should make few (if any) specific suggestions for relaxation or cognitive coping responses. Let the client experiment to see what works best.

As in session 7, the client's hand should stay raised until anger has completely dissipated. Only after successful coping should the scene be erased, and the entire process be repeated with the second scene. Continue switching back and forth between the two scenes with a goal of four to six repetitions.

It's a good idea to check in with clients about the effectiveness of coping thoughts after a scene presentation. If a counterresponse isn't working, drop it. Take a moment to look back at the Best Coping Thoughts Handout to see if something else might work better. Add any new thoughts that occurred to the client during the session.

Session Summary

The focus of this session has been gathering together the most effective cognitive counterresponses in one place (Best Coping Thoughts Handout), and developing new coping thoughts to fit into underused categories. Coping skills rehearsal has allowed the client to visualize high anger situations while simultaneously practicing relaxation and cognitive coping skills.

Feedback From Client

Explore any reactions to this round of coping skills rehearsal. How has the client fared since you've stopped giving specific coping instructions during the anger scenes? Is the client able to remember the coping thoughts? Is there difficulty putting the relaxation and cognitive coping skills together? If there are any reported difficulties, spend some time collaborating on a plan to solve them.

Homework

1. Clients should continue to practice relaxation without tension, breathing-cued relaxation, cue-controlled relaxation, and relaxation imagery five out of seven days between sessions. Results should be in the Relaxation Log.

2. Clients should continue looking for opportunities to use relaxation and cognitive coping skills in anger as well as in other stress situations. Coping efforts should be noted in Anger Log III.

3. Clients should develop two "worst anger" scenes (85 to 100 intensity). Explain that you really want "top of the chart" experiences, the worst the client can remember over the past few years.

   Encourage clients to develop counterresponses to trigger thoughts in each anger scene using the Creating Coping Thoughts Handout.

4. As always, remind clients that all significant anger experiences (40+ on the scale), whether or not there were coping efforts, should be recorded in the Anger Log.

5. Sometimes in the course of anger-management work, anxiety emerges as a second major issue. Coping skills training can easily be applied to high stress (e.g., anxiety arousing) situations. If you wish to add a session or two to treat specific anxiety problems, instruct the client to begin identifying a moderate and a high anxiety scene.

Best Coping Thoughts Handout

Cool Thoughts

"Just stay cool—getting all pissed off won't help."

"It's just not worth it. Take a few deep breaths and chill out."

"This too shall pass. Others have to deal with this kind of stuff without getting crazy."

Your coping thoughts:

Problem-Solving Thoughts

"It's not the end of the world, just a problem to be solved."

"It's okay to feel annoyed, but it's just a challenge to be dealt with."

"Develop a plan. So, the first thing I would want to do is . . ."

"Break the frustration down. I can deal better with it that way."

Your coping thoughts:

Escape Routes

"I can always walk away rather than totally lose it."

"It's okay to take time out. Move away, get your act together, then come back and deal with it later."

"Better to walk away than to be a screaming idiot."

"Bottom line, I'll walk before I hit or do something dumb."

Your coping thoughts:

Self-Efficacy Thoughts

"I can handle this, I've done it before."

"I'm hanging in and coping."

"I have what it takes to get through this hassle."

"I'm getting better at this anger-management stuff."

Your coping thoughts:

Reattributions

"They're probably just (scared, overwhelmed, not understanding, confused, out of the loop, hurting, etc.)"

"Cut them some slack. I'd hope they'd do the same for me if I was having a bad time."

Your coping thoughts:

See the Whole Picture

"Look at the other side."

"There are exceptions. For example . . ."

"Time to look for some of the good for a change."

Your coping thoughts:

Getting Accurate

"Cut the angry crap. Tell it like it is."

"Just the facts."

"Tell it simple and straight."

"I'm frustrated and disappointed, but I don't have to lose control."

Your coping thoughts:

Preferences, Not Shoulds

"It doesn't have to be my way, I just prefer it."

"What I want and what has to be are two different things."

"This is what I *want*, not a *should*."

"Nobody appointed me God. So give it up. Be human and focus on your wants."

Your coping thoughts:

People Doing Their Best

"They're only doing what they know how to do."

"They're coping the best they can, all things considered."

"I don't like how they do it, but they're just trying to survive."

Your coping thoughts:

Creating Coping Thoughts Handout

Complete the following for each significant trigger thought (automatic thought) in an anger scene or situation:

1. Trigger thoughts that inflame my anger:

    a.

    b.

    c.

2. Anger distortions that underlie my trigger thoughts:

    a.

    b.

    c.

3. Counterresponse plan for each of my trigger thoughts (e.g., looking for exceptions, alternative explanations, preferences not shoulds, and so on). Rewritten trigger thought based on each counter-response plan.

    a. Counterresponse plan:

       Rewritten trigger thought:

    b. Counterresponse plan:

       Rewritten trigger thought:

    c. Counterresponse plan:

       Rewritten trigger thought:

4. Helpful coping thoughts (see Anger Distortions Handout or General Coping Thoughts Handout in session 4):

    a.

    b.

    c.

Coping Skills Training — Worst Anger Scenes

Monitoring of Current Status

Have the client quickly complete the Anger Situation and Anger Symptom measures. Note changes compared to the initial assessment. If there is any change at all, give credit to the client for all the effort and hard work that went into learning anger-management skills. If the anger levels have remained relatively consistent, focus instead on specific skills the client has learned and several situations where those skills have been effective. Keep your attention on the positive, try to identify the coping responses that the client does use and finds helpful. Ask about the frequency of major blowups. Most clients will report fewer occasions of extreme verbalized anger. Supplement this discussion with a continued graphing of Anger Log frequency overall and the frequency and intensity of entries greater than 40.

Agenda

There's a lot to do in this session and you may require an additional meeting to complete the agenda. Early in the session you'll work with clients to summarize personal change. You'll identify and underscore new cognitive, behavioral, and relaxation coping skills. Next comes maintenance issues (see introductory chapter for an overview of maintenance and relapse-prevention strategies), teaching clients a way to keep applying their skills to new provocative situations. They'll need to do it without your help, so you'll teach them to make "anger plans," following a structure outlined in the Anger Plans Handout. Finally, you will continue coping skills rehearsal using the "worst anger" scenes.

Review of Homework

Take no more than a few minutes to review the Anger and Relaxation Logs. Focus on a single instance where the client effectively used coping skills. Verify that the client has prepared two "worst anger" scenes (85 to 100 intensity).

Concepts and Skills

Psychoeducation

Summarizing Personal Change

This is a key step in building your client's sense of efficacy. Start by getting out the Best Coping Thoughts Handout and briefly reviewing with the client some of the excellent cognitive counterresponses that have been developed. Point out that these coping thoughts have been proven effective in the coping skills rehearsal scenes.

Now take out all the Relaxation Logs the client has completed and put them down dramatically on your desk. Name each of the skills the client has learned and practiced, and acknowledge the work and commitment that relaxation training has involved.

Now explore with your clients behavioral changes they are making in provocative situations. What are they saying that is different? Are they walking away from situations that used to escalate? Are they making and following a problem-solving plan? Do they use a different tone of voice? Do they pause to relax and get control before saying anything? Praise anything the client reports as new behavior. Have your client write down the main points on the Best Coping Responses Handout.

Now ask your client about outcomes. Have there been changes in personal or work relationships as a result of using anger-management skills? Are people warmer and friendlier? Are things going more smoothly? Do people seem less apprehensive and avoidant with the client? Does the client feel a greater sense of belonging, of comfort with others? Some of these changes may be subtle, some may take longer than nine weeks to achieve. But if the client can see any positive changes in his or her relationships, emphasize that this is one of the big payoffs for all the work that's been done. These are tangible signs that the effort makes a difference.

Here's an example of how you might summarize personal change with your client:

I think you've achieved a lot over the past weeks, and I wanted to briefly summarize what you've done. First of all (pulling out the Best Coping Thoughts Handout), you've developed some effective coping thoughts to manage anger. They really work. You know that because you've used them again and again in the visualized anger scenes, and they've helped you calm down. And you've used some of them on your own when you were starting to get angry. They've helped keep things from escalating. This piece of paper (waving the Best Coping Thoughts Handout) *represents some very good ways for handling anger distortions and cooling yourself down. Long after therapy's over you can keep using these—and making new ones—to handle upsets.*

The relaxation skills you've learned (holding Relaxation Logs from previous weeks) *have taken a lot of work. But all of that work is paying off because now you can relax your body instead of getting angry. You've learned progressive muscle relaxation, relaxation without tension, cue-controlled and breathing-cued relaxation, and relaxation imagery. Every time you use cue-controlled breathing in provocative situations, it helps you calm down and be more effective. The work you put into learning relaxation skills is a real achievement, and it will keep helping you to stay cool months or even years after therapy is over.*

You've also learned some new ways of behaving in provocative situations. (Hand the client the Best Coping Responses Handout) *Here's something I'd like you to look at; it's a place to write down some of the new coping behaviors you've been using lately. See what it says there: "things you say that are different than before, changes in your tone of voice, walking away rather than exploding, making a problem-solving plan, pausing to relax and get control, etc." Let's think about some responses like these that you're doing now; things that are different from how you used to handle provocations before. Let's take some of the anger situations with your customers, for example. What are you doing differently there?*

The therapist and client continue to explore specific relationships and typical anger situations to identify new coping behaviors. The client writes each coping behavior down on the Best Coping Responses Handout.

So far we've focused on how you've *changed. But now I'd like to look at how your relationships have changed. This is really what all the effort's been about. We've been trying to improve relationships with family, friends, and at work. Let's take your roommate, for example. You don't blow up the way you used to when she doesn't do the dishes. Or when she and her boyfriend turn up the television volume. Is there any change in how things feel between you?*

The therapist continues to explore specific relationships, asking about changes in intimacy level, ability to cooperate, and so on.

Skill Building

Anger Plans

One key to maintaining therapeutic gains is to teach the client a structure for planning coping responses to new provocations. The Anger Plans Handout can give clients a simple framework to identify which coping responses would work best for a specific anger situation. The Anger Plans Handout is divided into five sections: anger thoughts, coping thoughts, relaxation, coping behavior, and problem solving. It is suggested that you fill in the Anger Plans Handout using a recent provocation as an example situation. Here's how you might do this exercise:

Let's do a sample anger plan for that recent situation where your coworker kept talking to her boyfriend on the phone instead of helping you at the cash register. What were your anger thoughts while she was talking on the phone? (Therapist has client write automatic thoughts in the space provided on the Anger Plans Handout)

Can you think of any coping thoughts that would help you in this situation? Is there anything that might neutralize some of the anger thoughts? (The client makes a suggestion) *Would you write that down in the space under coping thoughts? What about the Best Coping Thoughts Handout, anything there that would help?* (The client looks it over and selects another coping thought) *Let's write that one down, too. Remember that when you're doing this on your own, you can also get ideas from the Anger Distortions Handout and the General Coping Thoughts Handout.*

Now let's turn to the relaxation part of the plan. You're in a public situation where a coworker is really irritating you. What relaxation strategy would work here? (The client selects cue-controlled breathing) *How would you remind yourself to take a deep breath and use your cue word?* (A discussion follows about reminder strategies) *Okay, let's write that down, including how you'll remind yourself to relax the next time your coworker's talking to her boyfriend instead of helping.*

Let's think about coping behavior for a moment. Is there any way you could handle the situation differently so you don't have to get angry? Is there something you could say to her that isn't attacking but gets your point across? (The client decides to interrupt the phone conversation and ask her coworker for help) *Let's write that down under coping behavior.*

The last step in our plan is problem solving. Do you have any idea of how you could structure things to avoid this problem in the future? Could you put a sign on the phone that says "No personal conversations," or agree to end personal calls when the store gets busy? (Discussion yields a possible solution) *Okay, so you'll ask her to get off the phone as soon as there's more than one person in the store. That sounds good. Let's write that down.*

From now on, I want to encourage you to use the structure on the handout. When you run into provocative situations that occur repeatedly, and you're not controlling your anger well, it means that you really need a plan. If you plan in advance for the next provocation, you'll have far less chance of blowing up.

Coping with Worst Anger Scenes

Use the same rehearsal structure you employed in sessions 7 and 8. Write down sensory and emotional details of the two anger scenes. If the client hasn't already done so, develop with the client several cognitive counterresponses. Use the Best Coping Thoughts Handout as a resource. Have the client relax, then visualize the scene while using appropriate cognitive and relaxation coping strategies. When coping efforts have succeeded in eliminating the anger, erase the scene and repeat the procedure with the second scene. Try to cycle through each anger scene at least two or three times.

Session Summary

The main focus of the session has been summarizing personal change and working on relapse prevention using the implementation of anger plans. Coping skills rehearsal has now been completed, and the client has successfully coped with the "worst anger" scenes.

Feedback from Client

This is a good time to ask your client for feedback about the anger-management treatment as a whole. What has the client found most useful? What elements of the program have not worked particularly well? What did the client find the easiest and most enjoyable skills to learn? Which skills were the most difficult to acquire? Could anything have been done to make learning them easier?

Ask the client to take a copy of the Program Satisfaction Questionnaire (PSQ) to the waiting room after the session and fill it out. The PSQ appears on the next page.

Termination

Give your client feedback about some of the positive changes you have seen and express appreciation for all their hard work. Reinforce the idea that anger management is an ongoing project that will require commitment and effort long after therapy is over. Once again, encourage your client to make a structured anger plan in any situation where anger recurs. Make sure that the client knows how to contact you in the future. Implement any follow-up activities (e.g., phone calls, client sending in ongoing logs) or booster sessions (e.g., scheduled meeting in two months).

Program Satisfaction Questionnaire (PSQ)

Please evaluate the therapy program you have just completed by answering the following questions. Circle the number that best reflects your opinion. Your honest answer, whether positive or negative, will give us feedback to make the program better.

1. How effective was the therapy program in helping you with your problem?

   1   2   3   4   5   6   7
   Not effective   *Moderately effective*   *Extremely effective*

2. How helpful were the homework and exercises in this therapy program?

   1   2   3   4   5   6   7
   Not helpful   *Moderately helpful*   *Extremely helpful*

3. Were the skills you learned in this therapy program useful for coping with your problem?

   1   2   3   4   5   6   7
   Not useful   *Moderately useful*   *Extremely useful*

4. Overall, how would you rate the quality of this therapy?

   1   2   3   4   5   6   7
   High quality   *Moderate Quality*   *Low Quality*

5. If someone with a similar problem to yours asked for recommendations, how would you describe the usefulness of this therapy program?

   1   2   3   4   5   6   7
   Not useful   *Moderately useful*   *Extremely useful*

6. If you could go back to remake your decision about this therapy program, would you do it again?

   1   2   3   4   5   6   7
   No, definitely   *Uncertain*   *Yes, definitely*

7. How successfully were your goals met by this therapy program?

   1   2   3   4   5   6   7
   Goals met   *Moderately successful*   *Goals not met*
                               with goals

8. How would you rate your improvement in the symptoms that concerned you most?

   1   2   3   4   5   6   7
   Extremely improved   *Moderately improved*   *Not improved*

Best Coping Responses Handout

Write down coping behaviors that have been effective during provocations (i.e., things you say that are different than before, changes in your tone of voice, walking away rather than exploding, making a problem-solving plan, pausing to relax and get control, etc.).

Anger Plans Handout

Anger thoughts:

Coping thoughts:

Look at Best Coping Thoughts Handout for help.

Relaxation:

How can I use my relaxation skills in this situation (e.g., take a deep breath before I say anything, etc.)?

Coping behavior:

What can I say or do that will calm things down?

Problem solving:

Is there a way to solve this problem and avoid conflict?

Anger Log I

Date/Time	Situation	Reactions Rate 0–100

Anger Log II

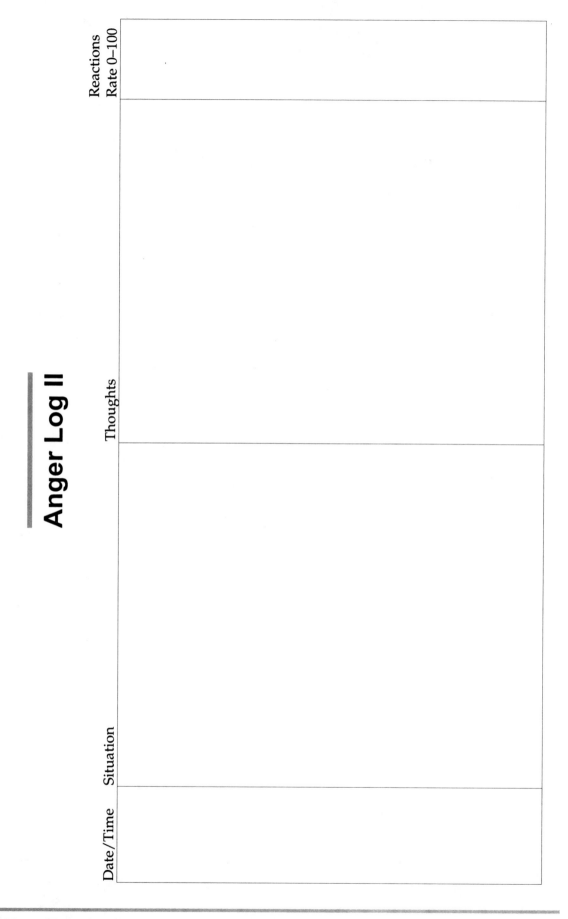

Date/Time	Situation	Thoughts	Reactions Rate 0–100

Anger Log III

Day/Time	Situation	Thoughts	Reactions	Coping Efforts (what did you do, how did it turn out? Rate 0–100 before and after

Appendix 1

Additional Self-Report Questionnaires

Although there are too many scales to review comprehensively, a few examples will be provided along with their potential clinical use.

The Buss-Durkee Hostility Inventory (BDHI; Buss and Durkee 1957) is an inventory that has had some utility. It is a seventy-five-item, true/false questionnaire that leads to eight, logically derived subscales assessing Assault, Indirect Hostility, Verbal Hostility, Irritability, Negativism, Resentment, Suspicion, and Guilt. Several factor analyses and other studies questioned the range of the subscale content. Buss and Perry (1992) undertook a revision that led to an improved Aggression Questionnaire (AQ). The AQ consists of four scales that assess general tendencies to experience anger, hostility, verbal aggression, and physical aggression. The clinician may use those four scales as general indices of these constructs, but may want to keep in mind that the scales are fairly highly correlated

Novaco (1993) described another multidimensional instrument. A twenty-five-item scale measures reported anger (four-point, Likert-type scale) in response to twenty-five different situations (i.e., how much anger the individual experiences in these different situations). This scale can provide a quick overview of general anger reactivity and can be used idiographically to explore what kinds of situations trigger anger and why others do not. The second, forty-eight-item scale contains items (rated on three-point scale) regarding the extent to which the individual experiences anger in the cognitive, arousal, and behavioral domains. The latter scale can provide a quick sketch of responding in these areas.

Inventories described to this point tend to be general in nature as they assess general tendencies to experience anger, express anger, hold hostile attitudes, and the like. There are very few instruments that measure anger in a specific situation or cluster of related situations. Yet, for many people, their problematic anger is found in very specific contexts for which there are currently no measures. The Driving

Anger Scale (DAS; Deffenbacher, Oetting, and Lynch 1994) is provided as an example of the kind of instruments that are needed to measure more situation- or context-bound anger. The DAS consists of a fourteen-item short-form and a thirty-three-item long-form. The long-form provides not only a total score, but six cluster analytically derived scores assessing anger in response to: 1) hostile gestures, 2) illegal behaviors of other drivers, 3) the presence of police, 4) being slowed down or impeded, 5) discourteous or disrespectful behavior of other drivers, and 6) traffic obstructions such as traffic jams and detours. The long-form provides a sensitive index to change in driving anger-reduction programs as well as an overview of anger in response to these dimensions of anger. The short-form provides a quick overview of driving anger and was constructed from the fourteen items that entered the best cluster analysis that had to include at least one item from each of the six subscales from the long-form.

Two other questionnaires, the Anger Consequences Questionnaire (Deffenbacher 1995; Deffenbacher, Oetting, Huff, et al. 1996; Morris et al. 1996) and the Worst Anger Incident in the Last Year (Deffenbacher, Oetting, Thwaites, et al. 1996) inquire about the consequences of anger. These two measures can be used in conjunction to provide estimates of the frequency and severity of anger consequences.

The Anger Consequences Questionnaire (see page 174) measures the frequency of anger consequences. It contains forty-two items and asks the individual to indicate (0 to 4+) times in the last two months that the individual's anger has led him/her to do, feel, or experience different consequences (e.g., break something or get into an argument). Cluster analyses yielded nine consequence dimensions: 1) five-item (#25, 26, 27, 28, and 39) Negative Emotions; 2) two-item (#36 and 37) Tense/Uptight; 3) three-item (#30, 31, and 32) Damaged Friendships; 4) three-item (#15, 35, and 37) Reckless Driving; 5) two-item (#9 and 11) Alcohol Use; 6) four-item (#6, 14, 41, and 42) Verbal Fights; 7) three-item (#5, 12, and 13) Physical Fights; 8) two-item (#22 and 40) Feel Like Hurting Self; and 9) three-item (#4, 8, and 20) Property Damage. Alpha reliabilities of .75 to .91 reflected good internal consistencies, whereas two-month test-retest reliabilities (r = .41 to .75) were somewhat lower due to low frequencies of some consequences. Individual items can also be used (e.g., getting into a fight with family or anger leading to becoming anxious or depressed) even though they did not form specific consequence dimensions. They provide the clinician with a sense of other types of anger consequences. Individual consequences and consequence dimensions tended to be predicted by different forms of anger expression. For example, emotional consequences (i.e., anger leading to negative emotional states such as depression, anxiety, negative emotions, and tension/uptightness) were best predicted by anger suppression, trait anger, and gender, with females reporting more of these types of consequences. Anger-related reckless driving, however, was predicted by expressing anger by physical assault on objects and by anger suppression, where as anger-related accidents were predicted by physical assault on objects. Fighting physically or wanting to fight physically were predicted by physical assault on people or objects and trait anger, whereas verbal fights were predicted by verbal assault and noisy arguing, and whereas anger-related alcohol use was predicted by trait anger and negative forms of expressing anger verbally. Thus, the Anger Consequences Questionnaire can help the clinician and client identify some of the most frequent anger consequences experienced by the individual and begin to link some of the ways the individual experiences and expresses anger to those consequences. These linkages can become targets for intervention in order to reduce negative anger-related consequences.

The Worst Anger Incident in the Last Year addresses more the severity of consequences in the extreme. It first asks the individual to describe in detail his or her worst anger-related incident in the last year (i.e., the event in which the person's anger led to the worst outcomes). He or she is then asked to indicate if any of the following happened—financial costs, physical or health consequences to the person him/herself or to others, property damage, relationship damage, problems at work or school, legal or other official consequences, and negative feelings about one self. If the person indicates that there was a consequence in any of these categories, then he or she is asked to explain or describe the consequences. Although there is a reliable coding system for judging the severity of consequences, the clinician can use the explanations to understand the nature and severity of consequences in this situation. Finally, the person indicates his or her overall evaluation of costs on a five-point scale (1 = no cost, 5 = extremely costly), which provides the clinician with a general sense of costs from the client's perspective. Empirically, generally angry clients experienced more frequent and, in some cases, more severe consequences than less angry individuals (Deffenbacher, Oetting, Thwaites, et al. 1996), providing evidence of validity for this measure.

Anger Consequences Questionnaire

Directions: These questions ask about what happens when **you become angry**. Please answer every question filling in the appropriate circle showing how many times in the **last two months** it happened to you because of **your anger**.

Number of Times It Happened

In the last two months being angry has made me:	Never	One Time	Two Times	Three Times	Four or More Times
1. Depressed	O	O	O	O	O
2. Anxious	O	O	O	O	O
3. Feel like hurting someone	O	O	O	O	O
4. Feel like breaking something	O	O	O	O	O
5. Get into a physical fight	O	O	O	O	O
6. Get into an argument	O	O	O	O	O
7. Have trouble with the law	O	O	O	O	O
8. Break something	O	O	O	O	O
9. Drink alcohol	O	O	O	O	O
10. Use other drugs	O	O	O	O	O
11. Get drunk	O	O	O	O	O
12. Hurt someone	O	O	O	O	O
13. Hit someone	O	O	O	O	O
14. Say nasty things	O	O	O	O	O
15. Drive recklessly	O	O	O	O	O
16. Do something dumb	O	O	O	O	O
17. Overeat	O	O	O	O	O
18. Withdraw	O	O	O	O	O
19. Hurt self physically	O	O	O	O	O
20. Hit a wall or something	O	O	O	O	O
21. Hurt my job	O	O	O	O	O
22. Feel like killing myself	O	O	O	O	O
23. Feel physically ill	O	O	O	O	O
24. Get into an accident	O	O	O	O	O
25. Feel bad about myself	O	O	O	O	O
26. Feel ashamed	O	O	O	O	O
27. Feel dumb	O	O	O	O	O

In the last two months being angry has made me:					
28. Feel embarrassed	O	O	O	O	O
29. Hurt my work/school work	O	O	O	O	O
30. Make my friends mad at me	O	O	O	O	O

31. Damage a friendship	O	O	O	O	O
32. Make my friends afraid of me	O	O	O	O	O
33. Get into a fight with my family	O	O	O	O	O
34. Feel tense	O	O	O	O	O
35. Drive too fast	O	O	O	O	O
36. Feel uptight	O	O	O	O	O
37. Drive unsafely	O	O	O	O	O
38. Feel nervous	O	O	O	O	O
39. Feel guilty	O	O	O	O	O
40. Feel like hurting myself	O	O	O	O	O
41. Tell someone off	O	O	O	O	O
42. Yell or scream at someone	O	O	O	O	O

Worst Anger Incident in the Last Year

Directions: Describe your worst **anger-related** incident in the **last year** (involving you being angry). Then there will be some questions. Fill in "yes" or "no" as your best answer and explain "yes" answers.

1. What happened? (Describe in detail)

2. How long ago did this happen? _____ months ago

3. Did any financial costs result from this incident? Yes O No O
   If yes, explain and give your best estimate of the total dollar amount.

4. Did any physical damage or health problems happen to you because of this incident? Yes O No O
   If yes, explain.

5. Did any physical or health problems result to anyone else? Yes O No O
   If yes, explain.

6. Was there any damage to objects or property? Yes O No O
   If yes, explain.

7. Was there any damage to a relationship? Yes O No O
   If yes, explain.

8. Did any problems develop at school or work because of this? Yes O No O
   If yes, explain.

9. Were there any legal or other official consequences? Yes O No O
   If yes, explain.

10. Did you feel badly about yourself as a result of this incident? Yes O No O
    If yes, explain.

11. All things considered, how costly was your anger? (Fill in one)

Extremely costly	Very costly	Somewhat costly	A little costly	No cost
O	O	O	O	O

Appendix 2

Guidelines for the CRCS
in Groups

This protocol describes the application of CRCS to individuals with anger problems. CRCS can be easily adapted to groups, and there are a significant number of studies that have demonstrated the utility and efficacy of group applications (see Deffenbacher, Oetting and DiGuiseppe 1999). A session-by-session description of a six week group CRCS protocol is available (McKay 1992). This appendix outlines a number of issues inherent to and adaptations for CRCS groups.

- CRCS is an appropriate, basic intervention for groups of angry individuals. As noted for individual intervention, CRCS reduces resistance to some intervention components and addresses both interpersonal and noninterpersonal sources of anger. It, therefore, addresses the range of anger issues that typically appear in a group. Even if skill deficits or other issues are discovered, a group CRCS intervention may be an efficient way to address some anger issues, prior to addressing skill or other anger-related issues.

- Consider implementing CRCS as a part of a larger intervention plan (e.g., along with parenting skills and realistic developmental information and expectations for abusive parents). If this is done, consider implementing CRCS early in the overall treatment plan. It should provide assistance in lowering anger and in making some other interventions easier (see comments for individual CRCS). If the clinician is integrating CRCS with other interventions, make sure that there is enough time for all intervention components. More is not necessarily better in overall intervention design. When more components are added within a fixed time period, personalized application and rehearsal activities are often the first things to be jettisoned. Yet, this personalization and rehearsal may be exactly what is needed for the angry client. Thus, when designing multicomponent interventions, make sure that there is enough time for quality implementation of all components.

- Consider using a single therapist. There may be some cases (e.g., integration of CRCS with marital or partner communication skills) where having male and female coleaders can be helpful. However, the literature is full of effective examples where groups were led by a single leader, and generally no therapist effects have been found in implementing CRCS.

- Consider mixed gender groups. Again, there are examples where this may not be feasible (e.g., in certain correctional facilities) or appropriate (e.g., in early stages of domestic/partner violence). However, in more general populations, mixed gender groups are effective (Deffenbacher, Oetting, and DiGuiseppe 1999), and there have been no gender main effects or gender by-treatment interactions in terms of outcome. That is, CRCS is effective for both males and females and equally so. Moreover, having both genders in the same group can sometimes have added benefits. For example, mixed-gender groups can provide both a male and female perspective on a given issue, a description of desired behavior by members of both genders, and greater possibilities for alternative cognitive responses and flexibility in discussions and role-plays.

- Set the group size at approximately six to twelve people. This provides a group large enough for good group interaction, yet small enough for attention to specific individuals' concerns and for individualization of intervention.

- Consider sessions of ninety minutes in length. This provides additional time to monitor and address issues of all group members. For example, this allows the initial time for going over homework to be extended by ten minutes or so in order to go over issues from all group members. This also provides additional time for in-session rehearsal.

- Consider lengthening the overall protocol by two or three sessions for groups. In general, the clinician has to pace the group in terms of the slowest members on a given task. For example, it may take an additional session or portion of a session to address relaxation-training procedures. It may take an additional session in the middle stages of rehearsal. Also, consider using one of these additional sessions as a follow-up or booster session, say at four to eight weeks after the last consecutive session. Many clients report that knowing they were going to meet again with the therapist and other group members helped them stay focused on and maintain anger reduction. Although this suggestion and that of lengthening the session to ninety minutes may roughly double the overall amount of time for a group version of CRCS, groups still represent considerable savings over individual CRCS, reflecting about two therapist hours per client.

- If possible, assessment and goal formulation should be done individually with referral to a CRCS group. This allows for a careful screening of the nature of the person's anger problems, readiness for treatment, and individualizing the linkages of the person's anger issues to the group. Clients who are inappropriate (see earlier guidelines) can be screened out more easily and motivation enhanced for those who are appropriate. If the group is psychoeducational in nature, then an individual assessment may not be feasible. That is, individuals with self-identified problems with anger may have little, if any, assessment before the first session. If this is the case, it is suggested that session 1 be reformatted to include the following procedures: 1) Have clients describe the nature of their anger problems and why they are attending the group at this time. 2) Have clients identify as clearly as possible their goals for the anger group. 3) Have clients spend some time describing how they and others experience (cognitive, emotional, and physiological elements) and express (behavioral component) strong anger in dysfunctional ways. Identify and record common themes. 4) Have clients spend some time describing how they and others experience and express anger when they handle anger well. Again, identify and record common themes. These activities will take most of the first session and yet address some of the issues that would normally take place in session 1 from the individual protocol. They also help identify potential positive cognitive, relaxation, and problem-solving strategies for use in future sessions.

- Address issues of confidentiality very early in the first session, even if they were covered during individual assessment. This sets clear expectations for both therapist and client behavior. That is, explain that confidence may be broken under conditions of dangerousness to self, dangerousness to others, and/or suspected child abuse. Also, outline the conditions of confidentiality among group members. Set a strong norm that material discussed in the group stays within the group and is not discussed with others. If applicable, link this to state legal guidelines for confidentiality among group members. That is, strongly encourage group members to share and discuss openly their anger concerns and issues, but only to the extent they feel comfortable and within guidelines of confidentiality. It is suggested that these guidelines be covered right after the therapist introduces him/herself and before clients even share their names, much less their concerns. This informs them fully of the ground rules before any personally identifying information has been shared. The clinician may wish to develop a list of guidelines for confidentiality and behavior in the group. Two copies of this can be distributed, with clients signing and returning one and keeping the other copy for their files.

- The clinician should be aware of the occasional client whose issues or behavior is so deviant from other group members that he or she should be removed from the group and referred elsewhere. For example, an occasional client will be an emotional monopolizer who wants all of the session focused on what he or she wants to discuss. Such a client should be removed from the group.

- Groups need not be homogeneous in terms of their anger concerns. To the contrary, sources of anger can be quite diverse. These differences can be accommodated by simply increasing the intensity level of anger scenes say by ten to fifteen units per session, by having clients develop individual scenes at that level, and by triggering those scenes off by general instructions to "visualize your first anger scene," or "visualize your second anger scene." This is done rather than the therapist providing a specific scene for an individual. In this manner, heterogeneous content can be addressed while retaining the efficiency of a group. If the group consists of individuals with a common anger theme (e.g., angry drivers), then it may be possible to develop and use common anger scenes (e.g., waiting as the second car in a left-hand turn lane and having the driver ahead of the client not accelerate when the arrow turns green).

- In presenting anger scenes, the time needed for anger arousal may vary from client to client. For example, one client may take ten seconds to reach full intensity of anger responding, whereas it may take another client ninety seconds. In individual CRCS, this can be accommodated by lengthening the exposure time slightly for the latter type of client. This cannot be easily done in a group. If this happens in a group, then it is suggested that the exposure time be lengthened slightly, to about forty-five to sixty seconds after the initial two or three scene presentations in session 3 or 4. This generally provides sufficient time for most clients to experience anger arousal, while ensuring some clients are not overwhelmed.

- During relaxation training, individual relaxation scenes should be developed. This can be done by the clinician interviewing two or three clients and firming up the details of their relaxation scenes much as would be done in individual CRCS. Once this is done, then the clinician can ask other group members if they have equally clear and detailed relaxation scenes. Individual problems can be discussed and clarified. When the therapist initiates visualization of relaxation scenes, he or she can provide a general instruction like, "Now switch on your personal relaxation scene," rather than providing greater description of any specific individual's relaxation scene.

- Make sure that signal systems (e.g., raising a hand) are clearly visible. For example, when clients are sitting in a circle, the clinician may want to use a general phrase like, "Signal me by raising the hand that is closest to me." Otherwise, clients will sometimes raise a hand that is not clearly visible to the clinician.

- In the cognitive-restructuring activities, use other clients in the group as a resource for identifying cognitive issues and for constructing anger-lowering cognitive responses. In nearly every group, there is at least one client who does not react with great anger to another person's high anger situation. Explore the differences in the thinking of the two. This provides a natural contrast from which to identify the importance of cognitive processes and to develop alternative cognitions.

- If groups are heterogeneous as most will be, then the therapist may want to introduce one or two cognitive distortions in a given session in order to focus the discussion and to develop specific types of cognitive counter-responses. For example, catastrophizing could be introduced one week and magnifying and overgeneralizing another, and so on. It is also suggested that if this approach is used, absolute thinking or "shoulds" not be the first type of cognition addressed. Clinical experience suggests that there may be greater resistance to addressing these and so preceding them with addressing other cognitions seems to lower this resistance. If groups are fairly homogeneous and common situations are being used for all group members, then the above approach need not be used (e.g., Deffenbacher, Lynch, Filetti, et al. 1999). All kinds of anger-lowering cognitions can be identified and rehearsed for a given type of situation. That is, in groups where members share common situational anger arousal, cognitive counters may be more situation driven. Over time, patterns of alternative cognitive counters are identified inductively and integrated.

Appendix 3

Anger-based Diagnoses/Conceptualizations

The overview briefly described the absence of anger-based diagnoses and sketched three parameters that could be used to define problem anger: 1) nature of the events triggering anger; 2) the presence of dysfunctional anger as defined by its emotional, physiological, and cognitive characteristics; and 3) the presence or absence of aggressive behavior. Five working diagnoses or conceptualizations were defined by the interface of these three dimensions—adjustment disorder with anger or angry mood, situational anger disorders with and without aggression, and generalized anger disorder with and without aggression. This appendix describes each of these in more detail and provides clinical examples.

Adjustment Disorder with Anger

Adjustment disorders describe excessive and/or impairing reactions to one or more stressors, typically psychosocial stressors. They appear within three months of the onset of stress and generally abate within six months. In DSM-IV (American Psychiatric Association 1994), three adjustment disorders are characterized in terms of the dominant mood or emotions. These are adjustment disorder with anxiety, depression, or a mixture of anxiety and depression. No adjustment disorders are defined in terms of anger. If anger is mixed with aggression (e.g., becoming verbally or physically assaultive) and/or with other forms of acting out that violate the rights of others or age-relevant norms (e.g., becoming heavily alcohol or drug involved, dropping out of school, running away, etc.), then an adjustment disorder with disordered conduct and emotion can be diagnosed. If the person is angry, but primarily acts it out, then an adjustment disorder with disturbance of conduct may be appropriate. However, if the person's dominant, maladaptive (either excessive or impairing) reaction is anger, then no DSM-IV diagnosis exists.

This misses a number of people who suffer major psychosocial stressors and who experience excessive, dysfunctional levels of anger, but who do not experience other disruptive negative emotions and who do not act their anger out in dysfunctional ways. For example, the following cases would appear to have no place within current diagnostic systems.

- A person has worked for a firm for many years and was, by all reports, a quality employee. The firm experiences a series of financial setbacks and closes the plant at which the person works. For the next several months the person is generally angry and irritable, often without reason, but particularly when in the presence of other former workers. He or she becomes very angry when the management of the firm, its policies and practices, or the plant closing are discussed. He or she is very opinionated and becomes loud and argumentative when discussing the company and its management. The person also spends considerable time in angry rumination about how unfairly he or she was treated by the firm. His or her anger disrupts sleep, appetite, much of his or her family relationships (because he or she is preoccupied with angry discussions about the unfair treatment by his or her former company). Several of the person's former friends do not like spending time with the person because of the unrelenting anger toward the company, and his or her job search behavior is sometimes disrupted and the quality of interviewing for new jobs is hurt because the person becomes angry when talking about his or her former employers. The anger is excessive and disruptive. However, the person has not acted out seriously in any way against the firm, its management, or others.

- Jim and Mary have been dating for two years when Jim breaks off the relationship and begins dating someone else. Mary experiences few signs of anxiety or depression, but is furious over the next several months. She used to be fairly happy and easygoing, but now is angry, irritable, and thin-skinned. She has little nice to say to any of her friends, often becoming angry with them, even when they are trying to listen to and console her. Her employer has even commented about how angry she is and once encouraged her to take a couple of days off. Anything that reminds her of or makes her think about Jim triggers off intense angry tirades in which she storms around her apartment or office mentally berating and cursing him out. She also is very jealous, having fantasies of embarrassing Jim while on a date. Although furious with Jim and easily angered by almost anything, she has not acted out seriously. However, she has engaged in some minimal aggression.

- At the beginning of his junior year in high school, James' family relocates hundreds of miles away from his friends, neighborhood, classmates, and the community in which he grew up. He was not at all happy about the move and did not want to go. At the time, he was angry and argumentative with his parents, accusing them of not taking his feelings or preferences into account. He has become sullen, angry, and terse, often withdrawing into his room and responding with a very angry retort when others try to interact with him, even for simple things like calling him for dinner. He also responds to parental requests by giving them angry icy stares and ignoring them. However, he only occasionally argues with his parents, and even then, he often breaks off the interactions, storming off to his room in quiet huff. In phone calls to his old friends, he describes himself as being "pissed beyond belief" and his parents are "too stupid to be of any help." In spite of the high, relatively chronic anger, his behavior has not shown serious disruption of conduct or aggression. He has continued doing well academically, has gotten a part-time job, and is making plans for college.

These cases have three things in common. First, all have experienced a significant psychosocial stress. Second, they are experiencing high levels of anger that is excessive or, at the very least, is disruptive and dysfunctional. Third, they have not engaged in significant aggressive or other dysfunctional behavior and, therefore, do not qualify for an adjustment disorder with disturbance of conduct. It could be argued that the anger is masking depression and, therefore, an adjustment disorder with depression, but this misses the salient, dysfunctional anger. Maladaptive angry emotionality is the primary presenting issue, and none of the criteria for other adjustment disorders apply.

Conceptually and clinically, it would seem best to acknowledge that anger is the primary presenting emotional issue and make it the focus of diagnosis and intervention. It is suggested that the clinician add a conceptual category of adjustment disorder with anger. It would in many ways parallel adjustment disorders with anxiety or depression, except that the dominant, defining characteristic would be anger. The person would have experienced one or more significant stressors and reacted with elevated angry emotionality and several cognitive and physiological elements of anger (see earlier description), which interfere with the person's life and/or elicited significant personal distress.

The above are the rule in criteria, but other diagnoses would have to be ruled out. Most specifically, it would have to be established that anger was the dominant emotional issue and that depression and anxiety were minimal, such that other emotion-based adjustment disorders could be ruled out. Also, the person would not have engaged in significant aggressive or other dysfunctional behavior that abridged the rights of others and/or violated age-appropriate norms so that an adjustment disorder with disturbance of conduct was not the most appropriate consideration. If there is a high level of dysfunctional anger and disturbance of conduct, then an adjustment disorder with disturbance of emotion and conduct should be considered. It is also for this reason that no adjustment disorder with anger and aggression is proposed. Anger and aggression may go together as a reaction to a stressor, but the DSM-IV description of disturbance of conduct is sufficiently broad enough to include aggression. Therefore, a separate adjustment disorder including both anger and aggression is deemed unnecessary. However, even in considering this diagnosis for cases with strong anger and aggression, the clinician will want to clearly distinguish between aggressive and other dysfunctional behavior leading to the "disturbance of conduct" portion of the diagnosis. Different behavioral patterns (e.g., angry verbal and physical tirades vs. binge drinking followed by calling into work sick) may require different intervention plans, although the same diagnosis is appropriate.

Situational Anger Disorder Without Aggression

This proposed disorder describes cases where anger is an intense reaction to either: a) a circumscribed situation (e.g., anger in response to discourteous drivers, to critical comments from a spouse, or to encountering mistakes in the work of subordinates), or b) a series of situations that share a common psychological theme or property (e.g., having one's authority challenged, or being made fun of). Anger reactions in this disorder are relatively delimited to a specific situation or a small number of situations. Anger is not a frequent response to a wide range of provocations or experienced as a kind of generalized mood state. Moreover, to qualify, anger reactions are not isolated reactions, but are consistent patterns of responding to these situations. Also, the situational anger reactions should be present for some period of time, say, at least six months (i.e., some length of time is necessary to establish a lasting, consistent pattern). Very often, people with such reactions indicate that their anger reactions have been present for a long time or that they have always reacted this way. Anger should not only be intense, but also should interfere with the person's normal personal, social, and/or vocational pursuits (e.g., triggers off tension headaches, disrupts friendships, or leads to difficulties at work) and/or causes significant personal distress (e.g., person strongly dislikes being angry because he or she feels out of control and has aggressive, retaliatory thoughts he or she does not like).

This conceptualization has two significant exclusion criteria. First, the person does not engage in frequent or severe enough aggressive behavior to qualify as aggression and thereby fit the next diagnostic category of situational anger disorder with aggression. That is, the person experiences elevated, dysfunctional anger, but behaves appropriately, suppresses overt reactions, behaves in dysfunctional but non-aggressive ways (e.g., inappropriate withdrawal or becoming intoxicated), or behaves in relatively low frequency, low magnitude aggression (e.g., mumbling and swearing to one's self or making a few negative or sarcastic remarks). The second set of exclusionary criteria include making sure that anger is not part of some other diagnosable condition which may be somewhat situational (e.g., anger in some cases of posttraumatic stress disorder where intense anger happens only in certain situations or contexts). It is also possible that some Axis II disorders, specifically borderline, narcissistic, and paranoid personality disordered individuals, might show anger that was primarily related to certain issues or people.

The following clinical examples would be consistent with situational anger disorder without aggression.

- A driver becomes enraged, experiences angry turmoil on most daily commutes, clenches teeth, tenses up all over, has an upset stomach, curses and makes negative remarks about the other driver to him- or herself, thinks about ramming someone with his or her car, yelling at them, telling them off, or giving them the finger. However, the person does not act on those thoughts, except occasionally mumbling curses to him- or herself and giving another driver the finger below the dash level.

- A business executive was about to be fired because of the way that he handled his anger. Whenever he felt that others questioned his integrity or blamed the "little people" (referring to the line level production workers) for management mistakes, he became very angry, felt a hot, tightening sensation in his stomach, felt muscle tension in his shoulders and arms, and thought very negatively about those making the offending comments. However, he did not express his anger in an overt aggressive manner. To the contrary, he became increasingly silent, narrowed his eyes, and stared at the offending person with an icy, steely glare, of which he was unaware. The latter demeanor made the CEO and other senior administrative personnel very uncomfortable and led the CEO to tell him that if he did not manage his anger he would be let go, in spite of excellent rapport with his staff and productivity of his unit.

- A woman who did design and drafting in a large firm worked under considerable time pressure and stress and her supervisor was highly critical and demanding. She reacted to her supervisor's behavior with strong anger, high levels of generalized autonomic arousal, especially tension in the hands and lower arms, experienced frequent tension headaches and teeth grinding following periods of anger, felt that the quality of her work suffered when she was angry, and often took her anger home with her in the form of angry ruminations about the mistreatment by her supervisor. Both her physician related her headaches and her dentist her dental problems to her unresolved, suppressed anger. Nonetheless, she suppressed her anger and continued to give her supervisor positive performance ratings because she felt her job might otherwise be in jeopardy.

Situational Anger Disorder with Aggression

Individuals with this pattern of reactions not only experience elevated anger, but also behave aggressively in response to specific situations. That is, the individual not only experiences anger sufficient to meet a situational anger disorder, but also behaves aggressively. The pattern of aggression may be relatively consistent (e.g., nearly always becoming verbally abrasive and intimidating), or somewhat variable (e.g., hostile glares and stares on one occasion, loud noisy arguing on another, and physically intimidating with pushing and shoving in another). Whatever the pattern of aggression, the individual shows aggression on a large number of the occasions in which he or she experiences anger arousal. He or she would not have to be aggressive on every occasion he or she became angry, but would do so with sufficient frequency or severity to have aggression contribute to his or her difficulties. Also, anger and aggression disrupt or interfere with his or her normal activities, relationships, or educational/vocational performance, and/or causes significant personal distress.

The following clinical examples are consistent with situational anger disorder with aggression.

- An individual became angry nearly every time he drove, sometimes experiencing an elevation in anger just getting into the car. He not only became very angry, but also had engaged in a number of aggressive behaviors in dealing with other drivers who offended him (e.g., tailgating or cutting another driver off in anger, flashing lights repeatedly at others, yelling obscenities, making a variety of gestures to other drivers, particularly giving them the finger, forcing another driver to the side of the road and going up to the car and pounding on the hood or windows while yelling at the other driver, etc.). He had received several traffic tickets for such behavior, had been arrested once for disturbing the peace, and had another assault charge pending. However, all of his angry and aggressive reactions occurred on the road.

- A mechanic who serviced a large industrial plant would become very angry when he was beeped on his pager several times before he had time to respond to previous pages. He experienced tension in the jaw, tension across the shoulders and stomach region, often experienced gastrointestinal upset during such times, had a significant number of thoughts about others trying to make his job miserable and implicitly telling him that he was not doing a good job, and of telling off his supervisor because of the plant being so shorthanded with people in his position. He had one relatively consistent aggressive behavior, which was to throw his tools or his beeper against the wall, resulting in several hundreds of dollars of damaged equipment.

- The owner of a consulting firm was a perfectionist and insisted that others be equally competent. He would become enraged at mistakes, even relatively minor mistakes, and become very verbally abusive, calling his employees names, putting them down, and indirectly threatening their jobs. Moreover, given his size and countenance, his nonverbal behavior was also very imposing and intimidating, as well. He had lost several good employees because of his behavior, and many of the rest lived in terror of him. This fear led employees not to seek his counsel, which only angered him more.

Generalized Anger Disorder Without Aggression

The anger reactions being described in this disorder are not contextual or situation specific, as was the case for situational anger disorders. Individuals with this type of problematic anger either experience anger as a somewhat chronic mood state or have anger elicited by a wide range of situations that are not related to some specific theme or issue. For example, anger may be prompted by a wide range of external events that do not appear to have anything in common (e.g., being angered at one's own imperfections, at political events, at other drivers, at having to stand in line or be slowed down, at one's spouse and children for messes and encroachment on his or her space, etc.). Anger might also be elicited by a variety of internal states or conditions (e.g., feelings of stress, embarrassment and rejection, memories of past mistreatment and injustice, ruminations about difficult or terminated relationships, reliving embarrassing or failing moments, etc.). Anger may be triggered by various aversive emotional and/or physiological states such as being fatigued, in physical pain or discomfort, sick or having chronic debilitating conditions (allergies or hay fever, and the like).

Whatever the sources of experienced anger, it is pervasive and chronic. As rules of thumb for judging the pervasive, chronic nature of the anger, it is suggested that the individual should have experienced significant anger more days than not for at least a year's period of time and that he or she has not been free of periods of anger and/or angry/irritable mood for more than a month in the last year. While these are somewhat arbitrary criteria, they are an attempt to capture the chronic, ongoing, widespread nature of the person's anger. It is not being suggested that these individuals experience nothing but anger. That is not the case. They may experience happy, positive feelings, and frequently do. However, what is characteristic is that their lives are permeated with frequent episodes of anger that does not appear to be related to some specific situation or theme. That is, they are frequently angered, no matter what their other feelings are.

Their anger must also eventuate in some kinds of negative consequences. The anger may interfere with their health, normal social activities, relationships, or work/school activities and/or cause the individual a significant level of distress. However, adverse consequences do not stem from aggressive behavior as this disorder is marked by the absence or relative absence of aggression. That is, the individual may occasionally respond aggressively (e.g., make cutting remarks, pout or sulk, or throw something), but the behavior is infrequent relative to the number of times he or she is angry and tends to be relatively mild when it happens. Thus, these individuals experience a great deal of moderate to more intense anger, but are not highly or frequently aggressive.

Finally, other issues and concerns should be ruled out as the source of this type of anger. For example, the possibility that the chronic, pervasive anger is part of a psychotic disorder, dysthymia, posttraumatic stress disorder, a cognitive or organic disorder, a substance-abuse disorder, personality disorders such as borderline, paranoid, narcissistic, or antisocial, or a chronic medical condition. Such possibilities should be considered and reasonably ruled out before the individual is conceptualized as experiencing a pattern that might be called generalized anger disorder without aggression.

Generalized Anger Disorder with Aggression

This pattern of anger not only involves the chronic, pervasive anger described above, but also the presence of frequent aggressive behavior. That is, the individual is not only angry frequently, but also often responds to that anger with aggression. Again, he or she would not necessarily behave aggressively on every occasion, but would behave on some occasions either with a consistent pattern of aggression or with several different types of aggression over time. Again, the pattern of anger and aggression causes disruption to the individual's health, normal activities, social relationships, or educational/vocational pursuits, and/or leads to significant personal distress. Finally, for generalized anger disorder with aggression to be ruled in, the types of conditions as potential contributing sources of anger or alternative conditions outlined for generalized anger disorder without aggression must also be ruled out.

Summary of Diagnostic Issues

Current diagnostic schemes such as DSM-IV do not include anger as a primary characteristic of any disorder. That is, there are no diagnoses in which anger *must* be present for a diagnosis. Yet, individuals for whom anger is a primary concern or presenting problem are clinically common. To aid in conceptualization and treatment planning, it was suggested that dysfunctional anger, much like some depressive and anxiety disorders, can be described in terms of a) the apparent triggers or sources of the anger, b) the emotional and experiential qualities, and c) a degree of life interference and/or personal distress. With these parameters in mind, three conceptually distinct anger disorders were outlined—adjustment disorder with anger, situational anger disorder without aggression, and generalized anger disorder without aggression. These three disorders focus on anger per se, and the consequences stemming from that anger. However, given the importance of aggressive behavior as a form of anger expression, as a source of negative consequences, and as an issue for treatment planning, two additional anger disorders were outlined—situational anger disorder with aggression and generalized anger disorder with aggression. A parallel adjustment disorder with anger and aggression was not seen as needed because current adjustment disorder with disturbances of mood and conduct were inclusive enough to include both anger and aggression. It is hoped that outlining these diagnostic and clinical descriptions furthers the clinician's understanding of problematic anger and assists in conceptualizing the case and planning for treatment.

Appendix 4

Treatment Plan

Problem: Generalized or situation specific anger that is excessive and/or dangerous.

Definition: A pattern of verbal attack and/or physical aggression that is a marked overreaction to precipitating stressors, and the severity of which damages relationships.

Goals: Reduce motor tension during anger provocations; replace anger triggering thoughts with coping thoughts; reduce overall levels and frequency of anger responses.

Objectives	Interventions
1. Daily monitoring of anger responses	Use Anger Log I, II, and III to identify anger triggering thoughts, outcomes, and develop coping thoughts.
2. Develop relaxation skills	Teach progressive muscle relaxation, breathing-cued relaxation, relaxation without tension, cue-controlled relaxation, and relaxation imagery.
3. Create awareness of the cognitive components of an anger response	Education regarding the six key cognitive distortions that underlie problem anger.
4. Cognitive restructuring	Guidelines and practice exercises for restructuring anger triggering thoughts and developing alternative coping thoughts.
5. Develop and practice combined relaxation and cognitive coping skills	Use coping skills training technique to practice relaxation and cognitive coping responses while visualizing anger provoking scenes.

6. Relapse prevention   Teach the use of situational anger planning to manage post-treatment provocations.

Diagnosis: See appendix 3, Anger-Based Diagnoses/Conceptualizations.

References

Achmon, J. M., M. Granek, M. Golomb, and J. Hart. 1989. Behavior treatment of essential hypertension: A comparison between cognitive therapy and biofeedback of heart rate. *Psychosomatic Medicine, 51,* 152-164.

American Psychiatric Association. 1994. *Diagnostic and Statistical Manual of Mental Disorders, Fourth Edition.* Washington, D. C.: Author.

Averill, J. R. 1982. *Anger and Aggression: An Essay on Emotion.* New York: Springer-Verlag.

Averill, J. R. 1983. Studies on anger and aggression: Implications for theories of emotion. *American Psychologist, 38,* 1145-1160.

Beck, R., and E. Fernandez. 1998. Cognitive-behavioral therapy in the treatment of anger: A meta-analysis. *Cognitive Therapy and Research, 22,* 63-74.

Beck, A. T. 1976. *Cognitive Therapy and the Emotional Disorders.* New York: International Universities Press.

Berkowitz, L. 1990. On the formulation and regulation of anger and aggression: A cognitive-neoassociationist view. *American Psychologist, 45,* 494-503.

Berkowitz, L. 1994. Towards a general theory of anger and emotional aggression: Implications of the cognitive neoassociationistic perspective for the analysis of anger and other emotions. In R. S. Wyer, Jr., and T. K. Scull, editors, *Perspective on Anger and Emotion.Vol. 6: Advances in Social Cognition.* Hillsdale, NJ: Lawrence Erlbaum. 1-46.

Buss, A. H., and A. Durkee. 1957. An inventory for assessing different kinds of hostility. *Journal of Consulting and Clinical Psychology, 21,* 343-349.

Buss, A. H., and M. Perry. 1992. The aggression questionnaire. *Journal of Personality and Social Psychology, 63,* 452-459.

Coccaro, E. F., and R. J. Kavoussi. 1997. Fluoxetine and impulsive aggressive behavior in personality-disordered subjects. *Archives of General Psychiatry, 54,* 1081-1088.

Cragan, M. K., and J. L. Deffenbacher. 1984. Anxiety management training and relaxation as self-control in the treatment of generalized anxiety in medical outpatients. *Journal of Counseling Psychology, 31,* 123-131.

Dahlen, E. R., and J. L. Deffenbacher. In press. A partial component analysis of Beck's cognitive therapy for the treatment of general anger. *Journal of Cognitive Psychotherapy.*

Deffenbacher, J. L. 1994a. *Anger and diagnosis—Where has all the anger gone?* Paper presented at the 102nd Annual Convention of the American Psychological Association, Los Angeles, California. August.

Deffenbacher, J. L. 1994b. Anger reduction: Issues, assessment, and intervention strategies. In A. W Siegman and T. W. Smith, editors, *Anger, Hostility, and the Heart.* Hillsdale, New Jersey: Lawrence Erlbaum. 239-269.

Deffenbacher, J. L. 1995. *Assessing Forms of Anger Expression.* Paper presented at 103rd Annual Convention of the American Psychological Association, New York. August.

Deffenbacher, J. L. 1996. Cognitive-behavioral approaches to anger reduction. In K. S. Dobson and K. D. Craig, editors, *Advances in Cognitive-Behavioral Therapy* Thousand Oaks, California: Sage. 31-62.

Deffenbacher, J. L. 1999. Cognitive-behavioral conceptualization and treatment of anger. *Journal of Clinical Psychology/In-Session: Psychotherapy in Practice, 55,* 295-309.

Deffenbacher, J. L. 1988. Cognitive-relaxation and social skills treatments of anger: A year later. *Journal of Counseling Psychology, 35,* 234-236.

Deffenbacher, J. L. 1990. Demonstrating the influence of cognition on emotion and behavior. *Teaching of Psychology, 17,* 182-185.

Deffenbacher, J. L. 1999. Driving anger: Some characteristics and interventions. *Proceedings of the 35th Annual Meeting: Prospective Medicine—the Tools, The Data, The Interventions, and The Outcomes* Pittsburgh: The Society of Prospective Medicine. 273-284.

Deffenbacher, J. L. 1993. General anger: Characteristics and clinical implications. *Psicologia Conductual, 1,* 49-67.

Deffenbacher, J. L. 1995. Ideal treatment package for adults with anger disorders. In H. Kassinove, *Anger Disorders: Definition, Diagnosis and Treatment* Washington, DC: Taylor and Francis. 151-172.

Deffenbacher, J. L. 1992. Trait anger: Theory, findings, and implications. In C. D. Spielberger and J. N. Butcher, editors, *Advances in Personality Assessment.* Vol. 9. Hillsdale, New Jersey: Erlbaum. 177-201.

Deffenbacher, J. L., P. M. Demm, and A. D. Brandon. 1986. High general anger: Correlates and treatment. *Behaviour Research and Therapy, 24,* 481-489.

Deffenbacher, J. L., M. E. Huff, R. S. Lynch, E. R. Oetting, and N. F. Salvatore. In press. Characteristics and treatment of high anger drivers. *Journal of Counseling Psychology.*

Deffenbacher, J. L., and R. S. Lynch. 1998. Cognitive/behavioral intervention for anger reduction. In V. E. Caballo, editor, *Manual para el tratamiento cognitivo-conductual de los trastornos psicologicos,* Vol. 2 Madrid, Spain: Siglo XXI. 639-674.

Deffenbacher, J. L., R. S. Lynch, L. B. Filetti, E. R. Oetting, and E. R. Dahlen. 1999. *High Anger Drivers: Characteristics and Cognitive-Behavioral Treatment*. Manuscript submitted for publication.

Deffenbacher, J. L., R. S. Lynch, E. R. Oetting, and C. C. Kemper. 1996. Anger reduction in early adolescents. *Journal of Counseling Psychology, 43,* 149-157.

Deffenbacher, J. L., K. McNamara, R. S. Stark, and P. M. Sabadell. 1990b. A combination of cognitive, relaxation, and behavioral coping skills in the reduction of general anger. *Journal of College Student Development, 31,* 351-358.

Deffenbacher, J. L., K. McNamara, R.S. Stark, and P. M. Sabadell. 1990a. A comparison of cognitive-behavioral and process oriented group counseling for general anger reduction. *Journal of Counseling and Development, 69,* 167-172.

Deffenbacher, J. L., E. R. Oetting, and R. DiGiuseppe. 1999. *Principles of Empirically Supported Interventions Applied to Anger Management*. Manuscript submitted for publication.

Deffenbacher, J. L., E. R. Oetting, M. E. Huff, G. R. Cornell, and C. J. Dallager. 1996. Evaluation of two cognitive-behavioral approaches to general anger reduction. *Cognitive Therapy and Research, 20,* 551-573.

Deffenbacher, J. L., E. R. Oetting, M. E. Huff, and G. A. Thwaites. 1995. A fifteen-month follow-up of social skills and cognitive-relaxation approaches to general anger reduction. *Journal of Counseling Psychology, 42,* 400-405.

Deffenbacher, J. L., E. R. Oetting, and R. S. Lynch. 1994. Development of a driving anger scale. *Psychological Reports, 74,* 83-91.

Deffenbacher, J. L., E. R. Oetting, R. S. Lynch, and C. D. Morris. 1996. The expression of anger and its consequences. *Behaviour Research and Therapy, 34,* 575-590.

Deffenbacher, J. L., E. R. Oetting, G. A. Thwaites, R. S. Lynch, D. A. Baker, P. S. Stark, S. Thacker, and L. Eiswerth-Cox. 1996. State-trait anger theory and the utility of the Trait Anger Scale. *Journal of Counseling Psychology, 43,* 131-148.

Deffenbacher, J. L., and P. M. Sabadell. 1992. Comparing high trait anger with low anger individuals. In M. Muller, editor, *Psychophysiologische risikofaktoren bei herzkreislauferkrakungen: Grundlagen und therapie,* Gottingen, Germany: Hogrefe Verlag. 153-169.

Deffenbacher, J. L., and R. S. Stark. 1992. Relaxation and cognitive-relaxation treatments of general anger. *Journal of Counseling Psychology, 39,* 158-167.

Deffenbacher, J. L., D. A. Story, A. D. Brandon, J. A. Hogg, and S. L. Hazaleus. 1988. Cognitive and cognitive-relaxation treatments of anger. *Cognitive Therapy and Research, 12,* 167-184.

Deffenbacher, J. L., D. A. Story, R. S. Stark, J. A. Hogg, and A. D. Brandon. 1987. Cognitive-relaxation and social skills interventions in the treatment of general anger. *Journal of Counseling Psychology, 34,* 171-176.

Deffenbacher, J. L., and R. M. Suinn. 1988. Systematic desensitization and the reduction of anxiety. *The Counseling Psychologist, 16,* 9-30.

Deffenbacher, J. L, G. A. Thwaites, T. L. Wallace, and E. R. Oetting. 1994. Social skills and cognitive-relaxation approaches to general anger reduction. *Journal of Counseling Psychology, 41,* 386-396.

DiGiuseppe, R. 1995. Developing the therapeutic alliance with angry clients. In H. Kassinove, editor, *Anger Disorders: Definition, Diagnosis and Treatment* Washington, DC: Taylor and Francis. 131-159.

Dua, J. K., and M. L. Swinden. 1992. Effectiveness of negative-thought-reduction, meditation, and placebo training treatment in reducing anger. *Scandinavian Journal of Psychology, 33,* 135-146.

Dryden, W. 1990. *Dealing with Anger Problems: Rational-emotive Therapeutic Interventions.* Sarasota, FL: Practitioner's Resource Exchange.

Eckhardt, C., and J. L. Deffenbacher. 1995. Diagnosis of anger disorders. In H. Kassinove, editor, *Anger Disorders: Definition, Diagnosis and Treatment* Washington, DC: Taylor and Francis. 27-47.

Edmondson, C. B., and J. C. Conger. 1996. A review of treatment efficacy for individuals with anger problems: Conceptual, assessment, and methodological issues. *Clinical Psychology Review, 10,* 251-275.

Ellis, A. 1977. *Anger: How to Live With and Without It.* New York: Reader's Digest Press.

Fava, M., K. Anderson, and J. Rosenbaum. 1990. "Anger attacks": Possible variants of panic and major depressive disorder. *American Journal of Psychiatry, 147,* 867-870.

Fava, M., J. F. Rosenbaum, J. Pava, M. K. McCarthy, R. J. Steingard, and E. Bouffides. 1993. Anger attacks in unipolar depression: Part 1. Clinical correlates and response to fluoxetine treatment. *American Journal of Psychiatry, 150,* 1158-1163.

Gerina, M. A., and P. Drummond. In press. A multimodal cognitive-behavioural approach to anger reduction in an occupational sample. *Journal of Occupational and Organizational Psychology.*

Hazaleus, S. L., and J. L. Deffenbacher. 1986. Relaxation and cognitive treatments of anger. *Journal of Consulting and Clinical Psychology, 54,* 222-226.

Lazarus, R. S. 1991. *Emotion and Adaptation.* New York: Oxford University Press.

Leibsohn, M. T., E. R. Oetting, and J. L. Deffenbacher. 1994. Effects of trait anger on alcohol consumption and consequences. *Journal of Child and Adolescent Substance Abuse, 3,* 17-32.

McKay, M. 1992. Anger control groups. In M. McKay, and K. Paleg, editors, *Focal Group Psychotherapy.* Oakland, CA: New Harbinger. 163–194.

McKay, M., P. Fanning, K. Paleg, and D. Landis. 1996. *When Anger Hurts Your Kids.* Oakland, CA: New Harbinger.

McKay, M., P. D. Rogers, and J. McKay. 1989. *When Anger Hurts.* Oakland, CA: New Harbinger.

McKay, M. and P. D. Rogers. 2000. *The Anger Control Workbook.* Oakland, CA: New Harbinger.

Meltzer, H. 1933. Students' adjustment in anger. *Journal of Social Psychology, 4,* 285-309.

Miller, W. R., and S. Rollnick. 1991. *Motivational Interviewing: Preparing People To Change Addictive Behavior.* New York: Guilford.

Moon, J. R., and R. M. Eisler. 1983. Anger control: An experimental comparison of three behavioral treatments. *Behavior Therapy, 14,* 493-505.

Morris, C. D., J. L. Deffenbacher, R. S. Lynch, and E. R. Oetting. 1996. *Anger expression and its consequences.* Paper presented at the 104th Annual Convention of the American Psychological Association, Toronto, Ontario, Canada. August.

Novaco, R. W. 1975. *Anger Control.* Lexington, Massachusetts: Heath.

Novaco, R. W. 1993. Anger as a risk factor for violence among the mentally disordered. In J. Monahan and H. Steadman, editors, *Violence and Mental Disorder: Developments in Risk Assessment.* Chicago: University of Chicago Press.

Persons, J. B. 1989. *Cognitive Therapy in Practice: A Case Formulation Approach.* New York: W. W. Norton.

Persons, J., and J. Miranda. 1991. Treating dysfunctional beliefs: Implications for mood-state hypothesis. *Journal of Cognitive Psychotherapy, 5,* 15-25.

Prochaska, J. O., C. C. DiClemente, and J. C. Norcross. 1992. In search of how people change: Applications to addictive behaviors. *American Psychologist, 47,* 1102-1114.

Prochaska, J. O., J. C. Norcross, and C. C. DiClemente. 1995. *Changing for Good.* New York: NY: William Morrow.

Rosenbaum, J. F., M. Fava, J. Pava, M. K. McCarthy, R. J. Steingard, and E. Bouffides. 1993. Anger attacks in unipolar depression: Part 2. Neuroendocrine correlates and changes following fluoxetine treatment. *American Journal of Psychiatry, 150,* 1164-1168.

Schlichter, K. J., and J. J. Horan. 1981. Effects of stress inoculation on the anger and aggression management skills of institutionalized juvenile delinquents. *Cognitive Therapy and Research, 5,* 359-365.

Spielberger, C. D. 1988. *Manual for the State-Trait Anger Expression Inventory.* Orlando, Fl: Psychological Assessment Resources.

Spielberger, C. D. 1999. *Manual for the State-Trait Anger Expression Inventory-Revised.* Orlando, Fl: Psychological Assessment Resources.

Suinn, R. M. 1990. *Anxiety Management Training.* New York: Plenum.

Suinn, R. M., and J. L. Deffenbacher. 1988. Anxiety management training. *The Counseling Psychologist, 16,* 31-49.

Trafate, R. C. 1995. Evaluation of treatment strategies for adult anger disorders. In H. Kassinove, editor, *Anger Disorders: Definition, Diagnosis, and Treatment* Washington, D. C.: Taylor and Francis. 109-130.

Zillman, D. 1971. Excitation transfer in communication-mediated aggressive behavior. *Journal of Experimental Social Psychology, 7,* 419-434.

Zillman, D., and J. Bryant. 1974. Effects of residual excitation on the emotional response and delayed aggressive behavior. *Journal of Personality and Social Psychology, 30,* 782-791.

BEST PRACTICES FOR THERAPY

Each of the protocols in this series presents a session-by-session, research-based treatment plan, including evaluation instruments, sample treatment summaries for use with managed care, handouts, weekly homework, and strategies to use for delivering key information. A client manual is available for each protocol, containing all the materials that the client will need.

Overcoming Agoraphobia and Panic Disorder
A 12- to 16-session treatment. By Elke Zuercher-White, Ph.D.

> Therapist protocol, *item 1462*
> Client manual, *item 1470*
> Client pack—set of five client manuals.

Overcoming Depression
A 10-session treatment. By Gary Emery, Ph.D.

> Therapist protocol, *Item 1608*
> Clent manual, *item 1616*
> *Client pack—set of five client manuals.*

Overcoming Generalized Anxiety Disorder
A 10- to 13-session treatment. By John White, Ph.D.

> Therapist protocol, *item 1446*
> Client manual, *item 1454*
> Client pack—set of five client manuals.

Overcoming Obsessive-Compulsive Disorder
A 14-session treatment. By Gail Steketee, Ph.D.

> Therapist protocol, *item 1284*
> *Client manual. item 1292*
> Client pack—set of five client manuals.

Overcoming Post-Traumatic Stress Disorder
A 15-session (or less) treatment. By Larry Smyth, Ph.D.

> Therapist protocol, *item 1624*
> *Client manual, item 1632*
> Client pack—set of five client manuals.

Overcoming Specific Phobia
A 10-session treatment. By Edmund J. Bourne, Ph.D.

> Therapist protocol, *item 1144*
> *Client manual, item 1152*
> Client pack—set of five client manuals.

Overcoming Situational and General Anger
A 9-session treatment. By Jerry L. Deffenbacher, Ph.D., and Matthew McKay, Ph.D.

> Therapist protocol, *item 1144*
> *Client manual, item 1152*
> Client pack—set of five client manuals.

Call toll-free 1-800-748-6273 to order. Have your Visa or Mastercard number ready. Or send a check for the titles you want to New Harbinger Publications, 5674 Shattuck Avenue, Oakland, CA 94609. Include $4.50 for the first item and 75¢ for each additional item to cover shipping and handling. (California residents please include appropriate sales tax.) Allow four to six weeks for delivery.

Prices subject to change without notice.

Some Other
New Harbinger Titles

The End of-life Handbook, Item 5112 $15.95

The Mindfulness and Acceptance Workbook for Anxiety, Item 4993 $21.95

A Cancer Patient's Guide to Overcoming Depression and Anxiety, Item 5044 $19.95

Handbook of Clinical Psychopharmacology for Therapists, 5th edition, Item 5358 $55.95

Disarming the Narcissist, Item 5198 $14.95

The ABCs of Human Behavior, Item 5389 $49.95

Rage, Item 4627 $14.95

10 Simple Solutions to Chronic Pain, Item 4825 $12.95

The Estrogen-Depression Connection, Item 4832 $16.95

Helping Your Socially Vulnerable Child, Item 4580 $15.95

Life Planning for Adults with Developmental Disabilities, Item 4511 $19.95

Overcoming Fear of Heights, Item 4566 $14.95

Acceptance & Commitment Therapy for the Treatment of Post-Traumatic Stress Disorder & Trauma-Related Problems, Item 4726 $58.95

But I Didn't Mean That!, Item 4887 $14.95

Calming Your Anxious Mind, 2nd edition, Item 4870 $14.95

10 Simple Solutions for Building Self-Esteem, Item 4955 $12.95

The Dialectical Behavior Therapy Skills Workbook, Item 5136 $21.95

The Family Intervention Guide to Mental Illness, Item 5068 $17.95

Finding Life Beyond Trauma, Item 4979 $19.95

Five Good Minutes at Work, Item 4900 $14.95

It's So Hard to Love You, Item 4962 $14.95

Energy Tapping for Trauma, Item 5013 $17.95

Thoughts & Feelings, 3rd edition, Item 5105 $19.95

Transforming Depression, Item 4917 $12.95

Helping A Child with Nonverbal Learning Disorder, 2nd edition, Item 5266 $15.95

Leave Your Mind Behind, Item 5341 $14.95

Learning ACT, Item 4986 $44.95

ACT for Depression, Item 5099 $42.95

Integrative Treatment for Adult ADHD, Item 5211 $49.95

Freeing the Angry Mind, Item 4380 $14.95

Living Beyond Your Pain, Item 4097 $19.95

Transforming Anxiety, Item 4445 $12.95

Integrative Treatment for Borderline Personality Disorder, Item 4461 $24.95

Depressed and Anxious, Item 3635 $19.95

Is He Depressed or What?, Item 4240 $15.95

Cognitive Therapy for Obsessive-Compulsive Disorder, Item 4291 $39.95

Child and Adolescent Psychopharmacology Made Simple, Item 4356 $14.95

Call **toll free, 1-800-748-6273,** or log on to our online bookstore at **www.newharbinger.com** to order. Have your Visa or Mastercard number ready. Or send a check for the titles you want to New Harbinger Publications, Inc., 5674 Shattuck Ave., Oakland, CA 94609. Include $4.50 for the first book and 75¢ for each additional book, to cover shipping and handling. (California residents please include appropriate sales tax.) Allow two to five weeks for delivery.

Prices subject to change without notice.

CPSIA information can be obtained
at www.ICGtesting.com
Printed in the USA
FFOW04n1443281114
9030FF

9 781572 242043